THE
SPECTATOR
ANNUAL

THE SPECTATOR ANNUAL

Edited by Fiona Glass

HarperCollins*Publishers*

HarperCollins*Publishers*
77–85 Fulham Palace Road
Hammersmith, London W6 8JB

Published by HarperCollins*Publishers* 1991
1   3   5   7   9   8   6   4   2

Copyright © *The Spectator* 1991

A catalogue record for this book
is available from the British Library

ISBN 0 246 13901 3

Set in Trump Mediaeval

Printed in Great Britain by
Hartnolls Ltd, Bodmin, Cornwall

CONTENTS

FOREWORD

Dominic Lawson

The Spectator has always prided itself on quality of writing above all else, and it is the sole criterion used in this anthology. Well, there *are* just one or two exceptions. Our interview with Nicholas Ridley – which to the magazine's considerable amazement precipitated his resignation and possibly contributed to the subsequent ousting of the Prime Minister – is included not merely on aesthetic grounds.

However, as A. N. Wilson shows, it is possible to create a monumental furore without sacrificing elegance of style. I refer in particular to his account of his dinner party conversation with Queen Elizabeth the Queen Mother, which gave a genuinely unique insight into the moods and manners of the most loved member of the royal family. This caused apparent anguish to the host of said dinner party, Lord Wyatt of Weeford, and the royal sycophant Nicholas Soames, but we did not receive a single critical letter from what one might describe as our 'normal' readers. Nevertheless A. N. Wilson took it upon himself to reply to his critics and we print his response.

Of course A.N.W. has been writing for *The Spectator* for years. But in this anthology you will find many pieces by outstanding writers who have only recently become regular contributors – in particular John Simpson, who subsequently became famous, and much admired, in this country for his television dispatches from Baghdad during the Gulf War. His accounts of the build-up and detonation of violent forces in the Gulf run like a burning thread through this volume. His description of the initial bombing raids is especially searing, although it is also combined with that peculiarly stiff-upper-lipishness which is in the great tradition of troubleshooting English foreign correspondents: nowhere more so than when he describes the sensation of discovering that a Cruise missile has just travelled five feet past the back of his head. While John was undergoing this ordeal, his close friend Roger Cooper was experiencing the far greater torment and misery of a fifth year of incarceration in Tehran. In April he was freed and he recalls again in this volume how he managed to survive his years in Evin gaol – partly by reading old copies of *The Spectator*.

Back in England, while John Simpson was ducking Cruise missiles, Vicki Woods was getting her house thatched. Her account, called naturally 'The Thatcher Years', is one of several articles by this writer, new to *The Spectator* but familiar perhaps to those who read the *Tatler* in the days of Mark Boxer. She is that rare thing, a journalist with entirely her own way of looking at the world and writing about it. (Her appointment as editor of *Harpers & Queen* was subsequently announced in June.)

The real Thatcher, rather than the one Vicki Woods employs, went down with all hands in December. No one was more disappointed than John Wells, who had been making a nice living parodying the former Prime Minister's husband. His article, 'So Farewell Then Denis', is the cry of an artist denied.

One new columnist, a worthy companion to such misanthropic writers as Jeffrey Bernard or, on some days of the week, Auberon Waugh, is the curiously named Theodore Dalrymple. In fact this is a pseudonym for a doctor working in the National Health Service, whose distaste for his patients is exceeded only by contempt for his fellow doctors. His first column we re-publish here by way of a taste of this macabre and depressed individual. If you want to read other examples, you will have to buy *The Spectator* every week. But then that applies to most of the writers in this book.

BIDDING FOR THE HOSTAGES

Charles Glass

A Lebanese friend of mine who was kidnapped told me his greatest humiliation came at the end of his captivity. This happened about five years ago, when, as now, the number of Lebanese held by other Lebanese and by Israel was far greater than the number of Western hostages. 'When they took me out of my cell, they drove me to the house of Sayed Mohammed Hussein Fadlallah.' Sayed Mohammed Hussein is usually described as the 'spiritual leader' of Hezbollah, Lebanon's Shi'ite Muslim Party of God. 'In front of the press and the television cameras, I had to thank Fadlallah for using his influence to obtain my release. I had to kiss him on both cheeks and show my gratitude publicly to the man I knew had kidnapped me in the first place.'

My friend is no longer alone. President George Bush and his secretary of state have joined him in making public displays of gratitude to the guilty. The parties they thanked on Sunday for using their 'influence' to obtain Professor Robert Polhill's freedom are the very people responsible for his kidnapping on 24 January 1987 and his detention for 1,183 days and nights. Even as his spokesman thanked Iran and Syria, President Bush insisted from his fishing boat off the Florida coast on Sunday that the United States had not negotiated directly with the 'hostage takers'. Why should it have? Why bother to talk to the monkeys in Beirut when you can deal with the organ-grinders in Teheran?

Despite the obvious hypocrisy surrounding the praise of Iran and Syria, President Bush had as little choice in the matter, so long as he wanted the seven remaining American hostages in Beirut to come home, as my Lebanese friend had. Sometimes, swallowing a little pride and maintaining a small fiction may be worth the price. Before anyone jumps to condemn my friend or President Bush, at the same time praising Margaret Thatcher's obstinacy in refusing to come to terms with Iran to free Britain's four hostages, let him spend a few months locked up alone in an empty room in Beirut's southern suburbs, not knowing from one day to the next whether the unlocking of the door means either the delivery of the day's breakfast or the prelude to an execution. Hezbollah murdered the American hostages William Buckley and Colonel William Higgins, and those who remain behind in Beirut now might just as easily be murdered as set free. The time has come to save their lives.

The hostages themselves, their families and the American administration have been forced to play along with what Robert Fisk, reporting from West Beirut in the *Independent*, rightly called 'a charade' in a 'theatre of the absurd'. The press, on the other hand, is not required to follow the government lead. Journalists do not have to accept Iran's terms of reference: the lie that the mullahs in Teheran, in exchange for a sympathetic approach from Washington, will attempt to 'persuade' Hezbollah in Beirut to consider releasing one hostage this week, perhaps another a few days, or months, later, then perhaps another. The press knows that Iran created Hezbollah, that Iran funds Hezbollah and that Iran stands in relation to Hezbollah as 'a mother to a son', in the words of one Hezbollah leader, Hussein Musawi. The press knows also that Syria and Iran co-operate in Lebanon, even though on some minor matters they differ. The press, unlike those directly involved, is not required even under the terms of the hostage game to pretend that the various sobriquets used by Hezbollah for different baskets of captives – Islamic Jihad for the Liberation of Palestine, Islamic Jihad, the Revolutionary Justice Organisation – are somehow distinct from one another, independent of Iran and unknown to the Syrian military and intelligence forces in West Beirut. 'We are never deceived,' Goethe reminded us. 'We deceive ourselves.'

The press must realise also that a deal is under way, just as surely as one was when negotiations in 1985 and 1986 between the Reagan administration and Teheran led to the staggered releases of the American hostages Benjamin Weir, Lawrence Jenco and David Jacobsen. That arrangement involved the illegal sale of American arms to Iran, sales that enabled Iran to continue its war with Iraq. This arrangement involves something else, and it is not unreasonable to ask what price is being, or is about to be, paid.

The most likely concessions that would please Iran without being unpalatable to the United States might be: (1) American withdrawal of export credits (in various forms totalling $1.25 billion a year) to Iran's enemy, Iraq; (2) more stringent application of American and other Western laws prohibiting the export to Iraq of sophisticated weapons and of 'dual use' technology (this appears to have begun already with the joint United States-British customs seizure of nuclear capacitors and the British confiscation of the so-called 'big gun' steel tubes); (3) condemnation by the United States of Iraq for its abysmal human rights record, certainly one of the worst on earth; (4) American release of Iranian assets frozen for the last ten years (this too has already begun, with United States-Iranian negotiations at The Hague making considerable progress); (5) an improvement in the Western approach to Iran that would allow it to receive international assistance and Western non-military technology to rebuild the country after the Iran-Iraq war; (6) American pressure on Israel to release its hostages, both Lebanese and Palestinian, as a way for Iran to pass some of the benefits on to its Lebanese surrogates in Hezbollah; and (7) a promise from the United States that it will resist the temptation, once all the American hostages are free, to bomb Hezbollah bases in Lebanon.

None of these concessions, however unpalatable they may be when made under duress, violates American law or is unacceptable in itself, unlike the previous arms sales to Iran. In fact, many of them might and probably should have been offered had Iran never ordered the kidnapping of Americans in Lebanon. The details and the architects of the US-Iran understanding remain to be revealed, but the inquiring journalist should not ignore the additional price of Syria's co-operation.

A friend in Damascus told me shortly before the release on Sunday of Robert Polhill that Syria was at last becoming media-wise. This was about two in the afternoon in Damascus, noon in London and, most importantly, seven of a Sunday morning in New York. At this stage, the kidnappers or the Syrians were keeping up the suspense by withholding all information as to which hostage was to be released and when. 'You know, Charlie,' my Syrian friend said, 'the government is beginning to understand that if they turn him over now, everyone in America will be asleep. But, if they wait a few hours, all the Americans will see it on television.'

And so, all of America did, when the American networks interrupted the usual Sunday afternoon basketball games and golf to show the Syrian foreign minister symbolically handing over Professor Polhill to the American ambassador. The Syrians were not entirely prepared: they had permitted camera crews to place their microphones on a table where Professor Polhill, the minister and the ambassador would make statements. They had, however, neglected to place chairs at the table, so, when the three men entered the room, they stood at the table, several feet above the microphones, and little they said could be heard on the live broadcast. No doubt they will iron that one out for the next performance – television producers outside the foreign ministry all day on their walkie-talkies, network satellite dishes to broadcast live from the ministry, millions of dollars' worth of communications equipment to send the image of a hoarse and weakened man thanking Syria for its role in obtaining his freedom. The Syrians nonetheless made the most of the unfamiliar technology. They put a correspondent from Syrian television in the car that took Professor Polhill from Lebanon into Syria. Syrian television then offered to sell the exclusive interview to each of the American networks for £100,000. When each in turn said it would not pay, Syria gave them all the videotape for nothing. The Syrian interviewer asked Professor Polhill only one question, a question he would never ask a Syrian in the street: 'What does the word "freedom" mean to you?'

For the Syrian government, 'freedom' for a hostage means hearing the Americans say thank you. President Bush thanked Syria. Secretary of State James Baker thanked Syria. Edward Djeredjian, the American ambassador in Damascus, thanked Syria. Professor Polhill, undoubtedly on embassy advice, thanked Syria. From the time the first American hostage, David Dodge, was released in 1983, everyone has thanked Syria whenever an American has come home. Syria wants recognition for its role as a regional power-broker. It wants also to be certain the United States goes so far in its gratitude as to support its policies in Lebanon and to ignore the evidence pointing to Ahmed Jibril, the Syrians' own man in the Palestinian movement, as one of the culprits in supplying the bomb that exploded over Lockerbie aboard Pan Am 103. That dossier will gather dust so long as the US needs Syrian help in freeing the remaining seven Americans in Lebanon. After that, the United States may be so grateful as to forget about Jibril altogether.

Syria did in fact help. Foreign Minister Farouq al-Shara flew to Teheran to discuss the issue. The Syrian military intelligence chief in Lebanon, General Ghazi Kenaan, drove Professor Polhill out of Beirut in his own car. Other than that, however, no one is saying what Syria did, but everyone is nonetheless exceedingly grateful.

Oddly enough, President Bush did not thank Hezbollah. Yet they too received thanks of a sort. Sources in Beirut told Ihsan Hijazi, a senior and respected New York Times correspondent, that Iran gave Hezbollah money and the sort of weapons no self-respecting Lebanese militia can do without: 'tanks, armoured personnel carriers and multi-barrelled rocket launchers', as payment for freeing Professor Polhill. My own sources in Beirut said Iran had given one Hezbollah leader, Sheikh Sobhi Tofailli, £1 million. It is a difficult story to check, but it does not sound unlikely. Iran paid Hezbollah to kidnap and hold foreigners. It might as well pay to let them go.

The bulk of the gratitude must go to Ayatollah Ali Akbar Mohtashemi, the former Iranian interior minister and former ambassador to Syria. While based in Syria just after the 1982 Israeli invasion of Lebanon, Mohtashemi helped to create Hezbollah. He personally directed the kidnapping of foreigners in Lebanon. He continued to run kidnapping operations when he moved back to Teheran, and he still commands the loyalty of the many men in Hezbollah who are paid out of his budget. It would be instructive to learn how Iran's president, Hashemi Rafsanjani, and others in the government who apparently want more normal relations with the United States persuaded him to give up a hostage. A scholar who studies Iran and has published an excellent book on the country suggested that Mohtashemi may simply have agreed to take a step back and say, 'Fine. Let some hostages go. If you can get something worthwhile for them, I will not oppose you. If you fail, we will keep the rest.' Or he may have decided at long last that now was the time to play the hostage card, because they were investments that had not paid dividends since the last Frenchmen were released. They appear to be paying dividends again.

28 April 1990

THE TROUT ALSO RISES

James Buchan

Livingston Manor, New York
Sometimes in the evening, when I'd fished the Willowemoc river in New York State for hours without catching anything, a pair of swallows appeared from somewhere and darted across the surface of the river. They were a good omen: if they were taking flies from above the water, then maybe trout would soon be rising. I retrieved my line, and prepared to cast with unusual delicacy, but I always fell into speculation. What if I cast, and a swallow mistook my artificial fly? What if I felt something snag on the back cast, and then saw, on the forward, a flash of blue? And how did I presume to take a fish from below the water but not a bird from above it?

I usually stopped fishing then, and walked to the covered bridge, or sat on the shingle and wished I still smoked cigarettes.

The Willowemoc is the second most famous trout river in North America. The most famous is the Beaverkill, which it meets at Junction Pool in Roscoe – Trout Town, USA – five miles from where

I was fishing. I fished the Beaverkill twice with Walt Zamansky, who taught chemistry at the State University of New York, and his son, Michael, who was trying to write a bestseller. They took me to the Cairns Pool, where Route 17 crosses the river on concrete stilts. It was early season both times, and we stood chest deep in the fast stream. Other guys stood so close that when I asked Walt what he thought of George Bush, he looked upstream and downstream, before saying quietly: 'I guess I'm what you call a liberal.' I looked up and saw a curtain of Hendrickson mayfly blowing upstream in the wind. The highway roared above us.

I liked the men who fish the Beaverkill. They used to ask me what fly-patterns I generally used on the Test and Itchen: I didn't dare say I'd never fished and never would fish these bonanza English streams. They liked to stand round their trucks on the highway, not smoking, and discuss advanced materials for tackle. Beneath their fishing vests, it was hard to know who worked in construction, who was a partner at Skadden, Arps. They all fished with a beautiful, lazy action: Michael Zamansky was so relaxed he took fish at his feet. I still don't know if this was because of the liberties guaranteed by the US Constitution, or because they dressed right.

What I didn't like was that you couldn't kill fish on this stretch. Walt said catch-and-release had saved the Beaverkill fishery, but to me it

'Sure I was relieved. But then I started thinking,
why did he throw me back?'

seemed an unusual torture for the fish. To feed on those Hendricksons, a trout had to run a gauntlet of men and sharp steel like an early Jesuit among the Iroquois. I took to doing much of my fishing on the Little Beaverkill, which is not famous at all and not no-kill. It joins the Willowemoc at a town called Livingston Manor.

A mile upstream from the town, there is a ruined railroad bridge and beneath the bridge, down a steep bank littered with Coke cans and automobile debris, a stretch of fast water opens out into a pool. You can be as dumb a fisherman as I and still know the pool would hold one or even two fish: you just had to crawl through the junk, roll-cast a fly 10 feet into the race and let it swim down into the pool. The only difficulty was to avoid any drag on the fly from rod or line: American fish abominate drag.

Returning with my fish, I passed a row of houses and trailers, some ruined, some started and not finished, some just a hole hacked out of the woods. One had wind-chimes on the porch; another, two armchairs spilling upholstery; another a washing-line with five pairs of jeans. Vehicles sat on blocks among the weeds. A child crouched in the road in her underwear. At the end, the road jinked sharply to pass back under the railroad and somebody had written in yellow paint, 'DANGER CHILDREN'. I gave up greeting people here.

A mile above this place, in the spring of 1989, my wife and I rented a house to go to at weekends. We found it in the *New York Times*. It had been a dairy farm, with a big, red Dutch barn all falling to bits, and a frame house covered in white plastic clapboard and shielded by Scots pines. From the house, grass fields ran off on every side and then gave way to woods, rising and falling until, to the north, you could see the peak of Slide Mountain where the Willowemoc rises.

We shared the house with the owner, Nina Pugliese, and her boyfriend, John Marrin. Nina had bought the house off the old farmer, and I think she wanted to subdivide, but then came 19 October 1987 and the stock market crashed and real estate went to hell. She paid $2,600 a month in mortgage payments and real-estate taxes and had a problem on the income side. In the morning, she passed our door in her car with a fixed look on her face.

Apart from us, she let out a trailer by the barn to a long-distance trucker and his wife. They had a dog with one brown eye and one blue eye and quarrelled so bad that once Nina ran up and intervened. Nina advertised for bed-and-breakfast guests, but this wasn't going well. New Yorkers were all talking about a new disease called Lyme Disease, which was supposed to be spread by a deer tick. One afternoon we had a barbecue, and I told a girl from Queens about how the deer came into the fields at sundown and stood, trembling and alert, like the unicorns in those tapestries in the Cloisters, and she stared right past me at her boyfriend with a look of undisguised hatred. We heard them talking late into the night and then, at two in the morning, they drove off, without paying Nina.

John Marrin ran a construction business, which had no work. He had a beard like Abe Lincoln, and was in demand for Civil War re-enactments at shopping malls. I once saw him mowing the verges in a frock-coat, string tie and stovepipe hat. I knew Nina wanted him to help get some cattle, because the real estate was so slow, but he said he'd grown up on a farm. To all these things – farming, the view from Slide, the wild raspberries in the wood-lots, the goldfinches that danced in front of the mower – he said the same thing, 'I've seen it all. I've done it all.' He did get an excavator and make my wife a vegetable patch, which she seeded with difficulty.

Our daughter was born in New York City at the end of May, and we came up a week later. The garden was green all over from peas, beans, onions and weeds. I used to take the baby for a while, so my wife could go out, blinking, to do the weeds. At night, while the baby cried in my arms, I used to count steps: 10 around the big table, 12 to the poster of the Woodstock Festival, 15 to the sink which ran only scalding water, eight and two up to the stairs where my wife banged her head so hard once she fainted. In the day, we used to go to Livingston Manor and park at the gas station and drink coffee from polystyrene cups and eat one doughnut each, which cost 13 cents from Hoos Bakery and were the best in the world. Then we went to Peck's supermarket. The men in the parking lot all looked tired out, or hadn't shaved, and had distressed-looking cars. The women wore slacks and pushed carts full of soda, potato chips and cigarettes. They screamed at children in tutus or padded football strip, who took no notice.

Because of the baby, I didn't fish much that summer. The river sank, and Walt said I had to use tiny black flies on hooks so small it took me hours to thread them. The water was clear and I could see the fish race upstream at each cast. Instead, we walked all over the farm, with the baby asleep in a pack. In the woods, we kept coming on ruined stone walls, or a rusty harrow, or a blackened chimney by a heap of tumbledown stones and a few apple trees covered in brambles. Once we blundered into a Ukrainian sporting club, deserted. Often on Saturdays, we saw Hasidic Jews, father, mother and children in descending order of height, walking along the road. Back at the farm, our tomatoes started turning red and Nina stole some for her bed-and-breakfast guests. We stole her zucchini squash. On the night of 4 September, there were 12 degrees of frost. Everything was killed, and there was peace.

On 7 October, in the morning, I heard a sound overhead and saw Canada geese flying in a straight line over the farm. I gave up counting after the first 400. Nina came by and, over the crying of the birds, said we could have the place for all of 1990 for $3,000 down now, or she'd have to let it out for the hunting season. In Livingston Manor, there was a fatal air of excitement. Guys in plaid shirts drove their trucks from the gas station to the supermarket parking lot, spun them round, and drove back to the gas station. At the farm, the man came out of the trailer carrying a rifle, fired four shots at the barn, and went back in again. We promised to be out by 15 November. John went round fixing things: the screen door, a gate down to the stock pond. Nina hinted there was some movement on the cattle thing.

The last weekend. I went down to my pool by the railroad bridge, but I didn't have the heart to fish. Climbing back up the bank, I walked up through the houses. A child was playing on a trike where it said 'DANGER CHILDREN'. I knew that this wasn't a warning but a fact. A child had died there, a year ago or five years ago, in the irretrievable American past.

In my memory, I get into the car and drive up the hill, past the last trailer, the lake, the hemlock firs and up where the fields run off on every side, and I see my wife and daughter coming back through the grass and, past them, hundreds of feeding deer.

5 May 1990

DIARY

A. N. Wilson

It was in this column that I was made crown prince of the Young Fogeys by Alan Watkins – what? nearly ten years ago. Not so young and not so fogey now. It makes me think of the Dylan song – 'But baby, I was older then, I'm younger than that now.' The other day, I went on a phone-in for a commercial radio station to discuss these serious matters. It is hard to shake an image. Asked by one caller what I should vote, I said Labour and expatiated, at tedious length, on the iniquities of the Tory Government. The next caller said, 'You right-wing bastards who write for *The Spectator* are all the same.' I saw what he meant, but for the sake of something to say, I expressed disagreement. 'Anyway,' continued this furious caller with what was obviously meant to be a deadly thrust, 'your books are not half as good as your father's.' I said that, as far as I knew, my father had not written any books. 'Aren't you Auberon Waugh, then?' asked this caller. 'You sound just like him.' I don't, actually.

5 May 1990

'We've got an indoor Bird bath.'

SELLING OUT

Michael Lewis

I should have guessed I was in for trouble from the uneasiness of my American publishers when they first raised the notion of a book tour. I was in a room with three editors when the most senior among them popped the question. 'Would you be willing', he asked me with a queasy smile, 'to spend a few weeks on a promotional trip around America?'

'Oh sure,' I said, 'that'd be fun.'

All three editors looked down at their feet to hide their expressions, like synchronised swimmers. It was as if I'd offered to shine their shoes for free, or lick the dirt from their floors. 'Well, he's certainly got the right attitude,' one finally said.

I was, I am told, easily promotable. I had written not just a scandalous exposé, but a scandalous exposé about *myself*, a first-person account of life in the financial world. Without anyone in television land having read a word of my book [*Liar's Poker*] I was invited onto several of America's most watched chat shows. If that sounds very cynical it is only because it was. The US publishing trade has struck a deal with the television industry in which it offers up its authors as fodder for ritual degradation in exchange for massive exposure of their books. But no one ever actually reads the book. As an unknown author of an unknown book, I regarded the exchange as more than fair. I reckoned anything I did to embarrass myself could be either passed off later as youthful indiscretion or blamed on my agent. Most things can.

Thus I debuted one morning in America, between 7.42 a.m. and 7.47 a.m., on a programme with about 25 million viewers, called *The Today Show*. At 7.18 a.m. I was ushered into the make-up room, where two ladies with tall hair were deep in conversation. One of them looked up at me and said, wearily, 'Who let the *Talent* in here?' Talent is what they call the guests on American chat shows. As the American television personality Michael Kinsley says, American television is the only industry in which the word talent is an insult.

I'd been on television exactly once before and poured sweat the entire three minutes I was on the air. They had to break for a commercial to save me from drowning. As I sat in the make-up room of *The Today Show*, I was more deeply nervous. My internal organs were sweating right along with my skin. Almost everyone I knew would be watching, as well as a few I didn't. A few minutes before I was due on the show one of the women wandered over and began to dust my face with orange powder. 'Why you sweating so much, darling?' she asked, soothingly.

To relax myself I began to imagine life at 7.48 a.m. The drug was beginning to work when I noticed the second woman standing in the corner of the room gripping a blow-dryer the size of a bazooka. 'Do you want me', she asked, 'to do something about that *hair*?' I didn't need to hear this. It was my hair, I said, and I thought it looked fine. 'Uh-uh,' she said, 'we can leave it alone, but if we do you're gonna look *really* stupid.' She began to smear a greasy substance across the top of my head.

The rest is too painful to recall except in barest outline. Suffice it to say that two women managed to transform perhaps the world's most innocent-looking muckraker into a slickhead faintly reminiscent of Gordon Gekko. I was then escorted onto the set to watch the show up close. To my horror the segment immediately prior to mine was a profile of perhaps the most wholesome and lovable character ever to appear on American television: a wise old hobo who had spent the last 40 years sleeping in railroad yards, and writing ballads. It was not a good act for a yuppie to follow.

Perhaps because the hobo had set a certain standard of moral decency my interviewer asked me none of the puffball questions for which I had been prepared by the show's producer. Instead, she asked why I had turned out so greedy. She asked me (I swear it is true) how my mother had raised me. Perhaps I exaggerate the depth of the humiliation I suffered. My younger brother, on the other hand, said, 'You looked even more scared than Dan Quayle in headlights.' Whom would you believe?

And if tens of thousands of books hadn't started to fly out of the stores (just as the publisher had said they would) I would have felt badly used. I learned to keep the ladies away from my hair but the other problems persisted as I was whisked across America. Only slight variations in technique distinguished the manner in which I was manhandled from one show to the next: rather than ask me how I was raised, for example, a radio interviewer in Los Angeles called my mother.

It seemed that wherever I went I was always either dull or despicable compared to the person directly in front of me. In Los Angeles I followed a married couple who wrote books about married sex and opened each interview with a graphic description of what they had been doing in their motel room two hours before. In New York I followed two women who had slept with Burt Reynolds, and a man who had invented a 943-day 48-hour-a-day calendar that had no advantage except the same number of days in every month. In Washington I followed a brace of henchmen and an agent who had just blown his cover with the CIA. In New York again (and again), I followed a furry mechanical rabbit that pounded a bass drum and scooted around the stage until a German Shepherd sprinted in from the wings and mauled it, loudly.

And I was forever being prepared to answer one set of questions, then asked another. The most dramatic moment occurred on something called *Late Night with David Letterman* (viewership 25 million). There is no British equivalent to David Letterman. He is perhaps what Terry Wogan might have become had he been beaten regularly as a child. David Letterman's producer called me four times before the show to rehearse the jokes he had decided I should tell. One of these required me to mention the phrase 'big swinging dick', a term of endearment in the financial circles in which I move. About five minutes before I went on the air, the producer raced to my dressing room in a panic to announce that all plans were off. 'No dick jokes,' he said, gasping for breath. 'David's got it into his head that his mother is watching tonight.'

The gruesome details form a graphic point of comparison with what I faced upon my return to England. I had agreed with my British publisher to tour England. I imagined, at first, that this would be much the same as the American experience, and my teeth were gritted as I stumbled from the back of the jumbo jet into the car, which took me straight from Heathrow to my first television show. And then . . .

Nothing. No hard questions, no tough acts to follow, no fiddling with my hair, no feeling of being a circus clown rather than an author. No one told me what I could or couldn't say on the air. It was okay to talk about big swinging dicks. In fact, no one really seemed to care what I did, or if I did anything. The BBC withdrew its invitation for me to appear on *What the Papers Say* because I had appeared on Channel 4 at noon the previous day and they felt I was over-exposed. Articles about my book in the *Sunday Times* and the *Daily Telegraph* led to accusations of over-hype from a reviewer in the *Independent*. I couldn't quite believe it. The American experience was still with me. For about a week I woke up in a cold sweat having dreamt that I had been asked to appear on Wogan to tell dick jokes. Gradually it dawned on me that it wasn't going to happen. And that the only way anyone was going to hear about my book was if he was told by a friend who had picked it up in a bookshop by mistake.

This raises an interesting question: which system of book promotion is more stupid, the American or the British? I should make clear that the difference in my two experiences had nothing to do with my publishers: they were equally diligent and competent. It had nothing to do with the nationality of the author: true, I am American, but I have lived in Britain for the last seven years. It had nothing to do with the nature of the book itself: it was set half in America, half in Britain. It was, in short, about as fair a comparison of the two systems as one could hope for.

And it seems to me that the fundamental difference between them is that no one expects an author to sell his work in Britain. The idea of the author as salesman (embraced in egalitarian America) is repulsive to the British. You can almost hear the British media retch at the mere scent of hype. The British publishing industry has yet to adopt the same author-degradation-for-book-sales deal struck in America. Just the reverse. No matter how hard you try it's nearly impossible to find a forum in Britain in which to really sell out (having one picture taken 50 times in tennis whites doesn't count as selling out, not by American standards anyway). I'm hardly complaining. My book sold well enough in small pockets in the City of London. And I cherish England as a rare place in which I have yet to make a fool of myself. My point is only that it's easy to scoff at the American hype without also seeing that it serves a legitimate function, for which unknown authors should be grateful. It affords them the luxury of writing for small British weeklies that pay them little.

12 May 1990

'No Julian, Mummy can't afford to save the planet this year.'

FAR EAST OF ETON

Murray and Jenny Sayle

Aikawa, near Tokyo

Neither of us is, strictly speaking, an expert on the newly fashionable topic of education in Japan. Your genuine pundit should, at least, have had some or all of his or her formal education in Japan, speak the language without accent, be deeply versed in the civilisation it expresses and be at the same time fluent in another language and well acquainted with its ideas and outlook, for the essential purposes of comparison.

We adult Sayles simply don't qualify. In fact, we only know each other's educational background by repute, and occasionally by results. One of us (*père*) was educated, more or less, at Erskineville Opportunity Class, Canterbury Boys' High and the University of Sydney, the other (*mère*) admirably at Woodford, Essex, Girls' High and l'Université de Nantes. One of us knows the Japanese system only as a parent (which, in Japan, still means a fairly high level of involvement) and, in Jenny's case, as an occasional teacher and participant.

We have, however, three full-time experts in the house, well qualified to fill the blanks in our knowledge. Alexander (named for the Macedonian military man and the better known former editor of this magazine), 11, is a sixth-grader at our local village primary school. His sister Malindi, nine, is in third grade. Their brother Matthew, pushing four, attends the local infants' school. Both these establishments are part of the ordinary, 'free', tax-funded Japanese state-run system, and their classmates are the children of our neighbours, ranging from those of the richest family in the village (who own the textile mill) through those of our doctor and dentist to the families of local rice farmers and factory workers. The language of instruction is, of course, Japanese. Our children were all born here in Aikawa-Cho, whose name, appropriately, means 'Love River Town'.

In recent years one or two Korean or Vietnamese children have been enrolled, but ours are the only blue-eyed, fair-haired youngsters who have ever attended our local schools, or, for that matter, the only ones their schoolfriends have ever seen in the flesh. We would like to report, straight off, that none of us has ever encountered any racism in the Japanese school system and that, on the contrary, teachers and neighbours have gone to considerable lengths to make our offspring feel welcome. Evidence: our daughter completed three years of kindergarten without ever having heard the word *gaijin* (outside person, foreigner). We asked her how she was referred to: 'as Alex's little sister, of course' she replied scornfully.

We should perhaps also explain here that we speak English at home, read *Winnie the Pooh* and *Skippy the Kangaroo* to our children, and that all three of them speak rather posh English, the influence, their father believes, of their mother. We are nevertheless living in deepest rural Japan, with many aspects of life, including the educational system, very different from the ones we knew. A sample day will perhaps bring out some differences.

Our day begins, summer and winter, at 6.30 a.m. School is six days a week, Saturday a half-day, with school activities from time to time on Sundays as well. On the equivalent of high days and holidays the sing-song bonging of a Shinto gong in the shrine next door will sometimes beat our trusty Japanese alarm clocks to the call. Breakfast is at seven, Japanese-style, which these days can be anything from rice and fish to toast, bacon and eggs (all firm favourites).

At 7.40 the group of children who will walk to school together is noisily gathering at our door. Walking to school is obligatory, part of the process of socialisation which is, of course, the central purpose of education. The obligation is reciprocal: the Japanese state has to provide a primary school within walking distance of every rate-paying habitation. There are schools in remote places with five or six pupils.

The walking group, up to eight, is in the charge of the oldest child who carries a flag and is held responsible for getting the rest to school on time, in principle 8.10, at the latest 8.25 a.m. The group waits outside one's door, cheerfully insistent, and occasionally the leader will, with parental permission, invade a house to drag sluggards out – but this is rare, peer group pressure normally being quite enough. For the past five years Alexander, an under-the-covers reader on scientific and literary topics and so a slow riser, has frequently needed a call of *Sayru-kun!* (an affectionate diminutive, along the lines of 'old chap!') to get him moving. This year he is the group leader and a lad transformed, impatient to get on the road with his sister, who is now part of his responsibility. He still, however, reads under the covers.

Here we see the first inculcation of key Japanese principles: flag-carrying, meticulous organisation, reciprocal responsibility and the self-policing of groups. The individual right, if there is such a thing, to travel by car is extinguished in favour of the higher interest in getting a group to function smoothly towards a common and, of course, externally mandated purpose. This sounds rigid, perhaps, but the system is softened by many humane and admirable touches. Handicapped children with Down's syndrome, crippled limbs and other afflictions are kept in the system on an equal footing with the others as long as possible, which includes the compulsory walk if they are physically up to it, and the friendships thus formed visibly enrich both sides. Alexander, for instance, has a particular, spontaneous friendship with just such a courageous brain-damaged boy.

Mutual help on the village level is evidenced in many ways. Our village is in the mountains and we can easily get a foot or so of snow overnight. In principle, parents are responsible for keeping a path clear for the walk to school, and the village chief (an informally-elected, unpaid, Buggins's-turn job) telephones the night before, warning that parents should be ready at 6.30 a.m., shovel in hand, if the Town Hall announces over the village loudspeaker system that school is open for the day. Total suspension of lessons is very rare. What happens if a parent fails to turn out? Solicitous neighbours would call with hot food, assuming an illness in the household. Good neighbourliness, taken for granted, is a mighty motivator.

The school building and playground are spartan but adequate, of a pattern uniform throughout Japan. On Mondays and Fridays there is a general school assembly, with some inspirational remarks by the headmaster. Some schools bow to the national and school flags on these days. Ours does not, but we would have no objection if they did. No other saluting or pledging allegiance is called for, and our neighbours don't see any point in such exercises – as another parent once told us, 'We don't really need to remind our children which country they're in.'

The periods of instruction are 45 minutes each, with intervals in the playground to blow off steam. Classes are currently limited to 40 maximum, a number which has gradually fallen with Japan's birthrate in the past two prosperous decades. It will probably be 30 to 35 a decade hence. The curriculum is set by the Education Ministry in Tokyo with little room for school or teacher variation, another rigidity which has certain advantages – on a given day every schoolchild in Japan will be studying much the same thing, so that a flourishing monthly children's newspaper and magazine, commercially published, are able to feature articles on the science subjects of the month and stories which introduce the new Chinese characters the children have just learned. The magazine comes with such useful giveaways as small plastic microscopes, test tubes and ant colonies.

The study of Japanese (the schools call it *kokugo* – 'national language') takes up six periods a week, the same as mathematics. Of these two pillars of the system Japanese is for us by far the more daunting. A mixture of some 10,000 basic Chinese characters, all different, many more compounds, two Japanese-invented syllabaries of 72 letters each and our own footling ABCs, the Japanese writing system has been defined as 'the greatest barrier to human communication ever devised by the mind of man'. Children have to master 996 characters by the end of primary school, 1,945 by matriculation, 3,000 to be considered passably literate.

We ignorant foreign parents try, in our cunning adult way, tricks and witty mnemonics to remember, say, the 19 strokes with which *ai*, the 'love' in our own postal address, is written, and in which order – this bit looks like a leaky roof, that part is dripping tears, and the whole emotion rests on *bun*, 'knowledge' (that's a laugh). 'Sit cross-legged, hand on heart' advises another rather condescending memory guide for foreigners. But as fast as we get one section right, another dissolves into the mist. 'No, Mummy,' advises Malindi, a straight-A student, over the kitchen table, 'you just have to get them into your *head*!' Japanese schools employ no flash cards, language laboratories, visual aids or other hi-tech would-be short-cuts. The poor little devils just have to learn them. One's admiration for one's children, another important function of education, can only grow.

Is it worth 250 hours a year for 12 years, with copious homework, just to read and write? This is a question we are often asked, and ask ourselves. The script is of course the rocky road into Japanese culture and beyond to its parent, the majestic civilisation of China. It is said to improve a child's visual imagination, if he or she has some to begin with. The characters are certainly elegant, especially after the

50 additional hours a year devoted to calligraphy with brush and ink, and once mastered they are read as effortlessly as, we hope, you are reading this. We are inclined to view them as the Asian equivalent of cricket – good exercise (for the mind) and, through mastery of an esoteric set of rules, the pass to a world-wide community. The truth they teach, however, is not, at least conventionally, so sporting: that nothing of value is to be had without hard, sustained, step-by-step work.

After this mental Everest, mathematics are, relatively speaking, child's play. Progress is fast with six hours a week and both algebra and geometry begin in the fifth grade. Great stress is placed on pencil-and-paper numeracy. Calculators are barred, although the centuries-old counting-frame (*soroban*) is introduced to help visualise big numbers – and, with a budget in the trillions of yen, Japanese numbers get very big. One result is a saucy Japanese invention, the electronic calculator with built-in *soroban* to check the machine's results.

Science (three hours a week) is taught imaginatively with experiments in electricity, magnetism, compressed gases and so on. Home-making gets two hours a week, and, the classes being mixed, Alexander has sewn a rucksack and an apron and cooked omelettes, hotcakes and potato chips well up to his sister's standard. Art (two hours) is the usual drawing, painting and model-building. The music-room (two hours) is the best-equipped in the school, with a Yamaha organ for each student and portraits of 30 composers, all Europeans. The theories of Shin'ichi Suzuki on early musical training are followed, and our older children have both played the piano in public to the restrained enthusiasm of Japanese audiences.

Social studies (three hours a week) get equal attention. This is a popular subject as it is mostly outdoors – I have just seen Malindi, for instance, blonde hair flying, in the forefront of a class of 40, marching to our local post office to study the working of the hyper-efficient Japanese postal system. Alex recently went with his class to see Mitsubishi cars being assembled, and another time to the factory where Nissan windscreens are cast from molten glass. Confucius's thought is plain here – children need *socially useful* knowledge, and should show interest and pride in the achievements of the community in which they live.

Respect for the past, another Confucian idea, is inculcated with visits to the rice farms, mulberry orchards and silk filatures which surround our village. Matthew will later this year get hands-on agricultural experience at something called an *o-imo*, 'dig-in' (the English words are used), in which his class will harvest a field of sweet potatoes they have just planted, and will tend during summer and autumn, each child bringing home a fair share.

Teaching is a profession greatly honoured in Japan. All teachers, even retired or administrative ones, are addressed as *sensei*, a term otherwise used only for doctors, successful politicians, gangster bosses and, very occasionally, writers. A primary teacher at 35 with two children can expect £15,000 a year, after tax, with extra allowances for housing, remoteness, cold climate (in Northern Japan) and a car where necessary. A headmaster or mistress will get £25,000 upwards (plus allowances). Women teachers get a year's maternity leave (three months unpaid) and equal pay and status, making teaching one of the few Japanese professions women can successfully combine with family responsibilities. Two-teacher families, very common, are opulent by Japanese, or anybody's, standards. When the Education Ministry recently recruited an additional 30,000 trainee teachers, 200,000 suitably qualified people applied, in contrast with the police and self-defence forces, neither of which can currently fill their ranks.

Teachers and parents are expected to collaborate. At the beginning of every school year parents get a visit from their child's 'home-room' teacher (we're expecting one next week) to establish rapport and discuss parents' worries, if any. We have, for instance, brought up the question of the racial and cultural differences between us and our neighbours, simply as something we are aware of, but have not found troublesome. At the end of the school year there is another meeting to discuss the children's progress. Five times a year per child, parents are expected (in Japan this is an expectation of iron) to attend demonstration classes, standing at the back and following the lessons.

Last Saturday, for instance, we both listened to a lesson in the mysterious subject *dohtoku*, 'morals and ethics', which before the war consisted of exhortations on hard work and unswerving obedience to the Emperor's (i.e. the bureaucracy's) commands. Malindi's teacher, Mori *sensei* (who has three children himself), instead produced a finger-bowl and explained that in some countries people used these utensils at table after, for example, eating asparagus, a vegetable little known in Japan. This led him to a disquisition on the variety of human folkways and the importance of recognising that none were inherently superior or inferior, an admirably liberal message. Other teachers use their hour of *dohtoku* to catch up on other subjects. There is no exam or grading in *dohtoku*, although serious subjects like science and Japanese are tested at least fortnightly.

There is no corporal punishment in Japanese state schools. Children who offend by noisiness or inattention can be sent outside the classroom for five or ten minutes, ordered to perform *zazen* (Zen meditation, supposedly on the vanity of earthly desires, while seated and staring straight ahead) for a like time, or in extreme cases sent to the teachers' room for a homily. Latecomers are sometimes shamed into 'volunteering' for unpopular jobs, like leading English conversation. Discipline is basically maintained by splitting the class into five or six *han*, squads (not the same one that walks to school) and holding every child responsible for the behaviour of his or her *han*.

There is a squad leader, the *hancho* (another Buggins's-turn job) whose duties include announcing at the beginning of each period, 'Now we are going to study arithmetic', or whatever, and at the end thanking the teacher for the lesson and leading the class in a deep bow. The system carries into adult life and you owe the quality control of your Japanese television or camera, for instance, to the group vigilance in the factory of something like a children's *han*. The responsibility is seen as being, not to the boss, but to each other ('don't let the side down, chaps') and it is justified by the most Confucian of all arguments. It works.

Nothing that could be called religion is taught in Japanese schools, and certainly not the doctrine that Emperor Akihito and all the other Japanese are descended from the Sun Goddess. In fact we lately monitored a lesson of Alex's on the *Yayoi* people, ancestors of the Japanese, who inhabited our village some 12,000 years ago. His teacher did not explain in so many words where the *Yayoi* came from, but when we asked him later, Malindi interposed in the weary tone bright young ladies use to dim parents, 'from Korea, of course!' Our children help carry the *mikoshi*, the portable shrine at village Shinto festivals, which Christian Japanese parents normally forbid on the ground that Shinto is idolatrous, but these are village, and not official, occasions. Our children think Shinto great fun.

Japanese schools are often depicted as hells of Darwinian competition but this is certainly not true of the primary system. There is no streaming, classes are balanced with the bright and not-so-bright, and marks, communicated to parents, are not made public. The school sports are, in fact, designed to avoid one-to-one competition, partly to enable the handicapped children to participate on equal terms. Japanese combat sports like judo and kendo, which all seem to have originated in killing people, are not taught. Instead, team sports like baseball, soccer and relay racing (on foot and in the school swimming-pool) are played. Handicapped students are often in the winning teams.

The theme of co-operation closes the school day, when pupils and teachers combine to clean the school, sweeping the classrooms and corridors, dusting the blackboards and scrubbing out the toilets. These jobs are done in strict rotation, teachers working with their pupils and, on appropriate days, parents summoned to weed and rake the playground. Schools in Japan, China, Korea and Vietnam employ no school cleaners, one of the great divides of the educational world which tells us much that is favourable about the attitude towards education of the countries of the Confucian tradition.

Where, then, do stories about the Japanese 'examination hell', the mental breakdowns and child suicides come from? As the American educator John Dewey teaches us, education is not a preparation for life, but part of life itself. The mutual help, the reasonableness, the concern for the unlucky and less gifted is very much part of Japanese life, although it is a part that foreigners seldom see (although, if we approach with an open mind, we are welcome to share its benefits and obligations). One result of patience with the less endowed has been to give Japan, overall, the best educated and most diligent labour force in the world, the basis of all Japanese successes.

The Confucian design has another side. The master taught that education should be as widespread as possible in order to find those, irrespective of class, most fitted to serve the state. Japan's productive, co-operative groups are directed by a bureaucratic hierarchy selected by examinations, perhaps the ablest and certainly the most arrogant of their breed to be found anywhere. Japanese industry, commerce, the military are all run by the same kind of snooty hierarchs. Up to the age of about 15, the end of the ninth year of compulsory education, the Japanese government schools are excellent. We would without hesitation recommend them to any parent, to those of less gifted children who will get at least as much respect and attention as the others, and to those with bright and imaginative children as well, because they are guaranteed a grounding in the hard subjects that just have to be learned. Tough as the syllabus is, some 95 per cent of Japanese children complete it, an unmatched national asset.

But, at that age (end of junior and beginning of senior high school in Japanese terms) the funnel starts to narrow, the pressure goes on. Schools compete with schools, classmates with classmates for the limited number of slots-for-life in the bureaucracy and business. Private, fee-paying schools proliferate at this point to serve the rich, while the notorious *juku* (after-hours cram schools) force-feed the children of ambitious parents with, as they promise, the secrets of passing exams. This is the area of scandal, of bribed examiners, stolen papers and suicidal children. Not surprisingly, individuality and creativity wither in this jungle. The Japanese universities, run on rigid hierarchical lines, don't do much to revive them, much to the alarm of concerned Japanese.

Our own children, for reasons of nationality and custom, have little prospect of ever being Japanese bureaucrats (although, in a fast changing world, you never know) and so we intend to send them to no *juku*, offer no bribes and hold them out of the Oriental rat-race as best we can. But, up to now, we have nothing but good to report of a system which has many, not always well-informed, critics. But then, none of us went to Japanese schools.

12 May 1990

IF SYMPTOMS PERSIST . . .

Theodore Dalrymple

We doctors have wonderful self-control. Our careers span four decades, yet never once in all that time do we tell our patients how disgusting they are. Is there another profession that equals ours in forbearance? The strain of keeping our disgust to ourselves is terrible: no wonder our suicide rate is so high.

The other day it fell to my lot, for reasons it is unnecessary to relate, to examine a lady's toes. The stench was awful, overpowering. It quite knocked me back against the white-tiled wall of the clinic.

'They'll have to come off!' I exclaimed, referring to her feet.

'But why?' asked the lady, thoroughly alarmed.

'The smell, the smell!'

Actually, this exchange took place only in my head. What I really said was: 'Thank you, Mrs Jones, you can put your slippers back on now.'

Why don't people wash before they consult a doctor? Why don't they wash full stop? After all, they never know when they might need to call a doctor in an emergency. The fat unwashed are particularly gruesome, the folds in their skin harbouring . . . no, I won't, I can't, describe it.

It's not that I'm particularly squeamish: I can wade in oceans of blood without turning a hair, or at least I could until the Aids epidemic.

Nevertheless, there are products of the human body, especially in ill-health, which still repel me, though I've seen a lot of them. For example, I have never been able to look sputum full in the pot. Chronic chest cases tend to treasure their output – Great Expectorations – and bring it to me in jars marked 'apricot jam' or 'English marmalade'. I don't much care for vomitus either, even when the patient considers it an indispensible aid to diagnosis.

I wish I could report that medical ethics always overcame aesthetic sensibilities, but in my case, even in matters of life and death, this has not been so. Mouth to mouth resuscitation I have never found attractive, and usually whenever it has been necessary I have managed as person in charge to delegate it to others. Once a highly agitated lady arrived at my clinic and I gave her an injection to calm her down. She calmed down all right: in fact, she stopped breathing. There was no one else around, so I braced myself for mouth to mouth. Then I saw the colour of her lipstick – mauve – and I simply couldn't bring myself to start. Luckily for me – I can't speak for her, she didn't seem to be enjoying life much before my injection – she began to breathe again.

On the other hand, I don't mind pumping someone's chest to stimulate their heart to beat again, even though I once caught scabies from a lady covered in the fulminating variety known for some reason as Norwegian. She died, but the scabies mite, *Sarcoptes scabei*, lived on.

Naturally, no reader of *The Spectator* will have cause to blush at my strictures. I refer only to non-readers.

'This is a very complex disease ...
you laymen have no business catching it.'

THE JEWS, AGAIN

Ian Buruma

It is the fate of empires that when, finally, thaw sets in, nasty weeds spring back to life. When Lord Mountbatten unfroze the British Raj in 1947, Hindus and Muslims slaughtered each other in masses. Now it is the turn of the Soviet empire to melt, and there is talk of pogroms. This is not to argue for the continuation of imperial rule, but we might as well know what we are in for.

Fanatics in Moscow have revived the bogus *Protocols of the Elders of Zion* and claim that Adolf Eichmann was in fact a Jew, conspiring to rule the world. In Hungary stars of David were daubed on the election posters of a party deemed to be led by Jews. In East Berlin the words 'Jewish pig' appeared on Bertolt Brecht's tombstone (he was not in fact Jewish, but his tattered reputation might be saved by his enemies yet). In Poland, where few Jews remain, tens of thousands took to the streets to demonstrate for a 'Jew-free Europe'. In Rumania there is talk of purging the sacred national soil of the polluting blood of Jews and Magyars.

It was perhaps bound to happen. But anti-semitism is not only on the rise in the former Soviet empire. It is here, too, in the wealthy societies of Western Europe. Last week in France Jewish corpses were desecrated in a cemetery near Avignon (an act of barbarism repeated in, of all places, Sweden). The body of an eighty-year-old man was impaled on a parasol, and a star of David was painted on the stomach of an old lady. Many French people demonstrated their disgust by marching to the Bastille and smashing up a restaurant where 100 Frenchmen had just celebrated Hitler's birthday. Further violence would have occurred if Simone Weil, the former President of the European Parliament and an Auschwitz survivor, had not intervened. Western anti-semitism was also frozen for a while, under the ice of guilty memories of the Holocaust. Now, as the memories fade and witnesses pass away, mass murder is becoming an abstraction, a passage in the history books, or as M. Le Pen, the French politician, put it, 'an incident'. The strength and swagger of Israel have helped to make anti-semitism more respectable again, as fewer and fewer anti-Zionists care to distinguish between world Jewry and the promised land of milk, honey and rubber bullets.

Anti-semites can point out that in this 'kinder and gentler' time of reaction against the 'greed and selfishness' of the Reagan and Thatcher years, the villains of Wall Street, the take-over artists and junk bond fixers, were almost all Jews.

But there is something else at work in the kind and gentle decade of melting empires, shifting populations and faltering capitalism: the unhealthy obsession with what the eminent German historian, Michael Stürmer, calls 'the healthy national identity'. He means an identity based on national pride, unencumbered by historical guilt, that is to say, the guilt of Auschwitz, Treblinka and Chelmno. Likewise, French revisionists are busy denying the Holocaust; for then, at last, the blood-stained hands of Vichy France can be washed, General Pétain can take his place again in the pantheon of national heroes, and France regain her healthy national identity.

The question of identity has become so obsessive that even the *Guardian*, organ of the urban liberal conscience, has taken to writing long agonised leaders about it, entitled, 'Who we are and what we ought to be'. The *Guardian*'s view of national identity is not, of course, the same as the one usually held by what Germans call 'identity builders'. The romantic view of nationhood, which is coming back into fashion, especially, but by no means only, in right-wing circles, is based not so much on politics or constitutionalism, which are matters of choice, as on ethnic and racial roots, on history and customs and folkways, on religious creeds and rituals, mostly, in short, on matters of birth. The great German patriot and inventor of mass calisthenics, Friedrich Ludwig Jahn, put this view across clearly in 1810:

> The people (Volk) will live as an actual people, not a people in name only; its outer national unity will reflect its spiritual union. Our people will not stray into rootless flitting about like Jews or Gypsies. . . .

One cannot deny the pull of historical and cultural ties, but modern societies are far too complex to be defined by them. For when such views of national unity, spiritual and racial, predominate, politics are regarded as divisive and the customs, creeds and folkways of others as threats to 'our' way of life, the fabric of 'our' society, 'our' national identity, or whatever we wish to call it. It is bad enough when the others are coloured and poor, but it is far more dangerous when they are rich and powerful and try to look and behave like us, for such people are like a fifth column in our midst, rootless cosmopolitans conspiring to undermine our civilisation and take over the world. Such fearful fantasies infected the 1930s, and the symptoms are recurring.

T. S. Eliot, who was much afraid that the spiritual and historical legacy of Europe would fall prey to modern barbarism, invented a prototypical rootless cosmopolitan, called Bleistein: 'Chicago Semite Viennese'. Bleistein stood for soulless greed, which spelled the end of civilisation. His presence and ill-gained wealth – 'money in furs' – were an affront to our spiritual heritage.

The spiritual nation, the *Kulturnation* – that is what Russian, Hungarian, Polish, Rumanian, German and other jingoists now, as ever, wish to establish. It has special appeal when political communities, or nation-states, are vague, non-existent or in a state of crisis. For when the state loses political legitimacy – as currently in the Soviet Union or Rumania – atavistic ideas of community take over. It is not surprising that right-wing romantics in Eastern Europe and Russia – such as Pamyat – have revived the spectre of the communist Jew, sometimes in league with international freemasonry. To be sure, this is partly because many Jews were attracted to communism and played prominent roles in communist régimes. They often did this because communism offered an alternative to the *Kulturnation*, from which they were excluded. They were often excluded in communist societies, too, of course, for communists are often as jingoistic as fascists, except that they call it 'national liberation'.

So when extreme nationalists speak about communist Jews today, they are not so much concerned with political ideology; it is Bleistein they are afraid of, the rootless cosmopolitan, whose 'lustreless pro-

'Take it from me, shampoo and conditioner combined!'

trusive eye' gazes covetously at the mystical community which he means to control by subterfuge. How deranged such fantasies can be was shown recently when right-wing Russian patriots criticised a theatre production of a Pushkin story in Sverdlovsk, because the actors allegedly used hidden Zionist, Nazi, Masonic and anti-Russian symbols.

Just as Russians and Eastern European jingoists associate Jews with communism, Western Europeans often look to rootless cosmopolitan America for their prototypical Bleistein, the Chicago Semite Viennese. Some romantics, by no means all anti-semitic or right-wing, have taken to dreaming mistily about something they call the 'European spirit', which is, to use another favourite term of such dreamers, 'organic'. Their Europe, with its traditional values, its ancient history, is forever being threatened by American materialism, selfishness and amoral, commercial greed. The Americans, in this view, have no traditional values, that is to say, Americans don't have a soul. As Jonathan Clarke, the Oxford historian, put it recently in one of his many articles for the *Sunday Telegraph*: 'The *real* American values are divorce, abortion, homosexuality and consumerism.'

Clarke is a man of the Right but it might surprise many an anti-American leftist that he or she is a direct heir to the reactionary ideas of Eliot. This is actually less strange than it might appear. Eliot was an admirer of Charles Maurras of Action Française, a prominent right-wing anti-Dreyfusard. But there were many socialists who were no less opposed to Dreyfus, since they too saw Jews, especially Jewish capitalists, as a threat to society. Anti-capitalism, anti-Americanism and anti-semitism can be highly congenial and sometimes indistinguishable bedfellows. Indeed, how close Bleistein can be to left-wing thoughts was illustrated famously some time ago when the *New Statesman* put Henry Kissinger on its cover, hook-nosed like Fagin, wielding, if my memory serves me well, a bloody butcher's knife. It was meant, no doubt, as an anti-American statement, but it came across as anti-semitic.

It is perhaps a sign of health in British society that Mrs Thatcher's earlier penchant for Jewish ministers and American-trained advisers did not elicit similar lampoons. So far, the anti-capitalist snobbery of the often well-heeled Left has confined its targets to yuppies, estate agents and other parvenus, who, unlike, say, artists and writers, are not entitled to their wealth. Any residual hard feelings about Jewish behaviour find a ready and respectable outlet in the outraged scrutiny of Israel.

Israel's role in the history of modern anti-semitism has been ironical, to say the least. The early Zionists sought an escape from their persecutors in Europe and Russia. And many of the founding fathers of Israel, like David Ben Gurion, were socialists in favour of an open society that embraced non-Jews. However, Zionists were never united in their aims, and the tension between those who favour an open society and those who seek to replicate the racial, spiritual communities of their persecutors has become a permanent fixture in Israeli politics. Today, Israeli fanatics, no less racialist than the anti-semites, are becoming an ever stronger force. To add irony upon irony, many of them come from America. One such figure is the notorious Meir Kahane, who described an American-born serviceman who killed two young Arabs at a sacred Muslim spot in Jerusalem as 'a hero who tried to liberate the Temple Mount from the foreigners' hands'. This is Kahane's idea of a healthy national identity.

Anti-Zionism and anti-semitism are often confused, both by the 'antis' and their targets. To Menachem Begin any critic of Israel would seem to be an anti-semite, which is of course absurd. Yet when one hears, as I did recently, a charming English journalist with strong anti-Zionist views denounce the New York Times because 'it's run by Jews', one begins to understand what Begin is up against.

This particular anti-Zionist fits into a long British tradition of phil-Arabism. He is an admirer of the ancient ways of bedouins and other sons of the baking sands, with their warrior codes, their racial purity and their manly spirituality. What is interesting about the phil-Arabists of this type is that they appear less contemptuous of the atavistic side of Israel – the mad rabbis and the Bible-bashing settlers – than they are of the modern, secular, indeed democratic side. Israel, to them, is the rootless, cosmopolitan intruder in the ancient world of spiritual communities, indeed a nation of Bleisteins. Naturally, English romantics of this kind are also invariably contemptuous of America, Bleistein's spiritual home.

What, then, can we conclude from all this? Not, clearly, that every anti-Zionist, or anti-American, or anti-capitalist, or even every dreamer of healthy national identities, is an anti-semite. But when these disparate elements come together, a climate of ideas is formed which is ideally suited to anti-semitism, or indeed to being anti-anybody who is not one of us, who does not – dare I say it? – pass the cricket test. This is unpleasant but not lethal in open, democratic societies with reasonably strong economies, for such bigotry can be contained in splinter groups and small political parties. But it can be highly dangerous when politics and economics are in a state of flux, when people are as unsure of their governments as they are of their next meal. And that is precisely the situation in parts of the crumbled Soviet empire. The least critical place – to pile on one more irony – is probably Germany, for East Germany can be contained by the largest democracy in Europe. It is most critical in the Soviet Union, where Russians are finding themselves increasingly isolated, humiliated and poor. The Russian writer, A. Yanov, is quoted in Stephen K. Carter's new book, *Russian Nationalism*, as saying that if *perestroika* fails, a brutal, anti-Western, fascist dictatorship will take over. One can imagine where their healthy national identity will lead, especially for Soviet Jews.

There is not much we in the West can do to influence Russian or other fanatics, except to keep our own obsessions about national identity at bay. The jingoists need no encouragement from us. As Saint Just, one of the heroes of the French Revolution, observed, 'There is something terrible about the holy love of one's nation, for it is so exclusive that it sacrifices everything to the public interest, without mercy, without fear, without humanity.' He knew whereof he spoke. Not long after he said this, his neck was sliced by the guillotine.

19 May 1990

HANGING GUARDIAN OF BABYLON

John Simpson

They seem to be thinking of turning the Hanging Gardens of Babylon into a recreation area. They might as well; there's little enough left of the original place now. My footsteps echoed on the new concrete paving of the palace where Nebuchadnezzar lived and Alexander the Great came to die. The only Iraqi I could see tried to sell me a cuneiform cylinder: perhaps he was a secret policeman. I could see that there was something not quite right at the base of a nearby wall, and went over to inspect it. The tidy new yellow brickwork, 25 feet high and crowned with olde-worlde machicolation, gave way to three courses near the ground which were crude and irregular. They proved to be the original mud bricks of Babylon, and they looked distinctly out of place in the gleaming new reconstruction. It requires real self-confidence to take an archaeological site like Babylon and rebuild it along the lines of an empty Safeway supermarket. Saddam Hussein has a great deal of self-confidence.

At the Saddam Arts Centre in Baghdad the artists in residence were putting in a heavy day's work, painting new portraits of their President: icons 15 feet high to decorate every major crossroads and every public building in the entire country. On either side of the road that leads past the Ministry of Information there are 36 such portraits, side by side. In some he appears as the stern father of his country, uniformed and thoughtful. But mostly he strives for the jovial effect. He smiles behind dark glasses in a variety of costumes, from hunting clothes to short-sleeved shirt and panama hat, he climbs mountains and kisses little children. Nature has given him a misleadingly pleasant appearance, much as it did to Nicolae Ceauşescu. But the brown pebble-like eyes are unsmiling and alert.

Yet these are not the bland, featureless portraits of Mao Tse-tung's China or Kim Il Sung's North Korea. Saddam presents himself to his people as real and approachable; he wants to be a part of everyone's life. His disarmingly pleasant, Westernised deputy foreign minister, Nizar Hamdoun, explained to me that the people's love for their President is such that in any private house his portrait is to be found not merely in the hallway or the sitting-room, but even in the bedroom. 'Most unusual,' I murmured.

In an expensive, impersonally furnished government office the incumbent minister looked mournfully at one of the armchairs, and turned to me. 'It's terrible to think that it's only a few weeks since Farzad Bazoft sat there,' he said. This came as a considerable surprise: we had not been talking about Farzad, though his execution for supposed espionage was much on my mind. Farzad had once worked for me, and I felt an obligation to defend him strongly. It appeared that on his last visit to Iraq he had tried to enlist the minister's support in getting to the weapons plant. He had already tried the Information Ministry, which had not been helpful. The man I now found myself talking to had not helped him either. Bazoft had told him, just as he had told the other government officials, precisely what he wanted to do. I had the impression from the minister that Bazoft had also warned him that he planned to travel to the plant, with or without permission. During the trial Bazoft tried to call the minister to give evidence on his behalf: no right-thinking spy would announce his intentions to a member of the government. But the court refused the application. I had the strong impression that the minister felt guilty about the whole affair, but in Saddam Hussein's Iraq it is more than a government minister's job, and maybe his life, is worth to defend a man whom the President has declared to be a spy. Perhaps the empty armchair was a continual reproach, and talking to me about it was a kind of quietus.

I spent seven troubled days with a camera crew in Iraq, during which we were followed, bugged, criticised and censored more intensively than in any country I can remember. Shortly before we left we were told that our video cassettes contained 'bad pictures', and that we would not be allowed to take them out of the country. The BBC's television audience will not therefore see schoolchildren being taught English by means of the chant 'Long live our President, Saddam Hussein! Long live our Party!' Nor will it see the full details of the extraordinary victory monument which was designed by Saddam himself to mark the end of the [first] Gulf War: two monstrous crossed scimitars held in hands modelled upon his own, with a tassel descending from each pommel and made up of a net containing hundreds of Iranian helmets, most of them bearing bullet or shrapnel holes. Between the two scimitars is a pathway studded with more helmets. In early Babylonian fashion one walks on the skulls of Saddam's enemies.

Baghdad, too, is like Babylon: rebuilt from scratch by Saddam in his own image, and thereby deprived of any real life of its own. It is quiet and dull, and the people do not want to talk to foreigners. It must be the only place in the entire Middle East where the shopkeepers fall silent when a Westerner comes along. As I wandered round a market-place, conscious of the minder following me, no one met my eyes or tried to sell me something or asked me in for a glass of tea.

In Saddam's Iraq there is no sign of independent thought, let alone opposition. In 1986 and 1987, when the war with Iran seemed to be going badly for him, the list of offences which merited the death penalty was lengthened to 29. It was already an offence punishable by death for someone to leave the ruling Ba'ath Party or to persuade others to leave it. 'A law is a piece of paper on which we write one or two lines and sign underneath it, Saddam Hussein, President of the Republic': Saddam Hussein.

History too is a piece of paper on which Saddam Hussein writes his own lines. At a school where the children chanted in praise of their President, the headmistress, a large lady with blonde hair, handed me some literature about Iranian war crimes. The school itself had suffered badly in an Iranian rocket attack two years before, and 43 children died. As a result it is a showpiece where visitors go to recharge their batteries of indignation. I leafed through one of the pamphlets. 'The inhabitants of Halabje,' said the accompanying text, 'were destroyed in an attack of chemical warfare by Iran.' Halabje is a Kurdish town in north-eastern Iraq. In 1988 it went over to the Iranian side in the war, and paid the penalty. I saw the results for myself when I went there two days later. The streets were clogged with the bodies of the inhabitants; Iraqi jets, not Iranian ones, had bombarded them with a selection of chemical weapons – mustard gas, nerve gas, cyanide. Now it is Saddam's crime no longer. His propaganda machine, like Stalin's after Katyn, blames it all on his enemies. Halabje, by the way, has been rebuilt and renamed 'Saddam'.

Nevertheless the more Western politicians and journalists criticise Iraq, the more support Saddam receives. I was in Baghdad to cover a pan-Arab conference to protest against the supposed campaign which was being waged against Iraq by Britain. Speaker after speaker, and by no means only those from the radical fringe, believed that Britain dragged up criticisms of Saddam and intervened to stop the flow of military technology to him because of Israeli pressure. The West, they said, was afraid of Saddam because he was strong and independent.

But if we help Saddam's cause by attacking him, what else can we do about him? To treat him as we treat Syria and Iran, and pretend he does not exist, leads nowhere. To wince at his misdeeds, but go on supplying him with the tools of his trade, is irresponsible. There may be a third strategy. During the war with Iran Saddam's régime reached new heights of repression and violence. But, now the war is over, he has promised to reform the constitution and allow a freer press and the legalisation of political parties. He doubtless intends the changes to be purely cosmetic – but it may be possible to encourage him to go further than he now plans. It is the only real hope.

My colleagues and I finally made our way through to the various controls and into the departure lounge at Saddam International Airport. We were glad to be leaving, but depressed at the thought that we had lost the videotapes which represented all our work. I wandered into the duty-free shop and distractedly looked at the display of watches. There lay a gimcrack pocket-watch in imitation gold; on it was the smiling face of Saddam Hussein, rebuilder of Babylon, victor of the Iran-Iraq war, the new Nasser of the Arab world.

'Do you sell many of these things?' I asked.

The woman behind the counter glanced at an Iraqi who didn't look like a passenger. She shrugged helplessly. Until there is real change in Saddam's Iraq, even the sale of political kitsch is best not discussed.

19 May 1990

'Whatever you do, don't drink the water.'

DEATH OF A PRECEDENT

Vicki Woods

The first job I ever had that wasn't paid by the day and in cash was as a junior sub-editor on *Harpers & Queen*. I was 20, and from a northern grammar school; everyone else was from St Mary's, Calne. It took *Harpers* years to train me to work on Mrs Betty Kenward's Jennifer's Diary column, where I had a crash course in everything pertaining to Society. I learned about correct forms of address, the Season, the order of precedence as laid down by *Debrett's* and how to plan a marquee wedding for 700 guests. It was a double life. I would leave my peeling squat in the Caledonian Road, walk to the office (*H & Q* paid very little) and spend long afternoons waiting for Mrs Kenward to get back from Ladies' Day and go through her galleys with me. Mrs Kenward would say baffling things ('She's a duke's daughter, so we'll put her here, d'you see?') and I would keep stumm – until I learned the form. The correct form. When I left, I knew how to find people in *Debrett's* and how to address a duke. 'Good morning, Duke,' I said, to the few dukes I met subsequently.

My next job (I left the squat, too) was on *Radio Times*, which was more . . . egalitarian, and the only really pressing problems were the newly fashionable anti-sexist ones: 'Above, Wogan and Gloria enjoying a joke – NB from VW: should this be Wogan and Hunniford or Terry and Gloria? Ed to VW: No!' and so forth. Until one day, I was asked to check the captions on some framed copper plates which were to be handed over in ten minutes' time to the all-time-great cover stars of *Radio Times*. I said, 'They're all OK, except this one, Lady Isobel Barnet.' The chief sub said, 'Yes, it's OK, she's I-S-O, one T. She used to be on *What's My Line?*' I said, 'Is she the daughter of a duke, marquess or earl?' and a baffled silence fell. 'Because if she isn't, it shouldn't be Lady Isobel Barnet. It should be Lady Barnet. It could be Lady (Isobel) Barnet,' I said, remembering the way Mrs Kenward used to solve her problems over the multiplicity of Lady Birdwoods. 'Or Isobel Barnet without the Lady, if that's how she's known professionally' – but the chief sub lost his rag completely and said it didn't matter a toss. That's what he said. To dukes' daughters it matters – I persisted, strong in my knowledge – and to anybody who cares about being correct. He said, 'Nobody cares about being "correct" any more. Christ, what year is this?'

It was 1975. But it has taken 15 years – until this month – for the editor of the *Times* to agree with the chief sub of *Radio Times* that nobody cares about being correct any more, and run its Forthcoming Marriages column alphabetically down the Court and Social page, instead of in a 'seemly order' based on the order of precedence of the United Kingdom as laid down in *Debrett's* and following through with the services in order of rank, unless the ranks are equal – then it's navy first, followed by army and air force. Up and down the land I hear the noise of the mourning of a mighty nation. 'When I saw Lord Mancroft halfway down the column, I *smarted* for him,' Peter Townend of *Tatler* told me, with his peculiar mixture of scandal and glee. 'And my poor friend Michael Naylor-Leyland, who's announced his engagement to one of old Prince Georg of Hanover's granddaughters! In the old days, he'd have been at the top of the column, obviously. At least Mr Wilson, no matter what his *tendencies* were, didn't meddle with the order.'

Simon Jenkins's tendencies are unknown to me, but he is getting very terse about this whining on about a 'seemly order'. He changed it on the *Times* because he felt it was no longer justified; and it's a terribly minor matter; and he hasn't had any cross letters from readers; and 'What do you mean, what did my social editor say? What would you expect her to say? I told her what I wanted done, and she did it.'

Is it a terribly minor matter? On the *Times*? The *Telegraph* still prints names in the old order; the *Independent* prints very few and those few alphabetically (the *Times* envies the younger, *moderne*, classless, meritocratic profile of the *Independent*). The *Guardian's* switchboard, asked for 'Social Editor', puts you through to the 'Society' page, which is about low-cost housing, cuts in the NHS and recreational play-schemes in the Wirral. 'We have never run a Court and Social page,' said the obituaries editor. Citizen Maxwell runs no Court and Social pages on the *European*. I wish he would; it would be dizzying. *Debrett's* is a breeze compared to *Almanach de Gotha*.

19 May 1990

VULTURES OVER THE BUNGALOWS

William Dalrymple

One of the great pleasures of living in New Delhi is that it is quite possible to forget that the second half of the 20th century ever happened. Sitting in the garden of one of the great Lutyens bungalows, a glass to hand, your legs raised up on a Bombay Fornicator (one of those wickerwork chairs with extended arms, essential to every Raj verandah), in front of you lies a long lawn dotted with croquet hoops; behind, the white bow-front of one of this century's happiest residential designs. Over the treetops there is not a skyscraper to be seen. You are not in some leafy suburb, but in the very centre of New Delhi. Its low-rise townscape is unique among modern capitals, the last surviving reminder of the town planning of a more relaxed and elegant age.

Sadly, it now seems as if the days of Lutyens's Delhi are numbered. The destruction has already begun. Ravi Bedi, a hawk-eyed Punjabi businessman, was one of the first to grasp the money-making possibilities inherent in its demise. In February 1984 he called in the demolition heavies. It took only two weeks to smash down the white neo-classical bungalow that his father had bought from the British. The two acres of garden went under concrete, to provide space for car-parking. The 42 identical concrete flats (christened Marble Arch Apartments) were ready by the summer of 1987. The going rate was then about $100,000 for a small flat, double that for a large one. Since 1987 the price of Mr Bedi's flats has risen by 100 per cent. Each flat is now worth as much as his entire bungalow was worth ten years ago.

Money on this scale cannot be kept quiet. Mr Bedi's neighbours have followed his lead, and the demolition bug has now spread all the way down Prithviraj Road and into the neighbouring streets. Most of the planners and architects I talked to agree that it now looks extremely unlikely that there will be a single private Lutyens bungalow left undemolished in New Delhi by the middle of this decade.

New Delhi is still one of the most elegant capitals in the world. With its undeviating geometrical layout and solid neo-classical buildings, Lutyens believed that he had built a 'symbol of the spirit and permanence of British rule'. And although it is the great monumental structures – Lutyens's Viceroy's House and Baker's two Secretariats – which are justly the most famous buildings in New Delhi, it is the smaller domestic buildings which give the city its character. From wide avenues shaded by neem, tamarind and arjuna, low red-brick walls give on to rambling white bungalows supported by broken pediments and tall Ionic pillars. Most of these domestic buildings went to senior government and military office holders and these still remain government property. The remaining 40 per cent were given away in perpetuity to the maharajahs, to the contractors who had helped build the new city and to some very senior Indian civil servants. It is these buildings, now the property of the original owners' children and grandchildren, which are currently being demolished.

Behind the demolitions lies the phenomenal growth of Delhi's population and the dramatic real-estate boom that this has brought. When Lutyens was planning New Delhi he envisaged a population of no more than 500,000. The mass influx of refugees from Pakistan following Partition put an end to such cosy schemes. By 1951 the population had grown to 1.3 million, and 30 years after that New Delhi was the home of nearly six million people. Planners expect the population to top 15 million by the end of the century. These people all have to be housed.

Already there have been some tragic losses. On Kasturba Gandhi Marg (née Curzon Road) only a couple of the original villas still survive. As was appropriate for a road named after Curzon, the houses here were of a most superior design: large, spacious two-storey buildings with lovely shady balconies covered with climbing jasmine

'Right Mr Jones, I'd like you to hot wire the ignition!'

and bougainvillaea. The backs of the buildings had bow-fronts, and gave on to spacious four-acre gardens. Of the two survivors, one is now in severe disrepair. Its plaster is peeling, its garden overgrown and in front of the gate stands a huge sign:

A PROJECT FROM THE HOUSE OF EROS
ULTRAMODERN DELUXE MULTI-
STOREYED RESIDENCE APTS.
COMPLETION DATE 1992

Sadder still is the loss of one very modest cottage in Aurangazeb Road. This is the house where Lutyens lived when he was first planning, then building, New Delhi. In any other country such a place would be a national monument, even a place of pilgrimage. In India the building was regarded as old-fashioned and uneconomic. When the cottage and its adjoining buildings changed hands five years ago, the bulldozers were called in. Along with it went a delightful two-storey folly, the remains of an early Mogul hunting lodge. The site is now occupied by one of the ugliest tower blocks in New Delhi.

Most conservationists now regard the battle to save the remaining private bungalows as lost, despite a temporary freeze on new applications for development. The question is for how long the government bungalows can be saved from a similar fate. The trouble is that the bungalows themselves strengthen the hands of the developers. When New Delhi was built the residential areas were considered to be a very uncertain investment. The Raj could easily have decided to move its capital back to Calcutta – after all new cities have a very bad track record in India: look at Fatehpur Sikri. As a result the contractors who built the city tended to economise on materials, just in case. Now 70 years after the first of them went up, they are all beginning to rot. Many people in New Delhi have stories of how they left the bedroom/bathroom/sitting-room just seconds before the ceiling fell in.

The other day I visited the house of a friend of mine. It is a massive, rambling affair with long lawns and jungly shrubberies – but it is badly maintained, and rapidly falling to bits. After a couple of drinks, I plucked up the courage to suggest that she should consider renovating the house.

'You can't have had it repainted for 20 years,' I said.

'Wrong,' she replied; 'we completely renovated, replastered and repainted it eight months ago.'

According to my friend it's not only the old buildings that are going to pass away within the next few years: the trees, all planted within a few months of each other in the early 1920s, have also come to the end of their life.

Meanwhile the vultures are gathering. Mr Kailash Nath is the father of high-rise Delhi. In 1966 he built Himalaya House, Delhi's first multi-storeyed building. Since then he has been ceaselessly campaigning for the lifting of all planning restrictions. 'Lutyens's Delhi is a passing phase,' he told me, sipping his imported whisky. 'You cannot allow people to have four-acre gardens while others are sleeping in the streets. At last people are beginning to see sense. By 2050 – at the very latest – it will all have gone.'

He rubbed his fingers in anticipation.

'The lot. Delhi will be a modern, multi-storeyed city at long last.'

19 May 1990

THE LOWER DEPTHS

Richard Lovelace

I have travelled quite widely, perhaps to 80 countries: except where there is famine, the worst poverty is in England. I do not mean worst physically, of course, but worst spiritually, for our poor are deprived both of the pride of achievement in having survived another day, and of any hope of improvement. And our poor are far more numerous than those in comfortable circumstances would like to suppose.

Recently I spent a couple of months as a doctor in the slums of Birmingham. They are very extensive, and appear to be spreading: streets with perfectly decent and spacious housing have been turned into slums, with boarded-up windows, graffiti, litter, potholes in the road, and unemployed young men standing on the corner looking malevolently at the world.

The first thing one notices is that the city is a visual inferno, from the litter swirling at one's feet to the Corbusierian tower blocks (all of whose entrance halls and lifts smell of urine) on the horizon, from the tangle of concrete flyovers above to the derelict factories below, from the patches of wasteground strewn with rubble, where scrubby bushes grow trailing tatters of filthy polythene, to the advertising hoardings enjoining the inhabitants to buy BMWs and avoid drugs. Many of the people on the street appear shrunken and prematurely aged, their health destroyed by poverty and a diet of pork pies and cigarettes, as they shuffle along in their jumble-sale clothes. Many are the dark little shops that sell dilapidated furniture and old clothing; those that sell food are eloquent testimony to the restricted tastes and pockets of the local residents. One striking feature of the landscape is that the worse the housing, the greater the number of satellite dishes that provide the junk food of the mind.

Alas, alas for England! In two months I did not meet one white patient who had been educated for longer than the minimum period prescribed by law, or who was encouraging his children to stay at school beyond the age of 16. No, not one; though I met several virtual illiterates – illiterate, that is, after 11 years of compulsory schooling. In this area, it was far more common for a man to go to prison than to university; and I met no one who showed the faintest understanding of the necessity for, or advantages of, education.

In case you imagine I am referring to an isolated pocket of the country, I should like to point out that 60 per cent of our people receive no formal education beyond the minimum. Let those who think, or once thought, that the teaching of grammar is a bourgeois tyranny imposed upon the working class, listen to the uneducated trying to express their emotions or frustrations in words other than expletives! Let them hear the broken fragments of sentences, the long silences during which patients struggle to find the words that will not come because they are not there, let them see the jaws of patients drop open when a word of more than two syllables is inadvertently used, and

then let them prattle about the glories of untutored self-expression!

Often patients came with a vague sense of dissatisfaction with the whole of their lives. Intelligent yet inarticulate, it soon became clear they wanted more from their existence than their birthright of vile food, unskilled work (if any work at all), the pub, domestic violence and squalor, and an old age of increasing poverty. But they had no notion of how to escape it; at school they had been subject to all kinds of social pressures actively to prevent them from learning; their children would follow the same path to perdition.

What is the solution to all this human devastation? More taxes and more public expenditure? Perhaps, but the Japanese, with the highest standard of education in the world, have schools with 90 children to the class; countries with fewer doctors than we do have better health. I do not see how faith in mass public housing can survive even a brief acquaintance with what has been done in this direction in the past. The problem, if it is any one single problem, is cultural, and thus not amenable to simple rectification. Improvement, if it happens at all, will be a prolonged process, more the result of a change of heart than of policy. Those who talk of a more *caring* society often appear to mean by it a society with larger and better paid bureaucracies.

As it happens, a model of improvement exists on the doorstep. I am referring to immigrants from the Indian subcontinent. Their cultural level is altogether higher; they are polite, they do not tattoo themselves from head to toe like Neanderthal tribesmen, they work hard, they aspire to something more than a video recorder on which to watch violent drivel. Above all they acknowledge an obligation to do the best they can for their children. They understand the worth, in more senses than one, of education, even when they are uneducated themselves.

They are not paragons of course: often the young women in their communities (and their communities *are* communities, not the euphemistic abstraction into which mental patients are being discharged from our asylums) are torn apart by a conflict between personal liberty and a strictly imposed cultural tradition, with dire consequences. And one notices not without a certain tremulation signs of sectarian and religious enthusiasm among them: painted slogans in favour of Khalistan, for example, or a butcher's shop more concerned with propagating an intolerant form of Islam, with displays of crude anti-Christian propaganda in the window, than with selling meat. But, taken all in all, they present the spectacle of people who require only opportunity to advance themselves, who will not always live in slums, and who will make a contribution to civilised life.

The young natives, by contrast, appear destined for a life of barbarism, or at least of pathetically reduced horizons. We seem to have bred half a nation of unemployables, covetous and resentful, aware of rights but disdainful of opportunity, lazy yet discontented with the fruits of laziness, prickly but without pride or self-respect, philistine and contemptuous of what they do not know, politically radical, perhaps, but unwilling personally to change. I fear for the future.

26 May 1990

THE COLONEL'S DAUGHTERS

William Dalrymple

To Kipling, Simla was a place of illicit romance. In story after story of *Plain Tales from the Hills*, the same plot repeats itself: after the boredom of a remote posting in the plains, the young Englishman goes up to Simla where, bowled over by the sudden glut of fair young English women, he falls in love with a Mrs Hauksbee or a Mrs Reiver – one of Simla's carnivorous memsahibs: 'He rode with her, and walked with her, and picnicked with her, and tiffined at Peliti's with her, till people put up their eyebrows and said, "Shocking!"'

Today it takes a tremendous leap of imagination to see the old summer capital as it was seen by the Victorians – to feel the sexual frisson they must have felt when they set out on their first promenade to Scandal Point. For Simla, although run down, is now a strangely prurient place. The Punjabi holidaymakers who today strut up The Mall seem to feel a bit out of place in the half-timbered mock-Tudor High Street, and they take refuge in a self-conscious formality. Everyone is on best behaviour. They dress smartly – in tweeds and ties and headscarves – and complement the outfit with a walking stick bought from the Lakkar Bazaar. Children who slurp their ice creams are told off: you don't slurp ice creams in Simla.

The constricting shadow of the English lies everywhere: in the shooting sticks and riding whips in the shops; in the net-curtained windows of the bungalows named 'Pine Breezes' and 'Fair View'; in the crumbles and custards on the boarding house menus. But of the English themselves there is only one well-stocked cemetery, and, as the manager of Clerk's Hotel told me, two frail old ladies, a pair of unmarried sisters, the last stayers-on in Simla. On my last day in the hills I decided to pay them a call.

It was not difficult to find them. At Clerk's I was pointed in the general direction of the old Viceregal Lodge (now the Indian Institute of Advanced Studies – a kind of Subcontinental All Souls). From there we were directed from chai shop to chai shop ('The memsahibs? Go straight, then turning left') until we came to their bungalow.

It was a rude shock. In my last summer at Cambridge I had earned a free trip to India by writing an article on the stayers-on for a glossy magazine. Then I had found, to my surprise, that most of the 200-odd stayers-on were in fact fairly well off. Contrary to the myth spread by Paul Scott's novel, it turned out that the typical stayer-on tended to own stud farms and polo ponies, ran gentlemen's clubs or tea plantations, spent his free time sipping chota pegs of pink gin and fussing over the health of his packs of labradors and King Charles spaniels. But the two sisters in Simla were clearly very different from this set – as one look at their tatty and peeling bungalow revealed.

The house had once been quite grand – a rambling, half-timbered affair with a wide verandah and cusped Swiss gables. It was surrounded by a scattering of out-houses of different sizes for guests and servants, and was reached through a gate-house looking out onto the deodars of Summer Hill, the seat of the Viceroy. But the estate had clearly fallen on hard times. Only thin, peeling strips of burnt sienna indicated that the house had ever been painted. A tangle of thorns had overcome the near-side of the verandah and docks and ragwort grew from between the paving stones of the path.

At first I thought no one was at home. But after ten minutes of knocking on doors and peering through windows, I was rewarded with the sight of one of the sisters hobbling across her sitting-room. She undid the multiple bolts of the door and slumped down in one of the wickerwork chairs on the verandah.

'And who are you?' she asked.

I explained, and to make conversation complimented her on the view from her front door.

'It may be beautiful to you,' she said abruptly. 'But it's not beautiful to us. We want to go back home.'

Doris Heysham was a frail old woman with mottled brown skin and unkempt grey hair. Her tweed skirt was extravagantly darned and her thick brown tights were shredded with a jigsaw of tears and ladders.

'We want to sell up,' she continued. 'We've been through a very bad time. There are prostitutes living all over the place – making life hell for us. They say we're English and shouldn't be here. After 78 years!'

Doris grunted angrily and began rapping on the front door with her stick:

'Irene! Irene! There's a boy here to see us. Says he's British.'

Then she turned around and began talking to me in a stage whisper: 'She had a fall today. The prostitutes put dope down the chimney. It makes her want to sleep. She fell on the fender – bleeding from 8 a.m. until after lunch. They're trying to drive us out you see.'

'It's not just dope down the chimney,' said Irene who had at this point appeared at the door. 'They come through the floorboards at night.'

'Through the floorboards? Are you sure?' I asked.

'Of course I'm sure. When we're asleep they put stuff in our eyes to make us go blind. Every day my sight gets a little worse. You have no idea what we've gone through.'

'You know something,' said Doris leaning forward towards me and continuing to speak in her conspiratorial stage whisper. 'They're all *Jews*. All of 'em. They're as fair as lilies but they wear these brown masks so as to pass off as natives. They've been persecuting us for 20 years.'

'Thirty years, Doris.'

'Since Partition, in fact.'

'But we're not going to give in, are we darling? We're not going to cut and run.'

At this point the drizzle which had followed me to the bungalow turned into a downpour. The water dripped through the roof of the verandah and we decided to move inside. From the sitting room I could see the half-lit bedroom. To one side of the bed was an upturned chest of drawers, on the other an inverted ironing board.

'That's to stop the Jewish prostitutes from coming in through the floorboards,' said Doris, seeing where I was looking.

'But they still come down the chimney,' said Irene.

'Oh – they'll do anything to drive us out. They've even started watching us bathe. They peer through the window as if we're some sort of ha'penny peepshow.'

We arranged ourselves around a table and Doris poured the tea.

'Just look at my hands shake,' she said.

'It's the prostitutes' dope,' said Irene.

'Makes me shake like a Quaker and dribble like a dog. I used to be hale and hearty, too.'

'Very hale and hearty, my sister was. Those prostitutes should be shot on sight.'

The two sisters fussed around with their teacups, trying to spoon in the sugar and the powdered milk before their shakes sprinkled the stuff over the table. At length, when this was achieved and they had relaxed, I turned the conversation towards their memories of Simla in the old days – what I suppose I had come to hear.

'Oh it was all such fun when we were young and blonde and had admirers. At night we went to the dances and drank champagne and by day we would sit up here and watch the soldiers riding past, four abreast. Those were the days.'

'But my God has it changed. Imagine – I now do my own sweeping . . .'

'. . . and the cooking and the cleaning and the laundry. Us – colonel's daughters.'

'Don't complain, my dear. We could do worse.'

'My aunt's husband was in the 23rd Punjabi's. I told the grocery boy last week. The twenty-thirds! He couldn't believe such grand people lived in such . . .'

'Simplicity,' said Irene.

'Exactly,' said Doris. 'Simplicity.' You know, Mr Dalrymple, you people today can have no idea what India was like before. It was . . . just like England.'

'Shut up, darling. The prostitutes – they'll report us. They've got microphones. Speak softly.'

'I will not. The wickedness! Tell them to go to the devil.'

'The wages of sin, Mac, have to keep pace with inflation.'

'Our brothers would have shown them. Charlie would.'

'So would Frank.'

There was a pause.

'Both dead now,' explained Irene.

The two sisters sipped angrily at their tea. They were silent for a second, but suddenly Doris sprang back to life.

'But you know the worst thing. Those Jewish prostitutes. They tried to . . .'

'Don't, Doris.'

'I will. You can't gag a Heysham of Heysham. They tried to put us in a madhouse. We were out for a walk and they started to drag us down the road. And I said: "This isn't the way home."'

'Damn cheek. A colonel's daughter.'

'The warders were very nice to us. We stayed there two weeks. Then a young police officer came and said: "Who put you here?" He went to the IG – the Inspector General – and by four o'clock we were back here. The IG ordered us to be brought home. All the other inmates were delighted.'

'Imagine putting two elderly people in a madhouse. Those prostitutes – they're from Baghdad you see. They were able to do it because they have a money-minting machine, and were able to bribe the inspectors.'

'They use us as a respectable cover for their operations. That's why we're going to leave this place – as soon as we can sell the house. We've had enough of Simla.'

'More than enough. We've had an offer for one lakh rupees [£3,000] from this man. If we can get two lakhs we'll be off home.'

'We thought we'd try Ooty first. Get a taxi to Delhi, then a flight to Coimbatore, then a car up into the Nilgiris.'

'It used to be lovely in Ooty. Just like England.'

'But if we have no luck there we thought we'd find a house in Wales. With two lakhs you could get a nice house in Wales, I'd have thought.'

Looking at my watch I saw it was time for me to leave: my train back to Delhi was leaving in less than an hour. Wishing them luck, I got up, said my goodbyes, and promised to send the English brassières and stockings they had asked for ('Indian women have the strangest shaped breasts'). They heaved themselves up and saw me to the door. But just as I was setting off down the garden path, Doris called me back.

'One last thing,' she said, clenching my hand in her claw-like grip. 'Just watch out.'

'What do you mean?' I asked, surprised.

'Look after yourself,' she said earnestly. 'Don't drink anything strange – or anything bitter. Watch out for the smell of bitter almonds. The Jews will be after you now – after you've tried to help the Heyshams. You're not safe.'

I thanked her again and opened the wicket gate. As I closed it, I heard her shouting behind me:

'Take it from a colonel's daughter.'

2 June 1990

PILGRIMAGE TO CALAIS

Nicky Bird

'A bigger f——ing shambles than 50 years ago,' grumbled a Rifle Brigade veteran. A true Rifleman – chirpy and profane, an indomitable whinger.

He'd stood for over an hour on the mole, the place where his regiment and the King's Royal Rifle Corps were landed on 23 May 1940. The ceremony was late and long, and the sun and the army's organisation threatened to kill the remnants Hitler had spared.

Thankfully the Duke of Gloucester came and went, shook hands, exchanged banalities ('Were you captured?' 'Yes.' 'What was it like?' 'Dull.') and left before any fatalities. The Greenjackets' chummy ship, HMS *Alacrity*, drowned out the address and the band. The march-past by the ancient survivors was more impressive than the shambling young French soldiers who followed. We seated relatives took photos of the veterans and they took photos of us. We clapped them as they marched and they looked embarrassed. Then it was off to the coaches and the Mairie for speeches, mutual flattery and champagne to make the *entente* more *cordiale*.

I am here because my father's brother, Lieutenant Edward Bird of the 1st Battalion Rifle Brigade, was killed at Calais on 25 May 1940. He was 24 and had been married four months. At the moment of Edward's death my father, who was in the desert with the 2nd Battalion, woke in the night and knew that Edward had been killed. My father and Edward's widow Elspeth are here with my mother and brother, who is named after Edward. We have never been quite sure how Edward died. We know he was killed while trying to rescue a lorry-load of wounded. But did he die instantly? Or later?

Local girls in traditional costume greet us at the Mairie, it is all a bit Ruritanian. The room is suitably gilded, vast and pompous. As we listen to the mayor's speech the champagne corks remain bolted to the bottles. This is not good for Anglo-French relations. Nor is the expletive 'bollocks' muttered behind me when mention is made of French gallantry during the defence of Calais. 'The only Frog soldiers I saw during the battle were the ones who clambered onto the ship when we landed, or the ones who shot at us from behind,' I heard an old 60th man say. Later that night several veterans claimed that fifth columnists behind them were 'a bloody nuisance'.

The Duke's speech was to end with a toast to something or other, so the concluding paragraphs were smothered by an explosion of popping, as the booze was belatedly doled out. Old soldiers never die, they just get to the bar first, as I found to my cost.

Commemorations of great military events or disasters honour the dead who fought 'to preserve our cherished freedoms'. 'Nonsense,' said a QVR man, 'Freddy died fighting for S Company, not for democracy. And he most certainly did not "give" his life like a donation to a cause.'

We like to believe that the dead died in 'a good show'. Calais was an accident and a cock-up.

The three rifle battalions were originally meant to link up with the 3rd Royal Tank Regiment, already in Calais, and push south-west of the town to harry the enemy. But on 24 May it became clear that the Germans were stronger than realised and the commander, Brigadier Nicholson, decided all he could do was to try to hold the port. The signal for evacuation came the same day but Churchill ordered the defence of Calais to the last round the next day – 'Evacuation will not (repeat *not*) take place.' Boats were needed at Dunkirk. Pressure of events had dictated strategy.

The strength and speed of the German advance and the chaotic docks conditions – few cranes, no tugs, no French dockers – scuppered the Light Division's mission. Crucially they had no effective anti-tank weapons.

Churchill justified the disastrous loss of élite battalions by calling Calais the 'crux' that saved Dunkirk.

'Of course,' said a retired regular, 'if we'd known how good Jerry was and what little equipment we'd get off, we wouldn't have gone. But we did. And we tied down two armoured divisions. The Graveline waterline was held. And Dunkirk was evacuated. My friends did not die in vain.'

Or as a CSM said to me, 'It was a balls-up, but we got a result.'

After the reception we toddle off to the buses for lunch, officers and relatives to the excellent Channel restaurant (menu à 200 francs), other ranks to the mercies of British Legion catering. Even in old age messing is separate. As we're getting into our coach Aunt Elspeth finds Sergeant Davey, now a Chelsea pensioner, who was with Edward at the end. My father asks him how he died.

'The lorry full of RB wounded was hit some distance from our lines and the driver disabled. The wounded were trying to crawl out. Your brother ran from his trench to restart the lorry but was hit in the head. Here.' He points to his right temple. 'He died immediately. When the fight was over I put his body in the back with the wounded myself. He was a good officer. He'd always tell you how to get off a charge. I've often wondered about his family. Goodbye, I won't see you again,' and he shook our hands and went to his coach, curiously comforted, as we were.

After lunch, in the hideous Place des Armes, Albert Speer's idea of a cosy square perhaps, the bands march up and down in the heat playing medleys from the Lloyd Webber songbook. There are snipers on the roofs to protect the Duke, and a lone bugler on the pizza parlour. 'What's he doing up there?' I ask a Greenjacket officer. 'Bugling.'

The bandsmen charge around the square at the traditional furious pace. It goes on far too long but the French seem to like it. Then it's back to our coach for the trip to the Rifle Brigade cemetery and a tour of the battlefield.

In the coach a lady from *Soldier* magazine sits next to Elspeth. She talks of Edward. Elspeth doesn't want to. 'Can I interview you?' says the lady. Pause. 'No,' says Elspeth and looks out of the window and is quiet.

The tour leader hands out a list of Rifle Brigade officers and men buried in the cemetery. Edward's name is not among them. But he will be there under a nameless stone, 'Known unto God.'

It is a hot evening in the cemetery, a dignified plot hedged off from vast grotesque local tombs. 'Bob's over there,' grunts one Rifleman to another and I glance in Bob's direction thinking I'll see a man with medals clanking. I see the grave of a man aged 19. Elspeth and Major Brush's widow stand in front of Jerry Duncanson's grave. He killed the last German of the battle and was then killed himself. Earlier he'd shot down an enemy plane with his Bren. He'd enjoyed his last days hugely. 'Did you know him?' asks Mrs Brush. 'Yes,' says Elspeth, 'he lent us his house.' 'I find this all very nostalgic and moving,' says Mrs Brush and I hide behind the memorial in case she cries.

It has not been a tearful occasion, more a jolly reunion. But as we are leaving an old bugler stands rigid in front of the cross and blows the Last Post. His puff is not what it was and it is agony and yet we are all terribly affected by his wavering tribute. He finishes at last, thank God, and salutes.

And at the end there is a telling moment. I ask a Rifleman who fought there to describe what happened 50 years ago.

'I haven't a clue,' he says. 'I hadn't then and I haven't now.'

2 June 1990

'And on the left we have the Tuileries.'

MR HONDA GOES TO WASHINGTON

Ian Buruma

Washington

The names are impressive, a veritable roll-call of big Washington players: Elliot L. Richardson, the former attorney-general, William E. Brock, ex-agriculture secretary, William Eberle and Robert S. Strauss, former US trade representatives, and the former Republican chairman, Frank Fahrenkopf. What they have in common, besides a predominance of German genes, is that all now work in some capacity for Japanese interests – Hitachi, Toyota, Fujistu – and all are under attack for doing so.

'Yep,' said the sharp young Washington lawyer, as we peered down at the White House from his office window, 'it's the best view in town.' We were talking about the so-called Japan lobby. Bill (not his real name) believes that the United States is at war with Japan, an economic war. And he is angry and frustrated that his fellow Americans fail to recognise this: 'It's a bit like Winston Churchill warning the British about the German threat in the 1930s. It's that serious.'

Bill is particularly incensed about what he calls 'the fifth column in our midst', the lawyers, Congressmen, former trade representatives, think-tank pundits, academics, and other assorted Americans who all, in one way or another, make a living defending Japanese interests. Almost every law firm in Washington has big Japanese corporate clients, most academic institutions studying Japanese affairs rely on Japanese funds, and Americans in government know that lucrative consulting jobs for Japanese corporations await them as soon as they resign from public office. In one famous instance, an official called Robert E. Watkins was sending out his CV to Japanese car firms, even as he was negotiating with the Japanese government about opening their market to American car parts. He was forced to resign.

But what about the other lobbies in Washington? I asked Bill. Surely the Japanese were not the only players in town. 'Indeed,' he replied, 'the Israeli lobby is more influential, but at least Israel isn't at war with us. The Japanese want to take over the world. They are buying everybody. They are *sui generis*, polluting the American system . . .'

The word 'polluting' reminded me of another critic of Japan I had interviewed in the capital of fixers, a well-known expert on international relations called Ronald A. Morse. He had used medical language to describe the gravity of the situation: the American economy was a dying body, being destroyed from within by a malignancy. The fatal germs included 'agents of foreign interests' lobbying for absolute free trade. This was eroding the independence and the wealth-producing capacity of the United States, since the country benefiting most from free trade, Japan, was not practising at home what she was preaching abroad.

But now for the other side of the story. Christopher Nelson used to work as an aide in the Senate. He is now a prospering consultant for a Japanese firm, or, to put it more crudely, a lobbyist. Nelson stated his case sharply and succinctly: Japan could not be blamed for America's ills; the real problem was American profligacy, the budget deficit; indeed, the Japanese were a great boon to the American economy – without their investments, their factories, and their cheap and excellent products, Americans would be much worse off. 'You know,' he almost whispered, 'much of this criticism is really racist.' There it was, the dreaded word. I knew it would come. And he knew it didn't quite wash, so he didn't mention it again.

It was of course perfectly clear where Bill and Christopher were, to use an Americanism, 'coming from'. Bill's law firm handles the affairs of some major American industries, while Nelson worked for what Bill called 'the other side'. Both men were playing the Washington game. It is the way the American system works. In principle, no person or institution can grab absolute power in a system built on the representation of conflicting interests. Lobbying, in other words, is the very stuff of American politics. It is more disreputable to lobby than it is to defend the interests of a client in a court of law. Sincerity is not the point, argument is, interests are. When I left Bill's office, he shook my hand and said: 'Send me your article, and if it's good I might pass it on to Senator Dole.' I told this story to a friend. 'Welcome to Washington,' he said.

So one might say that little is new. All that has changed is that whereas before it was mostly American interest that contended for government favours, the same game is now being played by agents of a strong foreign power. If one believes that free trade knows no borders, there is nothing wrong with this. Three cheers for the consumer and let the Americans put their own house in order. Unfortunately, it is not quite so simple.

The open society breeds its own forms of corruption, just as closed societies do. The fact that almost anything and anybody is for sale makes it difficult for a government to define its national interests. There are simply too many other interests, private and corporate, to consider. Indeed, the idea that there is not one national interest lies at the heart of the American system. So perhaps corruption isn't quite the right word. Certainly money alone does not corrupt. The heady access to power that is one of the most exhilarating aspects of American society (*Mr Smith Goes to Washington* and all that) has made influence-peddling almost as common an activity in American academe as fund-raising. As a result, analysis independent of political or financial interests has become a rare commodity in America, particularly on the East Coast, where much of the financial and political action is. And when the academics, pundits and experts, who are supposed to provide the ideas that might help to define national interests, become too dependent on funds provided by one source, Japan for example, the arguments tend to reflect this. So if the Japanese are screwing Uncle Sam, the old man certainly asked for it.

The money involved in the alleged buying of America's minds is indeed considerable – twice as much as the fee paid by Canadian interests, which follow Japan's in the league of lobbies. Pat Choate, vice-president of TRW, a firm that sells satellites among other things, believes that the Japanese and their American affiliates spend at least $100 million a year on lawyers, lobbyists and consultants in Washington. And Chalmers Johnson, the leading scholar of Japanese studies at the University of California, San Diego, estimates that three-quarters of American university research on Japan is financed by Japanese. Both men play prominent roles in the 'Japan debate': Johnson as a critic of classical free trade ideology, and Choate as the author of a book, which will appear in the autumn, fingering all the Americans working, overtly or covertly, for the Japanese lobby. The title of his book, which already is sending shivers up many Washington spines, is *Agents of Influence*. Even before its publication, those old emotive standbys, 'racism' and 'McCarthyism', are already being harnessed as a kind of preliminary defence.

Some of the more prominent agents of influence are already well known, some are not. It has been claimed, most recently by John J. Judis in the *New Republic*, that more than 110 former government officials have been hired by the Japanese, and that almost every important American ex-trade negotiator helps the Japanese in one way or another. The think-tanks, academic institutions and policy groups, generously endowed with Japanese money, include the liberal Brookings Institute, the Reischauer Center for East Asian Studies at Johns Hopkins University, the Center for Strategic and International Studies (CSIS), and the Committee for Economic Development (CED).

Nobody is suggesting that this money actually 'buys' opinions in the sense of making people express views they do not already hold. Some even argue that the Japanese are wasting their money, since it causes more paranoia and resentment than it's worth. But the fact that Toyota officials help appoint scholars at the CSIS and that Nissan has a hand in producing policy recommendations by the CED does seem to tilt the debate in one direction: free trade and more free trade in America, and never mind what the Japanese are up to. And the more dogmatic free-traders will even assert that the Japanese themselves exemplify free trade principles, both abroad and back home.

None of this means that the Japanese do anything illegal or that there is a conspiracy afoot in Washington. All one can say is that the Japanese are extraordinarily effective players of the Washington game, partly because they are flush with cash, and partly because so many Americans are prepared to play along with them. There is a third reason for their success: their plan of action is one that Americans would find almost impossible to emulate. A concerted, long-term industrial strategy, planned and executed by a combine of corporations, bureaucrats and politicians, is simply unthinkable in a free-trading, freewheeling society where the consumers are kings, bureaucrats come and go, and government, in theory at least, is not in the business of protecting American trade.

Japan has never been an open society. Japanese rulers, assisted by a co-operative class of scholars (not the same as an intelligentsia), have always imposed a kind of cultural propaganda on the population, which presented the status quo as benign, virtuous, unchanging, and blessedly native. In other words, it was virtuous to obey authority and not question one's lot, for that was the Japanese way. Or in more modern terms, it is virtuous for Japanese to pay more than foreigners for Japanese products (let alone foreign ones), to accept a de facto one-party state, and to sacrifice personal interests for corporate and national power: it is one's duty as a Japanese to do so.

If this causes problems abroad, it is said in Japan to be the fault of profligate, decadent foreigners. To think otherwise – as some critics are beginning to do – is to be un-Japanese. And when foreigners criticise this state of affairs, they clearly do not understand Japanese culture, or worse, they are racist. Because Americans in particular are terrified of being called racist, many will readily agree. And those who spend their lives as experts explaining the culture of others often end up as apologists for governments acting in the name of those cultures. So even though an American scholar of Japan like George Packard of Johns Hopkins probably gets well paid to write advertising supplements for the Japanese Chamber of Commerce, he will express the same opinions gratis, since he sees it as his duty to defend and explain the Japanese, right or wrong.

One can sympathise with Americans who are tired of seeing their own ex-government officials helping foreigners compete in the US markets. There *is* something called the Foreign Agents Registration Act but it was promulgated before the war to control Nazi propaganda. It was certainly never designed to make sure that lobbyists for foreign corporations were properly scrutinised. The Justice Department's Foreign Agents Registration Office has only a dozen employees and has yet to submit its report for 1987. Under the existing regulations advisers of foreign companies who don't lobby public officials directly, or lobbyists representing American subsidiaries of foreign companies, don't have to register at all.

It is easy to see how a strong nation which sees trade as a strategic weapon in the expansion of its power abroad can exert enormous influence on the Washington scene. But how much does it really matter? Ronald A. Morse observed that 'if you defect to the Soviet Union you get shot, but if you defect to Mitsubishi you get rich'. Again, one can sympathise, but is it apt to compare Mitsubishi with the Soviet Union, granted even that government and business are interlocked in Japan? The fact that the Japanese might see business as war, does not mean that it really *is* war. After all, Mitsubishi does bring palpable benefits, whereas missiles fired in anger do not. Is a Japanese company that provides jobs in America and good, cheap products to boot, good or bad for the national interest? Is it worse than an American firm which moves abroad for cheaper labour?

When one asks Americans who are worried about the Japanese economic threat quite what is so threatening, one soon enters a woolly terrain of perceived dangers to 'values', or 'our way of life'. I asked Morse what the difference was between the European fear of American power in the Fifties and Sixties, and the present American fear of Japan. 'Well,' he said, 'Europe was not the leader of the free world. America still is. And Japan, a nation without principles or values, cannot lead the world. They are predators . . .' But it is not immediately apparent what principles and values have to do with computers and motor cars.

In fact, what the Japan debate really boils down to is an American political debate, which should resonate in Britain, and which would take place even without the Japanese lobby. On the one side is an odd alliance of conservative Republicans and liberal Democrats, who believe in more government intervention in the economy, and on the other is a coalition of liberal free-traders, which also crosses party lines. Some right-wing Republicans, like Senator Jesse Helms, are afraid of Japanese power per se, and think the government should check the Japanese march into American markets for security reasons. Some liberal Democrats, like Labour economists in Britain, believe in protecting the principles and values of trade unions and inefficient industries, often in the name of patriotism. If this means shoddier goods, well, as Bill the lawyer said, 'I don't mind driving a worse car, if it's for the long-term good of my country.' Then there are the counterparts of Michael Heseltine who wish to have an industrial strategy along Japanese lines.

To keep open markets, even to the products of 'predators', or to have more corporatism, that is the question. The irony is that those who most fear the Japanese are most eager to emulate their methods, while the Japanese pay the wages of those who argue that we should not.

30 June 1990

'It's a nine cherub gale out there.'

MIRACLE-WORKER IN THE CHARM SCHOOL

A. N. Wilson

The Queen Mother is a largely mythological being. This is not to say that she is a bogus character – a hard, haughty aristocrat pretending to be a homely old body. It is more that her vision of her public role and her distinctive personal appearance exactly matched the job requirements – if not actually some profound need for a mother-figure on the part of the collective subconscious.

James Gunn's famous painting 'Conversation Piece' which hangs at the top of the stairs in the National Portrait Gallery is said to be Queen Elizabeth the Queen Mother's favourite royal icon. It was painted two years before the death of George VI and depicts afternoon tea at Royal Lodge. Cigarette in hand, the King slumps weakly in his chair, a snoozing corgi at his heels. The two princesses look like well-dressed doctors' wives from some southern suburb. Queen Elizabeth herself, with a hand on the teapot handle, gazes patiently towards her husband, as if coaxing him to tell her about his tiring day at the office. Though a portrait of George IV gazes down upon them all, the painting as a whole conveys to the observer the reassuring impression that there's some corner of a royal house which is forever Esher. In fact, Queen Elizabeth is one of the very last survivors of the pre-1914 aristocratic privileged life; she has never had to draw back her own bedroom curtains when she wakes in the morning; she has never had to prepare a meal; she never travels anywhere without two maids and two footmen.

It was in the first week of 1923, when newspapers were speculating about the future Edward VIII's choice of wife, that the *Daily News* carried the headline 'Scottish bride for Prince of Wales'. Although the paper did not carry the name of Elizabeth Bowes-Lyon, it was obvious that she was the girl in question. 'The future Queen of England is the daughter of a well-known Scottish peer, who is the owner of castles both north and south of the Tweed.' In his diary, Chips Channon described a party at the house of Lord Gage in Sussex at which he and Lady Elizabeth were fellow-guests. 'We all bowed and bobbed and teased her, calling her "Ma'am",' he noted. 'She is more gentle, lovely and exquisite than any woman alive, but this evening I thought her unhappy and distrait.'

It was soon clear that the rumour of her forthcoming betrothal to the future Edward VIII was untrue, but she has since admitted to friends that she was one of those many young women in the 1920s who was in love with him. She is very occasionally prepared to admit that this fact explains her icy refusal to forgive Wallis Simpson for marrying him. It is the classic example of the French adage that when love has gone, jealousy still remains. Those who seek, and therefore find, an archetypal cuddly grandmother-figure in Queen Elizabeth have been baffled by the vindictive pettiness which, for example, refused the Duchess of Windsor the right to place the initials HRH before her name. 'You think I am a nice person,' Queen Elizabeth once confided in a friend to whom she was speaking of these things. 'I'm not really a nice person.'

She is, however, a supremely charming person. I have only met her once, at a private dinner party in London, and it is probably the grossest impropriety to embarrass her, or her host, by repeating our conversation on that occasion. I do so, however, without very much compunction, since she never gives 'interviews', and I can think of no better person than Queen Elizabeth with whom to start off an occasional series of conversations with men and women who have lived through most of the years of this century – some obscure, some well-known – and whose memories stretch back far. I did not dare to discuss the Abdication with her, and since I earn my living by writing, it was inevitable that the talk should have taken a literary turn. She had been well-primed for our meeting, and politely said that she had been reading my life of Milton.

Queen Elizabeth: Oh, the research! The effort! All that work!
Self: It wasn't that difficult. Most of the facts are in other people's books.
Queen Elizabeth: But you're so young, and you've written all those novels and biographies and such lovely poems.
Self: What do you read for pleasure, ma'am?
Queen Elizabeth: I am very fond of detective stories. I like P. D. James, but it takes me about two months to finish one of her books. I really prefer Dorothy L. Sayers. Oh, and Barbara Pym I love.
Another guest: Princess Michael has done very well out of her books.

The Queen Mother threw up her hands and laughed.

Host: However rude people were about you, ma'am, it would be consoling to sell 100,000 copies of a book.
Queen Elizabeth: I can't understand a *word* Prince Michael says. He will mumble into his beard. As for Princess Michael ... [Another laugh.] But, golly, I could do with £100,000, couldn't you? Had such

an awful afternoon today with my bank manager, scolding me about my overdraft.

Like other limitlessly rich people, she spoke as if she was perpetually threatened with financial calamity. She is notoriously eccentric in her attitude towards money. When Norman Hartnell died, all the leading couturiers dreaded the prospect of being taken on by Queen Elizabeth. Was it, asked one of his more malicious customers, because of her distinctive, not to say appalling, taste in clothes? No, replied another couturier, it was because she had never been known to pay a bill.

At the dinner table, the talk turned to politics. It was in the days before the 'Gang of Four' had allied themselves to the Liberal Party.

Queen Elizabeth: I dislike this new socialist party of Woy's [*sic*].
Host: They're called the Social Democrats, ma'am.
Queen Elizabeth: Yes. Well, you don't change *socialist* just by leaving *ist* off the end. I say, it's a cheat to start something called the Social Party. I liked the old Labour Party. The best thing is a good old Tory government with a strong Labour opposition.
Self: Who did you like best in the old Labour Party?
Queen Elizabeth: (Sighs.) I remember Stafford Cripps coming to stay at Balmoral during the days of rationing and eating all our eggs for the week in one omelette. I remember my daughters scowling at him with hatred. Of course, you have daughters.
Self: Yes.
Queen Elizabeth: Can you get them to read?
Self: Difficult to make them stop, ma'am.
Queen Elizabeth: I remember dear Osbert – did you know him?
Self: Alas, not.
Queen Elizabeth: I thought the girls . . . you see, they were marooned in Windsor Castle for most of the war, and I was not sure that they were having a very good education and kind Sachie and Osbert said they would arrange a poetry evening for us. Such an embarrassment. Osbert was wonderful, as you would expect, and Edith, of course, but then we had this rather lugubrious man in a suit, and he read a poem . . . I think it was called 'The Desert'. And first the girls got the giggles, and then I did and then even the King.
Self: 'The Desert', ma'am? Are you sure it wasn't called *The Waste Land?*
Queen Elizabeth: That's it. I'm afraid we all giggled. Such a gloomy man, looked as though he worked in a bank, and we didn't understand a word.
Self: I believe he *did* once work in a bank.

When she withdrew, and went to sit with the ladies, I reflected that it had not felt like having a conversation with an extremely old woman. In spite of the ancient memory, she has the bubbly juvenile charm of a woman in her twenties. Her social manners are a throwback to old-fashioned whoopee, where everything was good for a lark, and subjects like poetry or politics, if raised at all, were more likely than not to have the company in stitches.

Yet, of course, there is much more to her than that. She did not marry David, she married (at the third time of asking) his poor, shy, stammering younger brother, and could be said, by so doing, to have re-invented the modern monarchy, long before the Abdication crisis had blown up. The early press cuttings about her activities as Duchess of York highlight the contrast between the Prince of Wales's cocktail-swigging fast set and her own sense of public duty. Two years before Mrs Simpson came on the scene, we read in the old scrapbooks of how 'the Duchess of York, accompanied by Lady Helen Graham, visited the offices of the National Knitting Appeal in Grosvenor Place, and saw some of the 8,000 garments which have so far come to hand for distribution in the distressed areas. She brought with her as a contribution a soft woollen scarf, knitted by her husband, the Duke of York.'

This in some ways fantastical response to the devastating unemployment problems of the 1930s set the tone of her public service for the next 55 years. Partly, no doubt, because of her reassuring physical appearance, partly because of her evident devotion to her husband and children, partly because of her physical courage – staying in London during the Blitz, etc – she became easily the best-loved figure in recent royal history. The simple explanation is her charm. There is no need to define this quality. As with Fats Waller's definition of swing, 'Lady, if you gotta ask, you ain't got it.' It may be that she has been to night-clubs less often than Mrs Simpson, but their lifestyles – pace Cosmo Gordon Lang's notorious broadcast after the Abdication which branded Mrs Simpson as a sort of Jezebel – were not fundamentally different. If one knew the amount of money that Queen Elizabeth had squandered on booze and race-horses, one might consider it miraculous that the British populace had not decided that enough was enough, and that the House of Windsor should be quietly put out to grass at Sandringham, Balmoral Castle or the Castle of Mey. By being a toughy who seems like a softy, and by never forgetting that soft woollen scarf for the unemployed, she has been able to charm an indifferent populace into a wholly unpredictable monarchical piety. No wonder Queen Mary loved her daughter-in-law so keenly. Queen Victoria had predicted that the monarchy would perhaps outlast her own death by 20 years. When Edward VIII was a young man, his parents could both see that the writing was on the wall, and that nothing short of a miracle could ever revive the popularity of the royal house. When one considers the charmlessness and talentlessness of the family into which Lady Elizabeth Bowes-Lyon married in 1923, there can be no doubt who the miracle-worker was.

30 June 1990

LETTERS

EMBARRASSED HOST

Sir: When your father was Chancellor of the Exchequer and said fascinating things at a private dinner party at my house no one present would have dreamed of recording them either accurately or inaccurately for press publication. I assume you would not have published such material to embarrass your father had it come your way. A. N. Wilson was at a private dinner party at my house in March 1987 on the well-known understanding that private conversations are private. Nevertheless you have published in the *Spectator* (30 June) what purports to be a detailed account of what one guest said. A. N. Wilson describes his action in giving you the material as 'probably the grossest impropriety'. He remarks that he does so 'without very much compunction since she never gives "interviews". . .' Thus he makes clear that he knew the interviewee was unaware she was being interviewed for press publication and obviously would not have permitted it. Knowing this, your publication of the deceitfully obtained and stolen 'interview' was a greater gross impropriety than A. N. Wilson's.

From your own background you must know that prominent people cannot ever go to a private dinner party and speak freely unless they are confident that mischievous use will not be made in the press of anything they may have said or may have been thought to say. This is particularly so with someone like Her Majesty Queen Elizabeth the Queen Mother who is unable to make any comments on, or correction of, what she has been alleged to say.

A. N. Wilson is proud of winning the 1975 Ellerton Theological Prize. His underhand behaviour does not square with the Christian ethics he professes. Nor with those of a gentleman, which I had naïvely thought him to be.

Over the years I have been at many private luncheons and dinner parties. This is the first time I have encountered a guest playing such a shabby trick on another guest. The free communication of social life would become impossible if A. N. Wilson's behaviour were not an isolated instance. He is boastfully shameless in being a scoundrel. But I hope you have enough decency to be ashamed of your participation in, and encouragement to, A. N. Wilson's squalid theft of an unauthorised 'interview'. It is worse than the much complained of invasion of privacy by downmarket tabloids. I am surprised at your giving ammunition to those who think the Calcutt Committee was not sufficiently stringent.

Wyatt of Weeford
19 Cavendish Avenue,
London NW8

7 July 1990

Sir: The 'interview' which Mr A. N. Wilson conducted with Her Majesty Queen Elizabeth the Queen Mother was, as your readers will have

realised, no such thing. Rather it was an intolerable betrayal of a privileged and private conversation. For Mr Wilson to have broken every convention of civilised society in this regard is bad
enough. Worse, it shows an appalling want of
chivalry from someone who has long set himself
up as a would-be moralist, and represents an absolutely fundamental breach of trust. You, Sir, have
condoned this deceit by printing such gossip and
in so doing have greatly diminished the high
reputation of your newspaper.

Nicholas Soames
House of Commons,
London SW1

'Not for me. I've got to remember which
number bus I have to catch.'

AFORE YE GO

Leaves from the commonplace book of Wallace Arnold

I have had the pleasure, nay, honour to be acquainted with My Lord Wyatt of Weevil ever since his days as a bookie's stringer working the Melton Mowbray circuit, but rarely have I seen him as angered as when his eyes caught sight of Ann Wilson's malicious and unseemly piece on the Queen Mother, bless her, in last week's *Spectator*.

I happened to be partaking of a little light luncheon with My Lord Wyatt of Weevil and a few choice guests when the letter-box snapped open and shut, depositing a copy of said *Spectator* in its wake. Within a trice, everyone around that table – from Bubbles, Lady Rothermere to Mr Roger Gleaves, the self-styled Bishop of Medway – was eagerly rushing towards the doormat, only too happy to have some diversion (and I know he'll forgive one for saying this) from the, at times, somewhat over-lengthy opinions of dear Wyatt.

As we all crowded around the new *Spectator*, leaving Wyatt sounding off to himself about this and that, I was the first to see the heading 'The Queen Mother's Table-Talk' beneath the ominous byline of Ann Wilson. 'Good Lord!' I exclaimed, and Wyatt looked up. 'That wretched woman's done the dirty! She's snitched on the lot of us, spilling the beans on our right royal evening!'

'Ding-dong, dong-ding.' Wyatt's sophisticated chiming doorbell, quite an icebreaker, pierced the air, and I made to open the door. There, fuming in pale blue chiffon with matching gloves, was HRH The Queen Mother, furiously snapping and re-snapping her delicate knuckles.

Offending article

'Out with it!' she said, marching into Wyatt's lounge-diner before removing his cigar from his mouth with a well-placed tug. 'What's the meaning of this, then?' She was brandishing a copy of the offending article. The conversation – for I was jotting it down with the utmost discretion – continued like this:

Wyatt of Weevil: B-b-b-but!
Queen Elizabeth: You've got a right nerve, coming over all hoity-toity, giving yourself airs and graces, when you're as common as the rest of 'em.
Wyatt of Weevil: B-b-b-but if I'd kn-kn-known she'd take notes, ma'am,

I'd have booted her out.

Another guest (Mr Kenneth Rose), noticing which way the tide is turning: Pay no heed to his protestations, ma'am. He has scant regard for the rules of propriety, and is not to be trusted.

Self (pointing to Rose): Nor he, ma'am! He too is a scribbler! He would welsh on his own dear grandma, if she were titled, which she is most certainly not, in fact quite the opposite!

From that moment on, guest was set against guest, contact against contact, scribe against scribe, as we all strove to reassure Her Royal Highness of our own superiority to the assembled company. Alas, the upshot of it was that, when the dust had settled and the shouting had died down, we realised with a start that our Royal visitor had vanished from our lives forever. A bitter blow to us all, and one which I trust you will all keep firmly under your proverbial hats.

7 July 1990

WHY ALL THE FUSS?

A. N. Wilson

Last week, Nato declared the Cold War to be at an end; Mr Gorbachev's fate hung in the balance at the Soviet Party Congress and with it the future of the USSR; thousands of Albanians fled to foreign embassies; Imelda Marcos was acquitted of conspiracy; Mr Scargill seemed poised to deliver a final death blow to the NUM by refusing to resign; Germany won the World Cup.

Something of a surprise, then, to find almost the whole of the Comment page in the *Sunday Telegraph* taken up with my dinner conversation with a spirited old lady whom I once met in St John's Wood. Not one article, but two; one, by Oliver Pritchett, making light of the affair, and the other, by Geoffrey Wheatcroft, denouncing me not merely as a cad for repeating the old lady's conversation, but also as a Tartuffe, a quasi-homosexual and an anti-semite – none of which is true or, surely, entirely relevant to the great issue under consideration. Since the *Daily Telegraph* had already carried two articles about my dinner with the lady, you might have thought it the moment for a blue pencil to scrawl, *'That's enough Queen Mother. Ed.'*

The *Independent*, not normally given to discussing Royal affairs, devoted the first column of its Diary to my *Spectator* article (30 June) in which I committed the solecism of repeating the spoken words of the Royal Family. No fewer than six Sunday newspapers also carried articles about it – one, the *Observer*, reprinted the entire conversation (plagiarism breaks no taboos in journalism) and there have, as far as I know, been one or two articles on the same subject in the *Evening Standard*.

It would be tedious to rehearse all the things which my fellow-hacks have been saying. The question which I ask myself – and them, nearly all of whom said complimentary things about the original piece – is 'Why all the fuss?' The Queen Mother is about to be 90 years old. The newspapers are full of 16-page, full-colour supplements all, roughly speaking, conveying the message, 'Gawd bless yer, ma'am.' None of the articles I have read have conveyed what it is like to meet her, or what she says. It seems strange that no newspaper except *The Spectator* seemed prepared to break the absurd taboo about never repeating the unrehearsed words of Royal personages.

When I said this to Alexander Chancellor, who used to edit *The Spectator*, I reminded him of an hilarious article he had written in which he had repeated the dinner conversation of Lauren Bacall. 'You're an anarchist!' he exclaimed – though not in the least disapprovingly. 'Lauren Bacall is a film star. The Queen Mother is ... the Queen Mother.'

Many people feel this distinction clearly, and I can't begin to see why. By the peculiar tribal codes which operate in England, I am fully aware that I have, in the apoplectic words of Nicholas Soames (*Spectator* Letters, 7 July 1990), 'broken every convention of civilised society'. 'Every convention'? If my article had been unkind or untrue, I should feel overwhelmed by remorse. As it is, I feel merely baffled. We have all read the accounts of primitive tribesmen who take it as a deadly insult if you don't belch, or don't attempt to seduce their wives after squatting for a meal on the floor of their mud huts. We recognise that these conventions exist, but few feel bound by them in the United Kingdom. Since I don't feel myself bound by the conventions either of Soames or of the mud hut, what possible harm could there be in writing as I did?

I am not suggesting that Lord Wyatt of Weeford lives in a mud hut – indeed his house is as far from a mud hut as any I ever visited – but I am puzzled that so urbane and 18th-century a figure should be so encased in Royalist superstition. In the era in which he feels at home, that of the four Georges and William IV, no one thought twice about repeating the frequently idiotic utterances of the Royal Family, and of pillorying their absurdities in the public press. Yet when I ventured to repeat some very harmless remarks made by the Queen Mother at his dinner table he resorts to a parody of outraged Colonel Blimp language, denouncing me as a 'scoundrel'.

Since I am fond of Woodrow, I hope he will simmer down, and one day come to dinner with me again. The best commentary on his letter of protest seemed to occur, quite by chance, a few pages later in the same issue of *The Spectator* in which Don Cupitt was commenting on Frazer's *Golden Bough:* 'We are not the lucidly self-conscious beings, capable of seeing things as they really are and of acting rationally in accordance with our true interests, that we fancied we were. We are hag-ridden. We human beings have always lived in magic worlds, our lives dominated by terrifying mythic Powers, forces and equivalences that we have unknowingly projected around ourselves.'

If Woodrow had entertained me to dinner with Marlene Dietrich or Barbara Castle or Elizabeth Longford, he would not have been remotely worried that I repeated their views of Stafford Cripps or T. S. Eliot. Nor would the papers have devoted, to date, about 15,000 words of newsprint commenting on the affair.

It is pure superstition and (same thing) snobbery which has everyone so excited. Queen Victoria attempted to suppress the publication of Greville's diaries because they repeated the near-imbecilic behaviour and conversation of her uncle, William IV. Thereafter, we have been hag-ridden by the 'conventions of civilised society' which decree that we should not repeat things said to us by members of the Royal Family. It is sometimes added that the reason for this is that they have no right to reply. But this is not true. If the Queen Mother wished to give her version of that harmlessly enjoyable evening at Woodrow Wyatt's house, there would be no shortage of newspaper editors prepared to print her story; but I dare say that she feels, as I do, that it is all a storm in a wine-glass, and not really worth so much wasted ink, nor so much true or feigned fury.

14 July 1990

SAYING THE UNSAYABLE
ABOUT THE GERMANS

Dominic Lawson

It is said, or it ought to have been said, that every Conservative Cabinet Minister dreams of dictating a leader to the *Daily Telegraph*. Nicholas Ridley, the Secretary of State for Industry, is, so far as I am aware, the only one to have done so. It happened when the late Jock Bruce-Gardyne, long-time writer of the *Telegraph*'s economic leaders, was staying with Mr Ridley. The then deputy editor of the *Telegraph*, Colin Welch, rang up to urge Jock to file a promised leader for the next morning's paper:

Colin Welch: Is that Jock?

N. Ridley: Yes.

CW: Where is your leader? We need it now.

NR: Right oh!

CW: I'll put you on to the copy-takers.

At which point Ridley delivered an impromptu pastiche of a Bruce-Gardyne leader, unfortunately too surreal to pass Mr Welch once he read it and divined its true author.

After I had visited Mr Ridley in his lair, an 18th-century rectory in the heart of his Gloucestershire constituency, I could see why he should have delighted in such innocent deception. As we ate lunch together I stared through what I thought was a window behind my host's left shoulder. But it was in fact a magnificent trompe l'oeil, painted by Mr Ridley in 1961.

The house's – real – garden, designed by Mr Ridley, a civil engineer by training, is similarly baffling. One secluded section turns cunningly into another, and from any one fixed position it is impossible to see where the next turn might lead.

But Nicholas Ridley's passion for illusion is most definitely only a pastime. In modern political life there is no more brutal practitioner of the home truth. Not even Mrs Thatcher – whose own views owe much to his – is more averse to hiding the hard facts behind a patina of sympathy or politician's charm. In a mirror world Mr Nicholas Ridley would be Mr Cecil Parkinson.

Even knowing this, I was still taken aback by the vehemence of Mr Ridley's views on the matter of Europe, and in particular the role of Germany. It had seemed a topical way to engage his thoughts,

since the day after we met, Herr Klaus-Otto Pöhl, the president of
the Bundesbank, was visiting England to preach the joys of a joint
European monetary policy.

'This is all a German racket designed to take over the whole of
Europe. It has to be thwarted. This rushed take-over by the Germans
on the worst possible basis, with the French behaving like poodles to
the Germans, is absolutely intolerable.'

'Excuse me, but in what way are moves toward monetary union,
"The Germans trying to take over the whole of Europe"?'

'The Deutschmark is always going to be the strongest currency,
because of their habits.'

'But Mr Ridley, it's surely not axiomatic that the German currency
will always be the strongest . . .?'

'It's because of the *Germans.*'

'But the European Community is not just the Germans.'

Mr Ridley turned his fire – he was, as usual, smoking heavily – onto
the organisation as a whole.

'When I look at the institutions to which it is proposed that
sovereignty is to be handed over, I'm aghast. Seventeen unelected reject
politicians' – that includes you, Sir Leon – 'with no accountability to
anybody, who are not responsible for raising taxes, just spending
money, who are pandered to by a supine parliament which also is
not responsible for raising taxes, already behaving with an arrogance
I find breathtaking – the idea that one says, "OK, we'll give this lot
our sovereignty," is unacceptable to me. I'm not against giving up
sovereignty in principle, but not to this lot. You might just as well
give it to Adolf Hitler, frankly.'

We were back to Germany again, and I was still the devil's – if not
Hitler's – advocate:

'But Hitler was elected.'

'Well he was, at least *he* was . . . but I didn't agree with him – but
that's another matter.'

'But surely Herr Kohl is preferable to Herr Hitler. He's not going to
bomb us, after all.'

'I'm not sure I wouldn't rather have . . .' – I thought for one giddy
moment, as Mr Ridley paused to stub out his nth cigarette, that
he would mention the name of the last Chancellor of a united
Germany – 'er . . . the shelters and the chance to fight back, than
simply being taken over by . . . *economics.* He'll soon be coming *here*
and trying to say that this is what we should do on the banking front
and this is what our taxes should be. I mean, he'll soon be trying to
take over *everything.*'

Somehow I imagined (and I admit it, because Mr Ridley is for ever accusing journalists of making things up) that I could hear a woman's voice with the very faintest hint of Lincolnshire, saying 'Yes, Nick, that's right, they *are* trying to take over everything.' I can at least recall, with no recourse to imagination, the account of one of the Prime Minister's former advisers, of how he arrived for a meeting with Mrs Thatcher in a German car. 'What is that *foreign* car?' she glowered.

'It's a Volkswagen,' he replied, helpful as ever.

'Don't *ever* park something like that here again.'

The point is, Mr Ridley's confidence in expressing his views on the German threat must owe a little something to the knowledge that they are not significantly different from those of the Prime Minister, who originally opposed German reunification, even though in public she is required not to be so indelicate as to draw comparisons between Herren Kohl and Hitler.

What the Prime Minister and Mr Ridley also have in common, which they do not share with many of their Cabinet colleagues, is that they are over 60. Next question, therefore, to Mr Ridley: 'Aren't your views coloured by the fact that you can remember the Second World War?' I could have sworn I saw a spasm of emotion cross Mr Ridley's face. At any rate he answered the question while twisting his head to stare out of the window:

'Jolly good thing too. About time somebody said that. It was pretty nasty. Only two months ago I was in Auschwitz, Poland. Next week I'm in Czechoslovakia. You ask them what they think about the Second World War. It's useful to remember.' It is also useful to know that Mr Ridley's trips to Poland and Czechoslovakia are efforts, in the company of some of Britain's leading businessmen, to persuade the East Europeans of the virtues of doing business with Britain. How very annoying to see the large towels of Mr Kohl and his businessmen already covering those Eastern beaches.

But, hold on a minute, how relevant to us, now, is what Germany did to Eastern Europe in the war? Mr Ridley reverted to the sort of arguments he must have inhaled with his smokes when he was a Minister of State at the Foreign Office:

'We've always played the balance of power in Europe. It has always been Britain's role to keep these various powers balanced, and never has it been more necessary than now, with Germany so uppity.'

'But suppose we don't have the balance of power; would the German economy run Europe?'

'I don't know about the German economy. It's the German *people.*

They're already running most of the Community. I mean they pay half of the countries. Ireland gets 6 per cent of their gross domestic product this way. When's Ireland going to stand up to the Germans?'

The strange thing about Mr Ridley's hostility to the Bundesbank and all its works is that, if he had ever been Chancellor of the Exchequer – a job he admitted to me he had once coveted, but no longer – then he would probably have matched the Germans in his remorseless aversion to inflation. But as he pointed out, 'I don't think that's relevant. The point is that when it comes to "Shall we apply more squeeze to the economy or shall we let up a bit?" this is essentially about political accountability. The way I put it is this: can you imagine me going to Jarrow in 1930 and saying, "Look boys, there's a general election coming up, I know half of you are unemployed and starving and the soup kitchen's down the road. But we're not going to talk about those things, because they're for Herr Pöhl and the Bundesbank. It's his fault; he controls that; if you want to protest about that, you'd better get on to Herr Pöhl"?'

There might be more financial discipline in a British economy run under the influence of men like Herr Pöhl, Mr Ridley agreed. But, he added, suddenly looking up at me through his bifocals, 'There could also be a bloody revolution. You can't change the British people for the better by saying, "Herr Pöhl says you can't do that." They'd say, "You know what you can do with your bloody Herr Pöhl." I mean, you don't understand the British people if you don't understand this point about them. They can be dared; they can be moved. But being bossed by a German – it would cause absolute mayhem in this country, and rightly, I think.'

The rumbustious tone of Mr Ridley's remarks and the fact that our conversation was post-prandial may give the misleading impression that the politician was relaxing, and not choosing his words too carefully. Far from it. Mr Ridley had the smallest glass of wine with his lunch, and then answered all my questions with a fierce frown of concentration, one hand clutched to his forehead, the other helping to provide frequent supplies of nicotine.

And although he has not been so outspoken on the matter of Europe before, it is no secret that Mr Ridley was a supporter of Enoch Powell long before Mrs Thatcher was ever a force in the political firmament. I reminded Mr Ridley that he had voted for Enoch Powell in the 1965 contest for the leadership of the Conservative Party, and asked him, 'If Mr Powell had been elected then, and become Prime Minister in 1970, would there ever have been a need for Margaret Thatcher?'

At this point, Mr Ridley's frown of concentration became an angry scowl, and to aid his pondering further he removed his spectacles and poked himself in the eyes with the ear-pieces.

'I think that is possibly . . . right. But then you have to put against that some extraordinarily correct but totally unreasonable belief that Enoch might have developed, which would have meant that his Prime Ministership would have been a failure.'

I must say that at this point I was overcome with admiration for Mr Ridley. Any other politician in the same position would either have said, to be safe, 'Yes, there would still have been a need for Margaret Thatcher', or less sycophantically, 'I don't think there's much point in answering such a hypothetical question.'

Similarly, when I asked Mr Ridley how he felt, as a self-described 'Thatcherite before Mrs Thatcher', seeing old Heath men like Kenneth Baker, Douglas Hurd and Christopher Patten gain greater preferment under the lady, he was quite unable to come up with the diplomatic evasion. Instead he produced an expression half-way between a smile and a grimace. 'I don't want to go into colleagues, and that. That's getting close to what you put in your memoirs. I'm not going to say things about current differences in the Government because I think on the whole it's a very good government. And of course everybody in it has slightly different views about things.'

'Slightly?'

'Well, less than slightly, but I'm not going to divulge those or talk about them.'

'Why not?'

'Because it would weaken the Government.'

'It might help to strengthen the Government.'

'Yes, but I'll do that my own way, not your way.'

'Don't worry, my wife's entirely on your side.'

'You think your way is successful?'

'Oh yes. I'm quite happy.'

'Does that mean you are still winning the important battles in Cabinet?'

'That presupposes that there are battles. We're moving pretty well along in the right direction. If I felt out of sorts with the whole thing I would resign. It's not an idle threat.'

That certainly will be believed. Mr Ridley is still serenaded by the Right as the only minister to resign from the Department of Industry after Mr Heath's famous U-turn of 1972. Mr Heath still insists that he sacked Mr Ridley. The truth – as usual in such matters – appears to lie somewhere in between.

Whatever, it seems that only Mrs Thatcher changing her views on Europe – a nearly incredible proposition – would cause Mr Ridley to leave the Department of Industry in such traumatic circumstances for a second time.

Or, as Nicholas Ridley put it to me with his habitual, but constantly surprising and un-English directness, 'I've been elected to Parliament nine times, I've been in office for 14 years, I'm still at the top of the political tree, and I'm not done yet.'

14 July 1990

DIARY

Dominic Lawson

It is time to reveal the role of Mr Charles Wilson, the former editor of the *Times*, in what has now become known as the 'Ridley Affair'. On the evening before we typeset last week's *Spectator* I was at a party at his home, thrown by his wife Sally O'Sullivan in her role as editor of *Harpers & Queen*. I arrived with a briefcase containing the galley proofs of the Nicholas Ridley interview. I left the party without the briefcase and went on elsewhere to dinner. It is an easy thing to do. It is a very annoying briefcase, actually. I bought it in the Leather Lane market for only £10, reduced because the lock is defective and has a habit of springing open of its own accord. When I returned home it was far too late to telephone the Wilsons and I had some difficulty in sleeping, trying to recall exactly where the briefcase had ended up, and wondering, if it had been stolen, what a thief would have made of its contents. But an early morning telephone call to C. Wilson confirmed that the thing was still lurking unopened in his hall, and Charlie sent his driver round to our typesetters with the UXB. Thank you, Charlie, and I'm sorry if I sounded a little tense on the 'phone.

It is time, too, to answer the question put to me by every taxi-driver I have met over the past week, viz (and I condescend) 'Didja know, Guv, when yer wrote yer article, that there'd be all this bovver?' The answer – embarrassing as it is to have to admit it – is, not entirely, and I think I can prove it, by way of a story. On Friday, the day after the sky fell in, I felt obliged to complain to Mr Kelvin MacKenzie, the editor of the *Sun*, because he had reproduced the interview over his centre pages in clear breach of our copyright. 'You may be a good journalist to get the story,' Mr MacKenzie informed me, 'but not good enough to realise just what a story you had. Otherwise you would have printed thousands of extra copies.' And he is right, although we did do a second print run last week, when the dramatic effect of the 'first edition' became apparent. By the way, Mr MacKenzie, since you obviously read *The Spectator* so attentively, can I ask you here to send us the cheque you promised as payment for reprinting our interview with Mr Ridley. Or is it in the post?

That edition of the *Sun* also carried a leader on the Ridley Affair written entirely out of its own intellectual resources: 'Your great strength, Mr Ridley, is that you speak your mind. You are no hypocrite. But next time, present those thoughts in more moderate language.' In particular the sensitive souls at the *Sun* objected to Mr Ridley's mention of Hitler in connection with the erosion of British sovereignty in Europe. Now where did I read this: 'Herr we go, Herr we go! We beat them in 1945. Now for 1990!'? Why, it was on the front page of the *Sun*, in block capitals, on the morning of England's World Cup semi-final match against West Germany. Mr Ridley is indeed no hypocrite. But what about you, Mr MacKenzie?

On Saturday I was playing cricket for my team, the Old Talbotians, against the Mihir Bose XI, when a man from ITN and a woman from the *Sunday Times* came running onto the pitch – I have notified the Test and County Cricket Board – waving pieces of paper and asking for my comments. They were holding Nicholas Ridley's resignation letter to the Prime Minister, in which he said that the views he expressed 'are very much in line with those of the Government. But I recognise the difficulties which my failure to use more measured words have caused.' It is precisely because I too thought that Mr Ridley's views as expressed to me were a trenchant rationale of the Prime Minister's opposition to speedy imposition of European Monetary Union, that I never dreamed as we went to press that she would ask him to resign because of our interview. The truth is that Mr Ridley has been expelled – to my enormous regret – for bad language, in particular about the Germans. And the fact that a British Cabinet minister has had to lose his job for being rude about the Germans is in itself evidence that Mr Ridley was right to warn us of the increasing German influence over our own political life.

In the last few hours before Nick Ridley's resignation a group described as 'friends of Mr Ridley' – actually one man, and not Mr Ridley, by the way – began putting it about that the remarks quoted in last week's *Spectator* were from a part of the interview that was off the record. Of the newspapers that I read, only the *Independent* swallowed this porky pie. In fact all the quotes came from a two-hour recorded interview agreed – almost a month in advance – to be entirely on the record. Furthermore all the quotes are on my transcript of the interview, which has been seen by the man calling himself 'friends of Mr Ridley', and he therefore knows very well that none of the remarks I quoted are prefaced or followed by the phrase 'this is not for quotation' which appears two or three times on the tape. I will offer

'I hate his more endangered than thou attitude.'

only one hitherto unpublished extract from the transcript and here it is, a response to one of my questions: 'I think I'd better not [answer] – you might publish it.' Not the remark of a man completely off his guard, or unaware that he is speaking on the record. Nor this, from the published interview, in response to my question about differences of opinion within the Government: 'I'm not going to divulge those, or talk about them.' Cabinet ministers speaking off the record rarely talk of anything else.

So what is the explanation for Mr Ridley's talking on the record about 'German takeovers' and 'French poodles'? Cast your mind back a few months to an interview given by Mr Norman Tebbit to a newspaper on the West Coast of America, in which he spoke of a 'cricket test' to judge the patriotism of blacks and Asians in the United Kingdom. That was no great shock for the inhabitants of Los Angeles – pledging allegiance to the flag is an American habit – but it was a shock for Mr Tebbit when the story was picked up by the British press. Similarly, I believe that Mr Ridley's remarks to me were well judged to appeal to the readers of *The Spectator*, as our post bag clearly testifies, but did not go down so well with the readers of the *Frankfurter Allgemeine Zeitung*. But could Nick Ridley, looking at me, imagine them? I certainly didn't, when I wrote the article out in longhand, on the day of *The Spectator* summer party. We were both naïve.

21 July 1990

LOW LIFE

A DOCTOR'S CALLING

Jeffrey Bernard

The build-up to this latest move had me cracking at the mental seams. I haven't known such anxiety and depression for an age. But at least the Gentle Ghosts did a good job. It was miraculous that they got my plaster bust of Nelson here without shattering it. Now I sit here surrounded by cardboard boxes and I haven't even got the strength or energy to put them out. They say that moving is third only to bereavement and divorce but, having been through three divorces, I think it is worse.

In fact, when my third wife divorced me I was rather amused. She cited my occasional spells of sobriety during which, she claimed, I was morose, sullen and uncommunicative. How very true. Why else should she have thought I drink? Anyway I have another wall to stare at for a year. It is a nice little flat this one, but it is a hundred miles from the West End. Public transport is not my cup of tea but a taxi costs the earth. But even with a decent flat, West Hampstead is not a place in which to loiter. There isn't a class food shop in sight and the only butcher here is an actor who murders scripts.

Anyway, I did venture forth to Soho yesterday and I met a very nice and rather extraordinary woman from Vienna who came into the pub to see me. She teaches English and speaks it fluently. Certainly better than any American I have ever met. She has been making herself busy collecting cuttings about me and getting photocopies made of this column. Now here's the funny thing and you're not going to believe it, but she has chosen me as the subject to write about to get her PhD. No, she is not mad but this has to be an incredible absurdity. I don't know whether to feel flattered or embarrassed. Both. In a way I am surprised that any Austrian can understand the back end of *The Spectator*. Rich fascist shits, The Coach and Horses and a speechless baby in that order. I'm not sure I can understand it either.

When the Austrian lady, Renate, talks about Vienna and Salzburg I feel strongly tempted to visit the place. By her accounts the countryside is quite beautiful and I would like to see the house in which Mozart lived but I am not a man for cream cakes and coffee, neither do I need to see a psychiatrist until I have to move house again. I also gather that Strauss must have been colour-blind if he thought the Danube was blue. I shall give it a try in the spring and laze by a lake, which will be a damn sight more soothing than staring at a West Hampstead wall.

And now I am preoccupied with the play again. Tom Conti is leaving and on Monday James Bolam is taking over from him. The third star making an Orion's Belt. When I met James the other day for the first time in an age he said not to come to his first night, but the second, or preferably the third, because he would be nervous. Who wouldn't be? I very much want to see James and think he is a splendid actor, just right for the part, but I shall nevertheless drag my feet to the Apollo. I have seen enough of myself.

Someone told me that he went to the show last week and sat behind two American women. One of them said to the other, 'I think it's very funny, but what a pathetic life.' I'm not sure I like that. I may not be a merchant banker or hot shot film director but I don't think the journey from the cradle towards Golders Green has been exactly pathetic, just manic depressive. Once I have got rid of these cardboard boxes it will hopefully be manic again for a while. But that is very typical of Americans. Had the play been called *Jeffrey Bernard is Eating Lots of Bran*, or *Jeffrey Bernard is Jogging*, they would have lapped it up. Well, he is doing neither. He is as sick as a dog, never mind unwell.

28 July 1990

'This is tricky. Everyone who got the placebo got better.'

LETTER

LOVE HIM, LOATHE HIM

Sir: As the 'very nice and rather extraordinary woman from Vienna' with a sense of the absurd and encumbered with the pleasurable task of doing a PhD thesis on Jeffrey Bernard (Low Life, 28 July), I would be most grateful if you could write to *The Spectator* stating why you love or loathe him (marking envelope 'Extraordinary woman').

Renate Sunkler
Schaumburgergasse 18/15,
Vienna, Austria

11 August 1990

LOW LIFE

NO MORE LAUGHTER

Jeffrey Bernard

The saga of Renate, the woman from Vienna who chose me as the subject for her PhD thesis, is over. So is the joke. She is dead. I received a telephone call from her boyfriend last Friday evening telling me of the fact. He wasn't very coherent but I got the distinct impression from him that she committed suicide. It would fit since she phoned me the week before in tears to tell me that she was in a mental hospital. It is a mystery. The week before that she was over here to see me and she spent some time in the *Spectator* offices looking up old cuttings and asking people about me. We had lunch and she laughed a lot at being teased about her thesis by people in the pub. She looked happy and well. I didn't realise that anyone could crack so quickly and suddenly.

I have a card in front of me which she recently sent me with the present of a book, *Mozart in Vienna: 1781–1791*, and she wrote, 'I hope the enclosed book will persuade you to come over soon and see it all before the actual Mozzamania starts. Best wishes, Renate.' That doesn't sound much like somebody on the brink. On that last visit to London she spoke of showing me Vienna and taking me to a lake in a forest which she loved and how we would have lunch on a boat there.

I may have made a mistake in writing about this in last week's *Sunday Mirror* but I repeat it here because I have had letters from *Spectator* readers who were interested in Renate's 'crazy' project. She loved *The Spectator* and she would read it in German to her pupils in the school where she taught English. But since the *Sunday Mirror* piece I have been badgered a little by other newspapers about the sad business. I should have expected that, but she was all I could think about last Saturday.

What a horrendous business suicide is. I first came across it about 35 years ago when my first wife, Anna, killed herself. We had been separated for some time and had lost contact. At the time I was living in John Minton's house in Chelsea. One day there was a knock on the door and when I answered it a man stood there, a newspaper reporter, and asked me, 'How do you feel about your wife killing herself?' What a bloody way to have news broken to you. I asked him to go away and he actually tried to force the door open.

Anna was no stranger to suicide. As a schoolgirl she had come home one day to find that both her mother and father had hanged themselves. Then it was in that house in Chelsea that Johnny Minton later killed himself with an overdose. He had been drinking more than I have ever seen anybody drink. He was a wreck and it had affected his brain but I still think that maybe it was a drunken mistake. Some people are unlucky enough to succeed in killing themselves. I know two people who have their own overdoses hidden away in case of getting some awful disease like cancer. I hope to God they are good diagnosticians. So, no more laughter with Renate. That rhymes and that is enough said about the tragic matter.

16 March 1991

NEW LIFE

TELEPHONIC HANG-UPS

Zenga Longmore

Although the weather last week was hot enough to fry plantains in their skins, it came as no surprise to see Uncle Bisi calling at my door clad in a three-piece suit, clutching a black umbrella. Olumba ran from the kitchen to give him a soap-sudsy handshake.

'Uh uh uh! Welcome Uncle.'

'Nephew – ah – I have come,' announced Uncle Bisi, over Omalara's screams, 'to discuss serious business.'

Flattered that his uncle was about to confide in him on important matters, Olumba ducked his head and simpered. 'Yes, Uncle? What would you like to discuss with me?'

'With *you*? Ha no. Heh heh! It is with my business associate on Onitsha, whether he has sold a house or not, that I wish to discuss munificently. I have to use your phone. There is a certain reason why I cannot utilise my own telephonic apparatus.'

'Why is that, Uncle? Is it tap-tappo? Can your business really interest the CIA or the KGB?'

'No, nephew; it is the cost of phone messages. If I use my own telephone, it will cost me much money on the bill. Have you any idea how much it costs to phone Nigeria? Chai! Hand me the phone.'

'Yes, Uncle.' Dutifully, Olumba took the phone from Omalara. For many months now, Omalara has found the phone an invaluable playmate. My friends all know they cannot call me until midnight, when Omalara is asleep, because I leave the phone unplugged. All day long, Omalara can be found shouting the only words she has mastered into the receiver: 'Up bedtimes!' On the rare occasions when I have left the phone plugged in, she has pressed the R button, and has got through to the person I have just called. A stunned gasp can be heard on the other end of the line, as 'Up bedtimes' is roared into the phone.

During Uncle Bisi's long and involved conversation in Ibo, Omalara was doing her best to wrest the phone from his grip. Finally, with an irritated 'chai!' Uncle Bisi dropped the phone into Omalara's eager hands.

'Well, Uncle?' asked Olumba, bringing in the tea tray. 'I hope everything went okayo with your business associate.'

'Hah! Unable to descry my monolithic logic, the rascal hung up on me.'

I was deeply impressed. How anyone even at the other end of a phone hundreds of miles away, could have had the temerity to hang up on Uncle Bisi, was quite beyond me. Such an heroic gesture seemed worthy of a medal for courage over and above the cause of business.

'Ah,' said Uncle Bisi, watching Omalara rattling the phone, 'to quote St Paul, "when I was, ah, a child, I did childish things, ah, because I *was* a child. But now I am a man, ah, I see through a glass darkly."' With that, he put on his sunglasses and left.

It was only then that I saw the phone had been unplugged from the wall, and that Omalara was earnestly chewing the cable. Could it be that, ever mindful of our telephone bill, the intelligent child had pulled the cord out some time during the beginning of Uncle Bisi's monologue?

28 July 1990

HIGH LIFE

HIGH STAKES

Taki

Gstaad

Back in the middle Sixties the then Prince Fahd was a regular chemmy player at Aspinall's wild game. Fahd was always accompanied by a young and beautiful Palestinian girl, and was extremely polite to us lesser mortals. Despite his wealth, however, he was a cautious gambler. Yet he was one of Aspers's favourites, the reason being, I suspect, the prompt payments he made. (During those good old days, punters gambled on credit, and worried about payment the next day.)

I particularly remember one night, when the game had as usual got out of hand, and I was down tens of thousands of pounds. Fahd had the bank and had passed three hands at the expense of Lord Lucan, later to become known for other things. When 'Lucky' did not call *suivi*, I asked for *banco*. I recall taking a large gulp of my whisky – again,

'Have you read my column?'

before the law prohibited us poor gamblers from the odd booster – and slowly looked at my first card. It was a four. I then quickly looked at the second one. It was also a four. 'Shredded,' I yelled, and showed my cards to the Saudi. Fahd smiled, and slowly turned his own cards over. I was in the habit of never looking at the cards being turned over, until I heard him softly say sorry. He had a nine.

I said well done, got up and went to the lavatory, where I was sick. My bride of three months gave me the kind of contemptuous look brave men give their executioner when asked if they need a handkerchief to cover their eyes. It was the beginning of the end of my marriage, not to mention my solvency.

Needless to say, I informed Aspers that the future Saudi king would have to wait, which meant that Aspinall's had to come up with the loot. But Aspers did not have to wait long. That winter, I ran into Harold Lever, back then still a commoner, and virtually took him to the cleaners: 50,000 big ones to be exact, enough to wipe out my debt to the Clermont. Although Lever was later to be knighted and ennobled, I don't think he ever got over my throwing three double fives in a row to win an unwinnable game that he had doubled me to 16.

After Fahd became king he turned into a ghost gambler. By this I mean he kept gambling but not against people who were liable to do an Andrew Wilson. But a private room at Aspinall's with unlimited stakes was always available when Fahd was in town. Which in a way is ridiculous. Gambling when one is as rich as Fahd is as futile an exercise as Arnold Schwarzenegger entering a strongman contest in a small village fair. Which brings me to the point I wish to make.

Fahd and the Saudis have the guts of a popinjay. They think that by going around bribing evil they can survive. Well, I've got news for them. If they don't fight now, they'll soon be gambling regularly with Taki *chez* Aspers in the very near future. What outrages me even more is the fact that they have the planes to do it. As Paul Johnson very correctly wrote, the Iraqis are novices in the air, and even without American help the Saudis – if they had any bottle – could establish air superiority after one week and then take the bully's armour out at will.

And what about King Hussein siding with his namesake and accusing the Kuwaitis of having too much? I guess the heat helped him forget his expensive hookers, his private planes and yachts and night-club bills even bigger than mine. He will also be joining us soon.

11 August 1990

DREAMING OF PORK AND PORN

Hilary Mantel

Gulfman will be sweating and hoping now. He will be tuning in to the World Service, for the foreign newspapers are censored and the local ones tell lies. If there is an emergency, if he has to throw his life in a suitcase and quit, it will be only what he has dreamed of doing, thousands of times, when the mosquitoes bite and the bureaucrats need bribing. And there has always been the threat of coup d'état or sudden deportation. With part of his mind, he has always seen himself scrambling for a seat on the last plane out. But then there is the other part of his mind, which sincerely wants to be rich.

Wherever in the world they are, British expatriates will always tell you, 'It's not what it used to be.' There was always a golden age, when life was tougher but less complicated, and everyone knew his place and stayed in it, playing his allotted role in the long drama of the Englishman abroad. In Arabia and the Gulf they look back to the age before shopping malls, when provisions were obtained in the souk and the roads were rough tracks and Islam didn't get on the nerves so.

Then in 1973 the oil price went up, the construction workers came. A concrete hell was born, with savage people in it. Salaries, fortunately, continue to go up too.

The first wave of 'Brits', as they describe themselves, were employed by the construction companies. These men with tattoos worked on short contracts, leaving their families behind. Bewildered, sunburnt and lonely, they got into trouble by smoking on the streets during Ramadan, or trying to chat up women. Often, one contract down and pockets full of money, they would jump ship. There were always more where they came from.

The second wave of expats were the professional experts – teachers, scientists, accountants, engineers. Their companies made an effort to retain them – housing them in what comfort was obtainable, paying them well and shielding them as far as possible from their hosts' strange religious and cultural susceptibilities. Families came out; a way of life was established, endurable but frail. It was dependent upon the successful functioning of air-conditioning units, and upon an ability to screen out many of the less pleasant features of Saudi life. In a land where people are stoned to death for adultery, it is dangerous to have a roving eye; in a land where the status quo is so precarious, it is dangerous to have an enquiring mind.

It is possible to make a photofit for Gulfman. He is 30–35, lower middle-class and embarrassingly aspirant. His education is redbrick/polytechnic. He believes himself to be shrewd, likes to say that he is a cynic. He reads Wilbur Smith and the free magazine that comes with his new Gold Card. Jewellery is worn – sometimes a Credit Suisse token on a chain. He despises the arts – he might go to the amateur Gilbert and Sullivan, if there is someone in it he knows. He likes to talk about camcorders, compact discs, kit-cars and tax shelters. His wife – very often his second wife – is deeply interested in nail polish. Her ambition is to open a nursery school.

Though it goes against his grain, Gulfman carries a sort of handbag for the many documents required to negotiate daily life in the Kingdom. Without these documents he is in peril; should he attract the attention of the police by, say, parking in the wrong place, he may be thrown into jail.

Gulfman curses his way early to the office, through traffic that knows no laws. The move towards 'Saudi-isation' has been under way for many years, so he will work alongside his hosts, and find them friendly, up to a point, but resentful of any criticism, watchful. At noon, he curses his way to the Gents; the floor is awash, for it is prayer-time, and ritual ablutions are required, and once again his Saudi colleagues have been washing their feet in the sink. Religion embarrasses him, especially in its public manifestations. He takes obscure comfort from the blatant hypocrisies of Saudi life – the gambling and womanising outside the Kingdom. He is not equipped to understand moral systems. He is not paid to do it. At three o'clock he goes home to a dip in the compound pool, to a piece of Dutch veal and a censored video; he goes to bed early, the air-conditioners rattling, and dreams of *Men Only* and pork sausages.

Quick in-and-out is the idea now; a couple of years max, he will say. But soon Gulfman is securely bound by his golden handcuffs. He always needs to do another year . . . just for more security, then for a bit more. He may be paying off a mortgage and putting his children through a private school, or his parents through their hip replacements. He may be paying alimony, or saving up to have his tattoos removed. He might go to Australia, when he makes the break; for the UK is so cramped and cold and Mrs Thatcher is such a leftist.

In daily life, he has everything he needs. The shops are well-stocked. Shopping keeps the family together; because of the laws that segregate the sexes few other joint and public activities are on offer. Nothing is cheap but petrol and flat Arab bread, but when he is in the Kingdom he lives frugally. He lives on his expectations; he likes to plan his holidays. His outlook, though, has narrowed over the years. His family look forward to going to Hong Kong, and other places where they have heard the shopping is very good.

Gulfman seldom sees his Saudi colleagues outside work. (Contact is not desired on either part. Saudis see foreigners as contaminators; they are necessary evils, paid inferiors, servants.) Unlike the classic expat, Gulfman has no club; social life is conducted almost entirely in private houses, and is lubricated by home-made wine and a colourless spirit called siddiqi. The authorities do not approve the viniculture but contrive to turn a blind eye. A familiar sight in any supermarket is a trolley groaning with grape juice, red and white, and stacked with bags of sugar; one room of his house stinks of yeast and rotting fruit, and murky brews bubble in plastic jerry-cans.

This double-think no longer bothers Gulfman. Daily life requires him to live by ill-defined rules which he does not understand, and which are always changing. In the Saudi system, which has to reconcile a mediaeval theology with the pleasures and horrors of the 20th century, all inconvenient features of the world fall into a black hole. The Saudi newspapers do not report crimes, only punishments. The English-language press excoriates the Americans as corrupt, effete imperialists, yet for years something commonly called 'the American missile base' has stood in the middle of Jeddah, proud behind its ostentatious golden gates. It has anti-aircraft missiles, people assume; they do not speculate about what else. It does not hide itself; everyone, obeying the custom of the country, simply pretends it isn't there.

18 August 1990

AFORE YE GO

Leaves from the commonplace book of Wallace Arnold

Though hardly as steeped in the rich, thoroughly British air of a Geoffrey, a Roderick or even, perchance, a Wallace, the name of Saddam Hussein seemed, at the time, more than acceptable to the goodly burghers of the Garrick Club.

I am talking now of the mid-Sixties (dread decade!) when the traditional gentlemen's clubs of London were considered by the young and ill-shaven insufficiently 'with-it'. ('With *what*, precisely?' I would declare in my richly stentorian tones over a leg of finest mutton, causing, needless to say, peals of mirth from my fellow guests – but I digress!) Nowadays, the Garrick is filled to the brim with the very greatest characters in the land – among them Mr Terry Worsthorne of the *Sunday Telegraph*, Mr Reginald Varney of *On the Buses* and several leading lights from *The Onedin Line* – but in that forlorn era it was a mere shell in which ghosts of the past seemed to hover in melancholy. By the fireplace, Mr Michael Miles might buttonhole one for the quick round of the Yes and No game before din-dins, and occasionally one would catch a glimpse of Mr Arthur Askey rehearsing his 'Buzzy Bee' routine *sotto voce* on the landing, but, by and large, the 'joint' no longer 'jumped'.

Never one to miss an opportunity, Saddam, at the time something of a big noise on the staff of *Burke's Peerage*, sought my aid in securing membership. Impressed by his robust handshake, pleasant blazers and rich fund of Gielgud anecdotes, the Committee elected him forthwith, honouring him further with the post of Entertainments Secretary.

No clubman he

Alas, it was soon to emerge that Saddam's instincts were far from being those of the natural clubman. This became evident at a Royal Variety Club dinner in honour of the three most famous Beverley Sisters, Dobs, Dibs and Dabs Beverley, with their youngest sister, Antonia Beverley – later to become known as the historian Antonia Fraser – in attendance, together with a galaxy of stars from stage and screen, among them Sir Alfred Sherman. It was to be a night of warm-hearted reminiscence and impromptu rendition presided over by honorary Gary – the term by which club members are known – HRH The Duke of Edinburgh.

It fell to Saddam to organise the various 'skits', dance sequences and folderols that were to accompany the speeches. Alas, members took it in bad odour when, shortly after an uproarious speech by the irrepressible Mr Terry Scott, who should march on to the floor but the Massed Bands of the Iraqi Fifth Airborne Division, trumpeting a tune in praise of Mohammed little-known to the assembled company, and frankly not catchy at all. When the exercise in Armed Combat which followed it resulted in severe injury to the Club Secretary some members decided to signal their disapproval by refusing a liqueur with their cigars.

Having lost his position at *Burke's* after dropping from inclusion all non-Iraqis, leaving but a single entrant (it seems that Lord Wyatt of Weevil originally hailed from one of the better parts of Baghdad), Saddam resigned his membership and went home. A sorry business, and one with repercussions that have since become all too evident.

18 August 1990

MARRIAGE A LA MODE

Nicholas Coleridge

A year and a month into marriage, free evenings – that is evenings with male friends unchaperoned by my wife – are few and far between. When we got engaged we sort of agreed that every fortnight or so we'd have a solo evening, but this has never really taken off. For one thing it was never clear what these free nights were intended for. I am not the kind of person who likes to spend an evening in a pub. Nor can I visualise myself roistering with old schoolfriends every second Thursday at the Pinstripe or Gaslight clubs, being fawned over by hostesses from Epsom who'd whisper soothingly, 'Don't worry if your wife doesn't understand you, duckie, she's not here now, is she?' before sliding over a saucer with a bill on it for £275.

The vicar in Gloucestershire who gave us an inspiring pep talk before reading the banns was a great enthusiast for free evenings. With an eight-year difference in our ages, he said, we were certain to have divergent cultural interests. These we could pursue, quite independently, on our free evenings. It was a charming picture. While one of us attended a sitar concert, the other would be all ears at a lecture at the Royal Geographical Society or the National Art-Collections Fund. What our inspiring vicar reckoned without, however, were the two great enemies of promise in modern marriage: late work hours and the widespread conspiracy among other newly married people that you can only be truly fulfilled when seated at their dining-room table with three other nice safe couples, admiring newly laid Amtico flooring.

Almost all the married couples I know well stepped out together for several years before they became engaged. Three years is about the average, though some went out for six or seven years. In retrospect it is hard to establish why they waited so long: most of the girls had jobs they enjoyed, so perhaps didn't want the disruption, and there was no great emotional or moral pressure to formalise a perfectly easy arrangement.

Increasingly often, though, at these dinner parties of happy young marrieds, there are spectres at the feast. An unmarried girl in her early thirties is there, who arrives alone and leaves alone. For the evening she has been fixed up by her hosts with a spare man, invariably divorced; often, for some reason, a German banker with granite-coloured hair and a plum-coloured smoking jacket and two small children aged eleven and nine. And what is sad about this lone girl is that, six months earlier, you would have placed a huge bet on her imminent engagement to her well-established boyfriend with whom she shared a flat.

How new is all this? People have, after all, been cheerfully enjoying sex before marriage since it was discovered by Philip Larkin in 1963, and then getting hurt by it. What I believe has changed, however, is two things. The first is the long, open-ended, unfurtive relationships – virtually dry runs for wedlock – that have characterised middle-class love throughout the Eighties. And now, as we move into the Nineties, we can suddenly see the consequences of it all. Marriages that would once unquestionably have gone ahead fail to proceed after five or six years of extended romance, during which time the couple have been inseparable and monogamous, spent holiday after holiday together, and been widely regarded as honorary marrieds. From my own observation, about a third of these long relationships now fall apart on the threshold of engagement, creating a new species of person: *the unmarried divorcee.* For the man in the relationship this is not so great a hardship (though often psychologically scarring to a surprising degree), for he can look to younger women for sexual and intellectual rejuvenation. For the girl, it can be bewildering. By the time she's 30 she has invested almost a decade in her career and one important relationship.

Gradually the affair has lost momentum, but so embroiled are they emotionally, and so carried along by the blithe conviction of their contemporaries that they would one day be man and wife, that it takes several painful soul-searching months to disengage. Clearly, since there was no longer sufficient momentum for them to become engaged, they were right to separate. But where does this leave the unmarried divorcee? Often vulnerable. Unless another unattached bachelor in his early thirties appears on the scene at the optimum moment (from where? The Far East? Hong Kong companies like Jardine Matheson still grant their unmarried 30-year-old employees a four-month sabbatical to come home and snap up a bride), then the statistical bias has shifted to older – and therefore probably divorced – suitors. One of the great trends over the last two years has been the number of intelligent, well-educated, grown-up girls in their late twenties who have surprised themselves by marrying one of the growing army of divorced males in their late thirties or early forties. Whether a biological craving to give birth is a significant – even the decisive – consideration in this, I cannot say.

When Shaw wrote, in one of his typically annoying aphorisms in *Man and Superman*, that 'it is a woman's business to get married as soon as possible, and a man's to keep unmarried as long as he can', he was reckoning without the modern faith in a consumer guarantee of satisfaction: 'If not completely satisfied please return to us within 30 days saying when and where you bought it.' The whole point – and the moral justification – of marrying later, having played the field, is that your choice ought to be better informed. You know what you are looking for, your eye is perfectly honed, and in your maturity you can better distinguish the spangly showgirl from the understated sophisticate who will become your wife. And there is, of course, a perfectly sound subsidiary argument for later marriage: the knowledge that, as we live longer and longer, our choice may have to last 60 or 70 years, so had better be well considered. Never take a melon home until you've squeezed it.

The latest *Marriage and Divorce Statistics* for England and Wales from the Office of Population Censuses and Surveys (HMSO, £8.75) show that between 1978 and 1988, the last year for which statistics have been collated, the mean age for bridegrooms at marriage had gone up by a year from $29\frac{1}{2}$ to just under 31 (for bachelor bridegrooms from 25 to almost 27). For brides the mean age had risen from 26.6 to almost 28.5 (for first-time brides 22.85 to 24.5).

In a late-marrying society, there is an increasing onus on both partners to get on with their spouse's numerous friends who have been collected in the 15 or so years before the couple met. What this generally means in effect is for the wife, being younger, to ingratiate herself with her husband's legion of school, university, work and sporting cronies. A very pretty soon-to-be-married girl told me that she was daunted by the roster of close friends of her fiancé – dozens and dozens of them – to whom she was taken for inspection when she got engaged; each one the subject of a long briefing beforehand in the car ('Adrian's great. I got to know him 11 years ago in Nantucket when I was going out with his cousin Rosie') and with whom she was expected to forge an instantaneous rapport. And not only with male friends but with ex-girlfriends too. We live at the start of a decade in which almost every marriage is haunted by the ghosts of long-established premarital lovers.

I am struck by the expedient new etiquette that has grown up on how to behave on meeting a former live-in girlfriend. Other than in the most general terms, it is regarded as improper to refer to a premarital entanglement. H. M. Bateman could have drawn a cartoon entitled, 'The man who reminded an old girlfriend – in front of her husband – of the creaky bed at Juan-les-Pins'. It is a studied, even mannered, etiquette, since I've never heard of anybody pretending that old lovers don't exist. Nevertheless a marvellous vagueness must descend on any conversation touching on that period. A conversational device I've observed is never making it plain that you were ever alone with another man's wife. This is achieved by inserting the word 'all' into every reminiscence, i.e. 'when we were *all* on safari in Kenya' or 'when we *all* stayed at that flea-pit on the edge of the desert'.

If marriage holds less mystery than it once did, then it ought to hold fewer nasty surprises too. The latest divorce statistics show that dissolutions granted on 'other' grounds (as opposed to desertion or adultery) are very low (7 in 152,633). 'Other' is presumably code for dressing up as a nanny on the first night of the honeymoon and chasing your wife round the bed with a ruler and a bottle of gripe water. There is little that is arbitrary about modern marriage. In *The Code of the Woosters*, Bertie tries to imagine what marriage to Madeleine Basset would be like, concluding, 'She is definitely the sort of girl who puts her hand over her husband's eyes, as he is crawling into breakfast with a morning head, and says, "Guess who?"' The modern Madeleine-suitor knows all this and more about her already.

A parallel development is the arrival of the pre-nuptial agreement; not a money-grabbing Hollywood 'prenup' (as they call them) where everything from the whirlpool spa to the towelling bathrobes is divided up before the wedding in anticipation of divorce, but a gentler, more tentative English contract that has more to do with agreement on how you are going to live your life than the division of possessions. Until the Sixties decisions about lifestyle hardly applied to conventional couples, since the assumptions you could make about how your married years would unfold were so clear-cut: questions like where you would live, what kind of work the husband would do, how long he would work, the care of children, even the kind of holidays you'd take. This is no longer the case. And a consequence of couples marrying later is that attitudes can be agreed in advance. A restaurant critic I know has made a firm pre-nuptial agreement with his wife that, however poor they become in the future, they will never live south of the river.

And similar pre-nuptial agreements are struck on matters such as education ('The boys can go to boarding school so long as the girls stay at home'), domicile ('I agree to stay in London until I'm 40, but that's it'), holidays ('I enjoy fishing in Iceland. You don't. Therefore I'm going fishing on the Laxa for a week every August on my own, and you agree never to give me a hard time about it').

For all this careful planning, are marriages becoming happier? My own apart, I don't believe they really are. There were 153,000 divorces during 1988, an increase of 1 per cent on 1987, and I knew three of them. Two of the couples had lived with each other before deciding to marry, but within two years were separated, neither for any good reason beyond unforeseen disappointment and peevishness. If you live with someone for five years before marriage, the seven-year itch comes early. But why isn't the divorce rate falling? Brides in the Twenties, who were generally obliged to select their husbands from a limited set menu of suitors, and with only a short time in which to dither, were playing a form of marital Russian roulette. Whenever Barbara Cartland speaks on the wireless about the 20 or so proposals she received from different men in one Season, I can't help thinking of the relief that the 19 spurned suitors must now be feeling. But the modern girl, choosing à la carte, is engaged in a different trial of nerves. In 1988, of the 256,221 spinsters that got married, only 25,000 were aged 30 or over. The downside of later marriage for girls is the increasingly discernible paranoia in many – not all – as time marches on and the temptation to marry whoever happens to be available and willing becomes compelling. You can always tell at a wedding, as you crane your neck towards the aisle to see the bride and groom processing back to the porch, whether it is a marriage made in heaven or in the spirit of compromise.

I am doubtful too that later marriage really induces the worldly tolerance, born of a greater understanding of human frailty, that it ought. Jekyll and Hyde behaviour, dormant until the ceremony of marriage is over, is something that even extended periods of living together cannot anticipate. A not-long-wed currency broker I know, in many respects a liberal enough man, announced to his wife on their return from honeymoon that he expected a three-course dinner every night, including Sunday, and that he had no intention of helping make it. When she pointed out that she, too, had a job, and would appreciate the same support in the kitchen that he'd given for the previous five years, he made such a fuss that she capitulated. I knew my wife for ages before we got married, so was pretty certain of her character, but I am startled sometimes by my own deep prejudices about the proper conduct of a wife. As it happens we share things like grocery shopping on a roughly 30–70 husband-to-wife ratio, but when supplies of black peppercorns or Tabasco run short, I am in no doubt who is to blame. On the other hand, marriage has reduced my yearning to dine at restaurants and I have come to appreciate eating at home.

'What's it feel like being married?' This is the stupid question you are asked three or four hundred times in the first year of being so. 'Exactly the same,' says a travel-writing friend in curmudgeonly tone. 'If we'd thought we'd feel different we wouldn't have got married.' In my own case, I confess to feeling 'different' only in the most commonplace ways: slightly more secure, pleased not to have to make quite so much effort or show off so much at parties, pleased to have a companion with a happy disposition who likes most of the things I like. And I confess too a measure of that awful smugness that besets married couples, and a proselytising determination that all other single people should marry too (never mind whom). 'Don't leave it too late,' I hear myself saying. 'Go on – take a chance.'

25 August 1990

GAMBLING WITH THE GULF

Charles Glass

Somewhere in Saudi Arabia

Before the interruption of a holiday with my children in the South of France, I read in *Le Parisien* that a hitherto obscure Saudi, an adviser to Prince Faisal named Sheikh Eynani, had made a few, shall we say, unlucky wagers. He dropped a mere 30 million francs in Monte Carlo, where he may earn the title 'the man who saved the bank', and another 84 million francs in Cannes at the Carlton Club. As I sit here watching American soldiers arrive at an airbase whose location the press has been asked not to disclose, I think of Sheikh Eynani and his 114 million francs, a mere £11.4 million. Are the American boys and girls I see here, as well as boys from Britain and Egypt, going to fight, kill and die so the sheikh can try his luck again with the casinos of the Côte d'Azur?

When the Iraqi dictator, Saddam Hussein, the man the State Department called a 'moderate' until this month, invaded Kuwait on 2 August, he must have been surprised at the American, European and Arab response. He had every reason to be. In 1980, the United States and most of the Western world endorsed his invasion of Iran. Throughout that war, France, West Germany and other European countries, not to mention the Soviet Union, supplied Saddam's army with the weapons it needed. In 1987 and 1988, the United States sent an armada to the Persian Gulf to rescue Saddam from the Iranian army that was advancing on Iraqi soil. (At that time, only Iran compared Saddam to Adolf Hitler and demanded as the price of peace his elimination.) When Saddam used poison gas on tens of thousands of Iranian troops, the world said and did nothing. When he murdered Iraqi deserters in the marshes of southern Iraq with the same poisons, the world looked away. When he used the chemicals again on thousands of Kurdish Iraqi citizens, the same world sent notes of protest. Until he invaded Kuwait, the United States was providing Saddam with financial aid – more than $1 billion in agricultural credits and $250 million in export-import bank loans – and was the main market for his oil. The US-Iraqi Business Forum, headed by prominent American businessmen and former diplomats, were praising Saddam's moderation and his progress towards democracy.

Nor was that all. West German and Austrian companies were assisting Saddam's chemical and nuclear weapons programmes. European firms were providing computers and other technology to assist in the production of Iraqi ballistic missiles. France sold Iraq the famous Exocets that had been used to such effect on British ships, and may be used again here, in the South Atlantic in 1982. The West, the Soviet Union, China, most of the Arab states and most of the Third World steadfastly ignored the massacres and deportations of Kurds in northern Iraq, the torture and execution of suspected dissidents, the murder of parts of families *pour décourager les autres* and the brutal torture of children. Why then should this world which had tolerated, which had in fact been implicated in, Saddam's earlier crimes bother about a little thing like Kuwait?

It would be comforting to believe that the United States and its allies are fighting for freedom, but there is a suspicion that an American former assistant secretary of defense, Lawrence J. Korb, touched the truth when he told *The Washington Post* this week, 'If Kuwait grew carrots, we wouldn't give a damn.' A friend of mine in the United States wrote to me a week after the Iraqi invasion, 'How come George Bush has been lavishing such loving care on the guy who now turns out to be worse than Hitler, though a few weeks ago he was a friendly moderate? Why is invading Kuwait an unspeakable violation of international law and morality, while invading Panama or Lebanon (by Israel, that is), or Timor is just normal statecraft, quite justifiable? How is it legitimate for Bush to set in action a programme to eliminate Saddam, overthrow his government, etc. with untold consequences, on the explicit grounds that Saddam threatens our potential economic welfare, but not OK for Hussein to take over Kuwait because it is undermining Iraq's current economic welfare? If Saddam ought to be brought to justice (as doubtless he should), or crushed like vermin, what is the right way to deal with Reagan, Bush and a few others who come to mind?'

Some day, our children will be taught that this battle, if it takes place, was fought to protect freedom and democracy. My generation was brought up to believe that Britain, France and the United States waged war against Nazi Germany to save the Jews and other non-Aryans in central Europe from extinction. Would that we had, but we didn't. The world tolerated Adolf Hitler's internal crimes and his invasions, just as it did Saddam's, until he crossed a line that had little to do with concern for humanity and everything to do with the balance of power. Hitler, like Saddam, just went too far. Yet even the most cynical among us must concede that, whatever Washington's motives, disposing of Saddam would be good, first and foremost, for Saddam's own people – just as Germans are better off without Hitler. (Anyone who doubts this must read Samir al-Khalil's *Republic of Fear: The*

Politics of Modern Iraq (Hutchinson Radius, 1989).)

The concentration of American, British, Egyptian and other troops in the Gulf may afford opportunities even greater than the ruin of Saddam Hussein. For the first time this century, there is the chance to undo some of the damage done to this region by the settlement of 1919, when the British and French dismembered the Ottoman Empire. In discussion with Turkey and a new government in Iraq, the United Nations and the United States may be able to bring autonomy and some justice to the Kurds, the stateless people who have suffered more than any other in the Middle East. The victory of the principle that territory shall not be acquired by force could pave the way to discussions between the Palestinians and Israelis (forgetting for the moment the Palestinians' temporary fascination with Saddam) on a settlement of the status of the territory Israel acquired by force in 1967. And the world, having saved Kuwait, Saudi Arabia and the other oil states from Iraqi aggression, could make it clear that these states, like those in eastern Europe, must now face the task of reforming their systems and moving towards governments 'of the people, by the people and for the people', and away from enriching the casino owners of Cannes and Monte Carlo. The question is not so much whether these things are desirable as whether they can be achieved. On that, we shall have to wait.

25 August 1990

'Somehow it's not the same now they're laser guided.'

THE IMPORTANCE OF BEING HONEST

Christopher Fildes

Lord Kylsant, chairman of the Royal Mail Line, stood in the dock beside his company secretary, charged with raising money on a false prospectus and false accounts. When the jury went out, the company secretary's wife telephoned Patrick Hastings, KC, for the defence: would her husband be late for dinner? 'Yes, madam,' she was told. 'About seven years late.'

Hastings did better than that – both men were acquitted. (Kylsant later faced lesser charges and went to jail for three months.) Ernest Saunders of Guinness, however, will be five years late. So he leaves the stage, blaming, to the last, everybody but himself.

If Guinness can still conjure up the Royal Mail case of the 1930s, the point is that such cases are rare indeed and their power to shock is durable. To label them as City scandals – skulduggery in the Square Mile – is to fall short of the mark. They were scandals in the conduct of major public companies outside the City – a shipping line, a brewer. Helped by evidence from Lord Plender, the great accountant of the day, the Royal Mail defendants had their honesty of purpose accepted. The Guinness defendants were less fortunate. They were not helped by the evidence for the defence; it may have been fatal to them all.

Their prospects seemed brightest at the end of the prosecution's case. Its chief witness, Olivier Roux, had cut a wretched figure. Seldom in a case of this seriousness can the prosecution have cared to depend on the evidence of a sworn liar. Mr Roux had to testify that, in giving evidence to the Department of Trade and Industry's inspectors, he had perjured himself. If his evidence were now to be believed, a former president of the Law Society would have to be lying. Mr Roux was succeeded in the box by Lord Iveagh, Guinness's president and former chairman. He was unimpressive, and in cross-examination he was asked whether he had had drink-related problems at the time of the bid for Distillers. He denied this.

Three of the defendants were content to leave it at that, giving no evidence and letting their counsel argue that the prosecution had not made out its case. Mr Saunders gave his evidence, and was thought to have insisted on it. His theme was familiar from *Nightmare*, the book published under his son's name – portraying him as an honest salesman ensnared by sophisticated financiers who used him, dumped him, and blamed him. There had indeed been a crooked conspiracy, he explained, but it had nothing to do with him. Day after day Mr Saunders returned to the box to swear that others were lying. In the end his own counsel could not invite the jury to believe all he had said.

Mr Saunders the salesman is part of the story, and a warning of the perils, which should be familiar, of making the salesman the boss. (Lord Stokes at British Leyland was a far better salesman than chairman.) Salesmen are always tempted to live by promising delivery next week, in the knowledge that next week they can promise something else. This particular high-powered salesman was headhunted out of Nestlé in Switzerland, to provide a new ingredient for Guinness. That, he delivered.

The Guinness of those days was a complacent and affable company, family dominated though not family-owned, living by its black but comely stout. Diversifications in hundreds of different directions had got nowhere. Guinness itself was unique, known and liked all over the world, but people were not drinking more of it – rather less, in fact. In the marketing men's jargon, it was an established branded product in a mature market.

Nothing like Mr Saunders had hit Guinness since its original yeast had bubbled up in 18th-century Dublin. He soon dominated the company. He held clearance sales of the job-lot diversifications, and tried to replace them with new profit earners – chains of newsagents, for instance. As for Guinness itself, he transformed the advertising (though it never sold any more stout), and his changes were symbolic. Gone were the days of 'Guinness is good for you'. Ernest Saunders stood for 'Pure genius'.

His supporters' club certainly thought so, and continued to think so through all the twists and turns of events which followed. I began to wonder when Guinness bid for Bell's. A whisky distiller? Another one-product company with an established branded product in a mature market? Surely the genius had diagnosed that as Guinness's trouble? I tried the effect of merging Guinness and Bell's in a glass and drinking the amalgamation. It lacked synergy.

The bid for Bell's got off to a bad start. Bell's share price suddenly shot up, and Patrick Weever, writing the stock market report in the *Standard*, had no doubt what was happening: heavy buying from Switzerland, he said, the bid from Guinness is on the way, help yourself. That was good advice; the bid came next morning. Some rough exchanges followed, but Bell's itself proved no more than a pipe-opener before the big one: Distillers.

Somebody had to do something about Distillers, that loose and ineffectual federation of producer baronies with its nine London head offices. The right people to do something were the owners, the shareholders – but the Edinburgh mafia of fund managers did not care to fire people whom they might have to meet on the links at Muirfield. They ducked, and let their shares trickle down towards London. Distillers is the worst instance of the British vice of management by takeover. That system in fact offered Distillers the choice of two managers, at the heads of the two rival bidders. One was James Gulliver, then of Argyll, later of Lowndes Queensway, which has just gone down owing hundreds of millions. The other was Ernest Saunders.

Mr Saunders won, at a price. Price is the battleground where bids are won or lost. Guinness's shares were the currency in which its bid was expressed, and all hung on what that currency might be worth. There are fair and unfair ways to influence it, legal and illegal ways, but this case has not served to define them, and did not, in the end, hinge on them.

When the scandal first broke, the imputation was that Guinness's money had been used to prop up Guinness's share price. The old Companies Act forbade companies to finance the purchase of their own shares, the new and ill-drafted Act says that it might be all right, in the United States and many other countries it is legal and commonplace. As the Guinness prosecutions trudged on, it was fascinating to see the Companies Act charges fading into the background. A fallback position, said Mr Justice Henry finally, throwing them out.

The charges which sent Mr Saunders to jail were that he had operated a slush fund with Guinness's money, covertly giving large fees or concessions to people who would support Guinness shares, and concealing this by a system of bogus transactions and false invoices. Ivan Boesky on Wall Street was in the slush, and in due course, seeking to modify his punishment, told what he knew. That information was crucial.

Victorious in battle, Mr Saunders promptly disavowed two formal undertakings which Guinness had made – that Distillers' headquarters would be in Scotland, and that the new chairman of the combined company would be the Governor of the Bank of Scotland, Sir Thomas Risk; instead it should be Ernest Saunders. Those, after all, were last week's promises. I thought it a danger signal, and said so in *The Spectator*, under the heading: 'Promises, promises – or, the importance of being honest', 26 July 1986).

The excuses put out from Guinness, I said, were neat eyewash, and shareholders who would take them would swallow anything. Mr

Saunders's faithful fan-club remained undismayed. He had a technique of endearing himself to one or two financial columnists, by giving them the sense that they, with him, were on the inside track. They in turn backed him uncritically, arguing that his pure genius must have whatever it wanted.

If the watchdogs of the press were silenced with bones, what silenced the watchdogs of the boardroom? Where were the Guinness directors, when Mr Saunders was running their company as his personal fiefdom? Were they just sitting back and enjoying the share price? In a properly directed company, could the chief executive put his hand in the till for £25 million of slush money without a word to anyone but his cronies? The directors bear a grave responsibility. They compounded it by letting their fallen favourite fight a ruinous law case, with his liberty at stake, without a penny of help. That was despicable.

In the event, it was Mr Saunders himself, overreaching, who made an entry for capable outside directors on the Guinness board. The Thomas Risk affair, and the cheap excuses put about for disowning an eminent banker, worried the Governor of the Bank of England. Mr Saunders called twice at the Bank, making a disastrous impression. A very senior official was heard to say: 'But that man is a crook.' The Governor secured the appointments of four new Guinness directors. Mr Saunders became chairman, but within months the new men had ousted him.

The Bank, then, was a City watchdog that barked – and indeed bit, tearing great holes in the trousers of Guinness advisers. Some lost their jobs, some lost their licences, some have lost both. The Takeover Panel, by contrast, turned out to be a stuffed owl – not a hoot, not a twitch! Later, given a good shake and a new chairman, the Panel came to life, and made Guinness pay £85 million in compensation to Distillers shareholders who had been treated unfairly. The trial judge and others have had much to say about the need to protect shareholders, but only the Panel has done anything for them.

The verdicts and sentences in the Guinness case have been taken as texts, to preach the laxity of City regulation, and the superior merits of criminal law and trial by jury. The texts do not justify the sermons. The regulators' legally-backed powers to judge and punish – to disgrace, to fine, to suspend, to put out of business, to enforce compensation – did not, for the most part, exist when the Guinness fund was slushing.

As for the criminal law, if the convictions prove it effective, what is proved by the previous sequence of acquittals in recent cases of financial misconduct? It is dangerous and unjust to argue that there must be something right with convictions and wrong with acquittals.

All that is proved is that the Serious Fraud Office, helped by some expensive commercial barristers and a good tip from Mr Boesky, has finally broken its duck.

Even this is an innings with faults. The case should never have taken five years from crime to trial. Defendants should not have to ruin themselves, in advance of the verdict and however it goes, in order to pay for their defence – seven figures is the going rate. Over the long-drawn-out proceedings there has hung the implication of a show trial, intended to prove determination to crack down on the excesses of the market. In the spring of 1987, a friend of mine close to what was going on at Guinness successfully forecast the date of that year's general election. 'It will', he said, 'be seven weeks after they arrest Ernest.'

Even now it is not all over. A second Guinness trial follows, no doubt in good time for the next election. This one has demonstrated a major scandal, not in the City, which on the evidence before the court was abused and deceived, but in the management and direction of a great company. Unchecked power corrupted. The worst casualty was that company's best asset, its good name. Guinness was bad for us.

1 September 1990

'I told the tooth fairy I wanted the money in Deutschmarks.'

INSIDE THE CASTLE

Dominic Lawson

Prague

When Mrs Thatcher flies into what is now called the Czech and Slovak Federal Republic, for her meeting on Monday with President Vaclav Havel, the following things will happen to her: her pilot will remind her that it is forbidden to take photographs over Czech air space, and that when she lands she must exchange foreign currency at the state bank at the airport. There she will find she is forced to buy Czech crowns at an invented rate of 30 to the pound, barely half the amount she would receive on any street corner in Prague. She will notice that any small change handed to her will still bear the imprint of the hammer and sickle. She will no longer be rendering unto that particular Caesar, but I think we would all recognise this as a socialist transaction. In fact probably none of these things will be forced on Mrs Thatcher – prime ministers are special cases – but they will be on the bevy of English journalists accompanying her, unless policies have changed since last week when I made the same journey, to interview President Havel.

The political table-talk in Prague is that while the finance minister, Vaclav Klaus, an unreconstructed supporter of Milton Friedman, is aching to introduce market economics to the country, even to introduce private sector restaurants, President Havel is obstructing him. Havel himself seemed almost affronted when I put this – hardly controversial – point to him.

'That is of course a mistake. It is a nonsense. Some people think it because that's the way it appears in our newspapers, but they do not reflect the real truth. Mr Klaus and I agree that the reform must be speedy and profound, although it is not really a reform but in fact a substitution of the existing system by a different one.'

Perhaps the argument therefore is at a different level, namely, what shall be the nature of the new system? When I asked Mr Havel if he was prepared to have capitalism in Czechoslovakia, he replied, with some asperity, 'I have never said that we should build capitalism in our country. We want to build a functioning economic system, on which prospering economies and trade have been based for millennia, that is, long before capitalism arrived on the scene.'

I'm not sure what Mrs Thatcher will make of that when she attempts to persuade the President of her ideas of a Pan-European Common Market, in which the newly liberated Eastern European countries would be full members of the capitalist club. Havel, as he put it to me, is 'a friend of various co-operative, collective forms of ownership, but at the same time I can see that purely private ownership has a legitimate right to exist parallel to them'. Switch the meaning of that sentence on its head, and you arrive at the view of the British Prime Minister.

The last time the two leaders met was at a dinner thrown in Havel's honour at 10 Downing Street. A fellow guest said later that he had never seen two people sitting next to each other with less in common. Havel grinned impishly when I recounted this remark to him, and then in his characteristic rumbling monotone attempted a serious response.

'Whether sitting at the dinner table next to Mrs Thatcher we are symbolising two different worlds' – here Havel broke off to stub out yet another cigarette – 'that is not up to me to judge. But it's always a useful experience for everybody – the confrontation with someone who may think in a different way.'

Is President Havel, the unwitting hero of the Right in the West, in fact a socialist? In 1968, when he was among a group dedicated to reviving the extinct Social Democratic party, Havel said in an interview, 'I was always in favour of socialism in the sense of nationalisation of the major means of production.' When I reminded Havel of this, he retorted, 'I might have said something like that, but my opinions have developed as I am learning to know the world. If I in the past accentuated the collective form of ownership more than I accentuate it today, perhaps it is because today I am some 20 years older.' So, come clean now, Vaclav, are you still a man of the Left or not?

'I have been refusing all my life to be identified as a leftist or a rightist. For many years I have been suspected by some of being a leftist, and by others of being a rightist, and at the same time both groups claimed me, and I just had to laugh.'

I was just about to remind Havel of Timothy Garton Ash's first law of politics in Eastern Europe post-1989: the man who says he is neither a leftist nor a rightist is a leftist. But then finally, after an agonisingly long drag at a cigarette held between thumb and forefinger, he answered the question: 'Nevertheless, I should probably say one thing: God created me in such a way that my heart is on the left side of my chest, and I will not deny my affiliation with the . . . let's say . . . liberal-minded international intellectual community, which is called by some left-wing.'

This conflation of God and the Left is in fact evident in the bookshelf in Havel's peculiarly modest and angular little office in the vast building overlooking Prague, known to all simply as 'the Castle'. Behind Havel and the clouds of smoke emanating from him I could make out, almost in a row, two copies of the Bible, a biography of Mother Teresa, and a plaque with the name of Olof Palme engraved on it. So, having established, at least to my own satisfaction, Havel's political credentials, I also had to ask, 'Are you a Christian?'

'I would not call myself a particularly good Christian, or even a practising Catholic, but at the same time I admit openly that my overall view of the world and its mysteries has been affected by my Christian upbringing and environment.'

It is tempting to see an element of the Christian doctrine in the reluctance of the new administration to launch into prosecution and sentencing of those who brutalised and oppressed the likes of . . . Vaclav Havel, during the period of communist rule. Whether or not there is an element of forgiveness in this, it is a matter of intense debate among those who once suffered as dissidents; one of them, now a member of parliament, told me, 'The Velvet Revolution has been velvet mostly for the beasts and freaks who used to run this

'I had no idea it was that permanent.'

country.' I repeated interrogatively exactly these words to Havel.

'First, we didn't invent the term Velvet Revolution. It was invented by Western journalists, and then it began to be used here as well. In my opinion it is not a very fortunate expression. As to your question, the situation is a complicated one. The revolutionary process is still going on while at the same time we are building the legal state. That means, as a matter of principle, that we want to avoid all acts of revenge, and to open the way for justice. The implementation of that justice is, I agree, not often as perfect as it should be. But if, on the other hand, we let the revolution take justice into its own hands we would join the fate of revolutions devouring their own children, responding to violence with violence.'

At this point the man sitting next to President Havel on the presidential sofa, sipping the presidential bitter lemon, nodded vigorously in agreement. This was none other than Prince von Schwarzenberg, Havel's Chancellor. And the Prince ought to know about such things. After all, he is a direct descendent of the Prince von Schwarzenberg who for his Habsburg masters put down the 1848 Revolution in Austria with such unsentimental efficiency.

Despite his name, von Schwarzenberg is in fact a Czech citizen, so I was able without embarrassment to ask Havel about . . . the Germans. Any visitor to Prague will seem to hear German spoken almost as much as the language of the natives, and bright new Mercedes and BMWs litter the streets of the city, dwarfing the Skodas which are all the locals can aspire to. As President, Havel himself is driven in a cavalcade of BMWs, at least one of them a gift from the German President, Richard von Weizsäcker. I recalled to Havel the remark he made in his inaugural speech as President, in January: 'Our state should never again be an appendage or a poor relation of anyone else.' Does that include Germany?

'I personally don't share the fear that Czechoslovakia could become a satellite and appendix of the uniting huge and rich Germany. We do not have to be afraid of a democratic neighbour. We can always reach an agreement with a democracy. There does exist in this part of the world a kind of historical genetically coded fear concerning the Germans, but it seems to me that this tradition should be patiently opposed. We should fight the subconscious fear, rooted in our tradition, of Germans as such.'

I don't suppose anyone in the room could altogether forget that we were sitting in what might have been the private office of Heydrich, when that Nazi was the 'protector' of Bohemia.

But why, I asked Havel, should the genetic trait only be a characteristic of those uneasy about German power? Why could there not be some undesirable genetic characteristics in the Germans themselves, as listed by Mrs Thatcher's adviser, Mr Charles Powell?

Havel's reply was so lengthy that it took almost an entire cigarette to get through: 'I should perhaps correct myself, and say that I use the word genetic in inverted commas. Of course it is not the result of genetics but of social and historical tradition. It is an expression of archetypes transferred from one generation to another. For example we can observe now the fears expressed by Poland about its western border, which seem to us excessive and unnecessary . . . I can't at the same time rule out the possibility that in some fraction of the German population there exists some sort of expansionist archetype, but it does not seem to me to be the policy of the new Germany or the will of the German public. I consider it a marginal phenomenon.'

So, no need to worry about undue German influence on the Czech economy. But I couldn't help noticing the inscription on the lighter with which Havel was fiddling throughout our interview. It was the logo of BMW. 'What's that then?' I asked Havel. He gave a wry little grin, and scuttled across his office to his desk, threw the lighter into a drawer, rummaged around for a few seconds, found what he was looking for, shuffled back, sat down, and banged another lighter down on the table between us. This one had the unmistakable twelve-starred emblem of the European Community. Then we all laughed, not too nervously.

15 September 1990

HAPPY FAMILIES

Hilary Corke

I see I've got Mrs Bun the baker's wife,
And Master Bun who was once a bun in her oven,
And Mr Chips the carpenter, and one
Of his young shavings, and Mr Boot the cobbler,
And Master Boot (Jack Boot) the Hitler youth,
And strict Miss Boot the disciplinarian.
Well that lot, I suppose, can be made to run;
But what shall I do with the wild card left over,
What do I do with Mr Desire the lover?

He's only wanting Miss Desire the beloved;
But I've asked all round and never a hide nor hair of her,
No one admits to being even aware of her,
They shake their heads or stall.
Either someone is lying, which wouldn't surprise me,
Or else she never was in the pack at all.

So we see it's not after all a simple diversion,
Completing a happy family: all's inter-reactive,
Where just what you need is denied you for just that reason,
And sticking to rule is usually counter-productive,
And the cards change faces even as they change places;
And even when the game's over no one has won.
Happy Families is easier said than done.

15 September 1990

VOYEURISTIC EDITORS

Vicki Woods

How many times a night one likes to have sexual intercourse is not a permissible topic at dinner; nor is it a fit subject for a columnist on the *Times* or the *Independent*. Sex talk – Doing It, Loving It and Bragging About It – is for the lower classes, isn't it? and the grimy papers they read. Sex and violence and smut and sleaze: it brightens up their dull lives and keeps them going between Giro cheques. The lower classes bonk away in an uncontrolled manner in their underprivileged housing – 'I Had Sex at 13 and I've Never Stopped' and grubby men in raincoats write about it for the grubby papers – 'Are there orgies down your street? Tell us any day 10 a.m. to 6 p.m. on 071 782 4498.' These headlines are from last Sunday's *News of the World*.

The shoe-wearing classes are assumed to keep this sort of thing well tucked in, like a shirt-tail, and undiscussed, except sotto voce

'Have you a copy of The Lady?*'*

with a close friend, or wordlessly, like Sicilian mafiosi using only eye-contact and raised eyebrows. Sex is very powerful, of course, and will sometimes burst the confines even of the pinstriped trouser, which is why the middle classes, especially men, have a great fear of being discovered *in flagrante* themselves by the *News of the World* or the *Sun*. It isn't so much a fear of being discovered to have bonked (almost everyone bonks, after all, and one's wife may forgive) but a fear of being for ever tarred by those shudder-making lower-class headlines saying, 'Ooooh, Five Times a Night!' and the pictures of Sex Mad Karen or Debbie (as it might be) who looks like one's cleaning-woman or her daughter and the copy beneath written in the same curiously dated demotic as the *Beano* and the *Dandy*, about toffs and blokes and pals and kids and boozing and kinky stuff and fancying sex-mad raving nymphos like crazy. No man in public life or a decent shirt, no merchant banker, no Harley Street doctor, no moderately successful television scriptwriter even, wants to see his own haunted photograph slammed up alongside that of Mrs A. and Mrs B. posing and smiling in their favourite undies.

Newspapers with downmarket readerships, then, print as much about sex as they can, in order, presumably, to keep Kevin and Sharon in a permanent state of arousal. And newspapers with upmarket readerships have to get their attitudes to bonking and undies pretty firmly sorted out, or they run the risk of losing not readers – never that – but class.

The *Daily Mail*, which I once worked on, prides itself on its upmarket readership despite its tabloid shape and it has a unique line on sex stories. The *Mail* knows full well that 'tits' and 'bums' and bonking are horribly lower-class, but it also knows that sex sells. So – write about it. Often. But do it with 'taste' (no hard language) and decorum (no dirty pictures) and flag the sex feature with urgent straplines that tell your readers they will learn important lessons about themselves and the human condition by reading it: the Rape Story Every Woman in Britain Must Read, for example, of Jill Saward's account of her assault at the Ealing vicarage, or What Pamella's Story Tells Us About Men of Power, of Miss Bordes's life and times with Arabs and newspaper editors. In the case of Jill Saward's book, the important lesson about the human condition failed to come across. My neighbour the headhunter's wife bought the *Mail* every day last week, in sympathy with a young woman who had been horrifically treated, she felt, both by drunken intruders and then subsequently by the judiciary (the trial judge observed that Jill Saward's 'trauma . . . was not so great' – after she was raped by various means including a knife-handle – and gave the rapists astonishingly light sentences). My neighbour the headhunter's wife was disappointed with her purchase. She learned no important lesson. 'I couldn't work out why they'd bothered to print it. I wanted to understand how on earth she coped with it, and with life afterwards, but I didn't understand any better after reading every word.' What the *Mail* bought, for its £250,000, was a flawed book: Miss Saward, who has suffered greatly, wrote her story 'to help other women', but she doesn't write well enough to make her readers feel her suffering as she did, or to learn from her suffering. Apart from cutting out 'most of the God bits', the *Mail*'s adaptation was fair, but the book itself is unemotional, flatly written and pedestrian. Therefore, what the *Mail* bought was simply the chance to run scaremongering (for women) and titillating (for men) copy for five days on the trot headed, 'RAPE: Every Woman's Nightmare.' And the circulation bumped up by 30,000 extra readers.

Not many women work on the *Mail*; almost none in positions of power. It's an old-fashioned, woman-fearing place: women working there are treated with top-heavy gallantry by Sir David English and his male colleagues. The *Mail*'s favourite sex stories reflect these attitudes precisely: they have a unique, Sapperesque moral line that can be summed up briefly in the words, Beware, chaps! There are *loose women* out there and they can sap a chap's strength.

Of course, each paper deals with sex in its own way. The *Times* can review a new ludicrous sex book by Shere Hite as well as anybody; it can report marriage break-ups (sex), 'Satanic child abuse' (sex) and the divorce rate (sex) in carefully-written prose. There are still, as ever, those closely detailed sex-crime stories on the home news pages of the *Telegraph*; there are social-worker sex stories in the *Guardian* about underprivileged people who live in unfortunate housing schemes and have to put up with all sorts; and there are fashion pages in every paper which show young models looking sulky-mouthed and sexy in knickers and bras or clingy evening frocks. What would you? We are not monks. But what the upmarket papers do not do is to write firsthand about sex itself: Why I Love It Five Times a Night. That's titillation, simply. If you want to read about mucky things, read a mucky tabloid.

Or you can read the *Independent*. The *Independent* is the most serious-minded of Britain's newspapers, and its readership, to the *Daily Mail*'s frustration, is both upmarket and young/female as well as young/male. It's so serious-minded as to appear gratifyingly stuffy: no smut, no sleaze, no salaciousness, no Royal Family. Which is why its coverage of sex is so baffling.

Readers of the *Independent* are used to finding, on the 'Living' or

'Health' or even 'Law' pages, just as explicitly written articles on How Much, How Big, How Often as readers of the *Sun* and the *News of the World*. On the Health page of 1 May appeared, 'Frank testimony of a child sex abuser', straplined: 'Is there a cure for men who sexually assault children? Here, an offender writes about his crimes and his treatment. His wife shares the pain of her experience.' The illustration shows a big heart made of sponge leaning on and squashing a little heart made of sponge. Each heart has the biological symbol for a male on it. The copy is as gruesome as you might expect. Here, the writer describes 'fooling about' with a 12-year-old boy: 'It happened that my hand fell in his lap and I began stroking, almost in fun.' It's the 'almost' that gets me, and the illustration.

Readers of the *Independent* gaze, week after week, at giant female condoms the size of freezer bags; lasciviously positioned 'anatomically-correct' dolls with a man's eye locked on the dolls' genitals; little putto-like babies' thighs with the one eye of (this time) a woman child abuser gazing at the baby's fleshy bottom. The drawings are well-executed, but rather lubricious. And what's the point of them, except to titillate? In August, the Health pages of the *Independent* ran an article on vaginismus – painful intercourse – from which 27,000 women are supposed to suffer. I suppose there is a place for cogent, reasoned help on this painful condition on a paper's health page. Why not? But the *Independent* ran the feature with a big (five inches by eight) illustration. Now – how on earth do you illustrate a feature about painful intercourse, in an upmarket newspaper? You draw a man's finger pushing at a woman's tightly-curled fist. And then, in the background, you draw a stone phallus with an Assyrian's head on the top of it, and a massively erect stone penis in the middle of it. Get it? You bet we do.

Last weekend the *Independent* had a centre-page article from America on Saturday, headlined, Dial a Dream Girl for Safest Sex. The next day the *Independent on Sunday*'s lead feature in their Review section was called 'Damaged Goods'. It was an unpleasant tale about the life and times of a violent Londoner who took cocaine every night and beat people up. Having read it once on Sunday and twice since, I still can't work out why they printed it, stuffed full as it was of blood, beatings, bruises, bricks in the eye, broken knees, blows with hammers. It was the sort of feature that is given as a present to the chief crime reporter by his local nick: a feature about how dogged 'honest coppering' finally gets Chummy slammed up for a good long stretch. It was written in the ingenuous style of *True Detective* ('Theories – the police had plenty') and was depressing to read on a bright September Sunday. Why was it there? Because the man was a pimp and the people he beat up were prostitutes. Equals *sex*, of course, and the illustration showed the backside of a naked woman in bed with the ominous shadow of a man holding a stick creeping up on her.

As I say, if you want to read mucky things, read a mucky paper.

22 September 1990

HAVING THE NOSE FOR IT

John Whitworth

The taste of blood's medicinal teaspoonfuls,
Slow trickling down your throat, was sweet and warm,
And it meant three quarters of an hour off school,
Flat on the floor of an echoing cloakroom.
As I lay unmoving, bare legs to the cool

Linoleum and eyes screwed shut, I tried
To summon solitude and silence. If
You concentrated, all the airy, wide
Contingencies of life beyond the cliffs
Of scarf and burberry on either side,

Milk-bottle clunks, loud whispers, giggles and
Occasional crumps of anger, simplified
Themselves into a tapestry of sound
Like the swish of leaves and birdsong. Then you died,
Then you caught your fluttering soul in your cupped hand

And loosed it down a dust-filled shaft of sun,
The poet habit, hammered from defeats.
So the four-eyed twats, unhandy with a gun,
Drowsing deliciously could feel like Keats
And, had I heard of him, I would have done.

22 September 1990

DIARY

John Wells

'I wunnasee a mediaeval city like it wuzz – *nutt like this!*' The small, wizened and intensely angry old American tourist in the yellow short-sleeved shirt and the tiny straw hat was having his tantrum just beyond the portcullis in Carcassonne, bobbing among the dazed human flotsam that swills slowly up and down between the ice-cream shops and plastic swords and dayglo cuddly toys, and it was hard not to sympathise with him. Mérimée and Viollet-le-Duc probably wanted to see a mediaeval city like it wuzz when they began the 40-year job of knocking up this early French Disneyland in 1844, and they can hardly have imagined it was going to be peopled in perpetuity with lepers, hunchbacks and extras dressed in codpieces and pointy shoes pouring boiling oil over each others' heads from the ramparts. What has happened here is that a rather humourless exercise in Gothic Revival has become a colossal smash hit, like Mont Saint Michel or Les Baux, with pilgrims from all over Europe and beyond coming to take their cultural punishment like they do at *The Mousetrap*. More sensitive souls like the old American tourist drawn here perhaps by the magic of the name, perhaps by some dim memory of Henry James and Edith Wharton raving about it in their quaint convoluted way before the First World War, find themselves in a minority. The only refuge, apart from one quite good restaurant and a couple of semi-serious antique shops, is one expensive hotel with Puginesque panelling, heraldic wallpaper and milk-jugs designed to match the gothic chairs. On the gothic shelves of one of its vast reading rooms, among the complete works of Molière and Wilde and Diderot, some of them in the hotel's own bindings, I found one of the London Library's lost copies of *The Sacred Fount*.

29 September 1990

THE LAST NICE
PRIME MINISTER

A. N. Wilson

Many of the younger delegates about to assemble in Bournemouth for the Tory Party conference do not remember the year in which Alec Douglas-Home was the Prime Minister. He is perhaps best known as the man who accompanied Chamberlain to Munich in 1938, or as the brother of William Douglas-Home, the famous comic dramatist.

I thought of these things as I motored over the Lammermuirs on a gloriously bright autumn day to meet Lord Home at the Hirsel, his Berwickshire seat. By English standards, the estate is huge and one drives through acres of well-kept farmland before reaching the enormous house. It was here that Chamberlain and his wife came to recuperate after the horrors of Munich, when Alec Home, then Lord Dunglass, was the Prime Minister's Parliamentary Private Secretary. It is an unlikely setting in which to spend two years reading the works of Karl Marx as Home famously did, and when he came forward to greet me, I wondered whether I was meeting a serious political thinker, or one of the more amiable characters in his brother's stage comedies.

He wore an old green jumper, rather good tweed trousers and on his feet, somewhat surprisingly, a pair of trainers. We paused in the hall, a room which would dwarf many an English parish church, to help ourselves to Dubonnet and examine a glass case containing relics of various bloodthirsty figures from Scotch history. The sword of the Bruce. The hawking-glove of Mary Queen of Scots. The cap worn by the Earl of Argyle on the scaffold in 1685.

Home: An ancestor of mine, who was very properly beheaded.

Alec Home's family on both sides – his mother was a Lambton – are famously eccentric, and I asked him if this had been a handicap in pursuing what had been a conspicuously straight political career.

Home: Not at all.

Self: Are you more of a Home or a Lambton?

Home: Oh, more of a Home. Do you ever see Lucy [Lambton] on television? (*laughs*) She's a natural. It's very entertaining, it really is, whether it's the history of loos or 'Up the Great North Road'. That was the one which amused me more than anything. And, of course, she loves to laugh at her own jokes so infectiously . . . But Tony [Lord Lambton] . . . he's quite an able fellow; but if you're visiting a lady of the streets . . . (*Pause for almost helpless laughter*) you don't leave your official car outside the door; which (*more affectionate laughter*) is what he did.

Self: All the same, it was rather absurd to make him resign for a thing like that, surely?

Home: Oh, yes. But I think he was always too eccentric for the Conservative Party. I like him very much. He's very amusing, and a very kind character. He'd go out of his way to help anybody.

Self: Both your brothers went to prison, I believe.

Home: Yes, they did. Henry went to prison for a motoring offence. My mother was rather pleased. Said it was just what he wanted! (*More laughter*) I used to go and see William during his year in Wormwood Scrubs. [He was court-martialled after refusing to join the Allied attack on Lé Havre in 1944 because he believed – correctly – that large numbers of civilians would be killed.]

Self: I have enjoyed his plays.

Home: They're rather dated now. I had to veto a play of his about Margaret Thatcher the other day. If you're going to write a play about Margaret Thatcher, it's just *got* to be funny . . . He's a genuinely funny man, but the drawing-room comedy has rather gone out of fashion.

Self: Is that because they are too innocent for nowadays?

Home: I suppose that's it.

Self: It's very good-humoured of the Thatchers to allow these plays about Denis, isn't it? They make him out to be a drunken buffoon.

Home: I know. I happened to go to one of them on the same night (*more laughter*) as they did. He *was* portrayed as a drunkard. It can't be awfully easy to laugh it off.

Self: Denis Thatcher was in the audience?

Home: And her too. Both of them.

Self: Laughing?

Home: Not immoderately.

Self: Did Mr and Mrs Thatcher take you to the play?

Home: No, no. We just happened to coincide. But some things are *really* funny. I think those 'Dear Bill' letters are the funniest thing.

I noticed that every time Mrs Thatcher's name was mentioned, Lord Home laughed. It was not a malicious laugh; indeed, I should guess that there was not an ounce of malice in his nature. Rather, the laugh suggested the gulf between the present time and the era in which he himself had exercised political power. He several times expressed the loyal certainty that Mrs Thatcher would win the next general election.

Self: I forget – were you in the Cabinet with her?

Home: Just. Ted Heath always used to get very impatient with her.
Self: Why? Was he impatient because she was so efficient?
Home: I think partly.
Self: In those days, he could not possibly have guessed what was going to happen?
Home: I wouldn't have thought so, no, although I did come back to my wife from the first Cabinet which Mrs Thatcher attended in Ted's government and said to Elizabeth, 'We'd better look out, because that woman has more brains and more energy than the rest of us put together.'

There could scarcely be a greater contrast between Mrs Thatcher's unabashed enjoyment of power and the nonchalant manner in which Home appeared to have drifted into the highest office of state. People don't, however, become Prime Minister just by accident, and I asked myself why he had bothered to leave his agreeable life in the Scottish borders in order to go into politics, and why he had been so conspicuously successful.

Home: It was the unemployment in the mining areas around our house in Lanarkshire [Castle Douglas] which really decided me to go into politics. I thought that the Conservative proposals for reducing unemployment were good, and that I should have a shot at standing there. Mercifully – well, that's the wrong word – the sitting member died and I stepped into his shoes.
Self: Stanley Baldwin has not enjoyed a reputation as a man who cared much about the unemployed.
Home: No, he hasn't, but I think he will.

I thought of the Jarrow Hunger March, and of the odium with which Baldwin and the Conservatives were regarded among the unemployed in the 1930s, and I wondered how this reversal of reputation would come to pass. Then we fell to talking about Baldwin's unrehabilitated contemporary and fellow-fighter against unemployment, Adolf Hitler.
Self: Was Hitler physically revolting when you met him?
Home: Yes, I thought so. Squat, and a nasty-looking fellow. I noticed something which I never heard anyone else mention at all. I happened, after the signature of the agreement, to walk behind him down a very long passage and both his arms swung together. Anybody walking normally swings their arms alternately, left and right, but his arms swung together; rather an ape-like thing, with long arms that swung right down to his knees.
Self: Mrs Thatcher went to Prague recently and apologised to the people of Czechoslovakia for the Munich Agreement. Do you think she was right?

For the only time in our conversation, a faintly perceptible iciness descended.

Home: I don't know about that. I remember, not long before Munich, Chamberlain saying to me, 'It's no part of a Prime Minister's duty to take a country into a war which he thinks you can't win.' I was very much behind him. In the circumstances, I thought he was right to make the settlement which he did.

It could be said that the three greatest moral blots in the record of the Conservative Party in this century were Baldwin's failure to tackle unemployment, Chamberlain's betrayal of Czechoslovakia and Eden's mishandling of the Suez crisis. I asked Lord Home his views of Suez.

Home: I was with Eden on Suez. Incidentally, the present Gulf crisis goes some way to justify Eden's view of Nasser. One of those Arab boys – not that Nasser was an Arab, he was an Egyptian – but they can upset the whole area, one of those boys.

Self: So you do not incline to Ted Heath's view of the Gulf crisis?

Home: No, I don't. I'm rather sad about it, because I think Ted has lost a lot of his influence by reason of his own performances really. You must not seem to pursue a vendetta with a woman, and certainly not this one.

Self: Why do you think 'this woman' is so unpopular in Scotland?

Home: I can't quite work it out. You would have thought that Margaret Thatcher's insistence upon self-reliance and self-discipline would be right up the street of the Scotsman. But, of course, there's always been a strong radical, Liberal streak in Scotland.

Self: But don't the Scots feel alienated from England at the present time? It's not just Mrs Thatcher. They dislike the whole idea of being governed from Westminster.

Home: Yes, there's an element of that. And there's also the fact that Mrs Thatcher is a woman who leads from the front. We're not used to that in Scotland.

Self: I seem to remember that your first ministerial post was in the Scottish Office?

Home: Yes. It was not long after Yalta, and Winston asked me to take over the Minister of State's job in Scotland, with the instructions, 'Go and quell those turbulent Scots and don't come back until you have done so.'

Self: How many Scottish Tories sat in the House of Commons in those days?

Home: 52 members.

Self: And how many now?

Home: Only ten now.

Self: And many Conservatives believe that at the next general election all those seats might be lost to Labour or the Nationalists, so that there might be no Conservative MPs left in Scotland.

Home: I don't think that will happen. I would bet on gaining two or three more seats at the next election.

Was this a seriously held view, or was it wishful thinking? Lord Home's views on Scottish devolution have been equivocal. In 1979, he appeared to support the measures for Scottish devolution, but then, before the referendum, he made a public speech advising people to vote against it. This provoked one malicious Scot to say that Home had begun his career by selling one small country down the river, and had ended it by selling another. Now, he seems to favour a moderate form of devolution, perhaps as a way of keeping the Scottish Nationalists at bay.

As he spoke of his very long career in public life I wondered if it was possible to analyse why he had succeeded, where others, ostensibly more able, had failed to become Prime Minister. I had lately re-read

Iain Macleod's classic *Spectator* article 'What Happened' (16 January, 1964) about the manner in which Home had beaten any possible contenders to the leadership after Harold Macmillan's resignation. Reginald Maudling, Lord Hailsham and Rab Butler were the names discussed by members of the Cabinet and the parliamentary party. Home's was the name that Macmillan passed to the Queen.

The choice of his successor was in Macmillan's gift. Macmillan was so prodigiously snobbish that he would have felt disposed to appoint an orang-outang as Prime Minister if the ape could boast a sufficient number of quarterings. But could it have been as simple as that?

Home: He liked his Dukes, certainly. It was a fairly harmless sort of hobby. Cabinet having what you might call an aristocratic bias did not seem to matter then.

Self: Had you foreseen, before that famous Blackpool conference, that you would be the next Prime Minister?

Home: No, I was absolutely taken by surprise. I was very happy at the Foreign Office and I did not in the least want to change. If you are approached by so many people, as I was, and asked to stand, it was almost impossible to refuse. I wish I had now, on the whole. I think we really allowed ourselves to be hustled at the Blackpool conference, when Harold was ill. It could have been Butler, Quintin or me.

Self: But Quintin Hogg made rather an ass of himself at Blackpool didn't he?

Home: He made every possible mistake, unfortunately. He threw his hat into the ring in a very ostentatious way and marched about with labels on. It was largely due to his exuberance, I think. All I wish was that we had waited. We could have waited. Harold wasn't as ill as all that.

I pressed him to say what it was about himself which enabled him to succeed where the others had failed. After all his protestation, it was clear that, if forced to a choice between Butler, Hailsham or Home as Prime Minister, Home would have chosen Home.

Home: I've never been afraid of saying 'Yes' or 'No'. Possibly that is the reason I got on. I think in particular that is what a Prime Minister has to do, because nobody else will. I never minded getting out in front and saying what I thought was necessary.

There was always more steel, and more intelligence, in Lord Home, than he would have liked his supporters to notice. He is also – something of an asset – a very nice man, the last Prime Minister in history who could, strictly speaking, be described as nice. Once he had been installed at Number 10 Downing Street, it seemed, like his fellow peers in Gilbert and Sullivan, that he 'did nothing in particular, and did it very well'. I asked him if he had found the job tiring.

Home: I didn't have time to know. In a year you can't tell. There was a year in which we had nothing to do, because we had finished our programme and you couldn't do anything except await the election.

We strolled out into the garden in the autumn sunshine. The first frost of the year had umbered the roses. We spoke of women in politics and I asked him why he thought so few women, with one notable exception, had made successful politicians. 'I think they've been as good as men,' he said, 'not that that's setting a very high standard.' When we parted, it was hard to resist a faint feeling of nostalgia for the days before drawing-room comedy went out of fashion, when Prime Ministers could speak rather proudly of having done nothing much for a whole year.

6 October 1990

UKRAINIAN POWDERKEG

Anne Applebaum

Kiev

When the Chernobyl nuclear reactor first began to overheat, it was because a few engineers were experimenting, quite normally, with the control levers. Very quickly, things got out of hand. Very quickly. In only four seconds the reactor reached a temperature one hundred times higher than normal. Then it exploded.

In Kiev, the capital of Ukraine, they should know about the dangers of experimenting with control levers, because Kiev lies downstream from Chernobyl on the Dnieper river. The memory of Chernobyl floats in the city's air like an invisible radiation cloud, but now, in Kiev, there is a whole new experiment going on. This experiment has several names: *perestroika, glasnost,* the Shatalin Plan, 'Reform in 500 days', Ukrainian independence. This week, it took the form of an all-Ukrainian pro-independence strike. Moscow started it, allowing Ukrainian communists to back a hollow declaration of sovereignty, but Moscow doesn't seem to have realised quite how dangerous Ukraine has become politically, how difficult to reform economically, how easily it will explode.

Or, more precisely, Moscow doesn't realise quite how dangerous and difficult they – the Russians – have made it. It took 350 years of Czarist domination, several decades of Stalinist purges, two collectivisation-induced mass famines, two world wars, and the refusal to teach Ukrainian children how to speak Ukrainian, along with the systematic elimination of anyone who might be thought a leader, an intellectual, a capitalist, or even a wealthy peasant. But they did it. The Russians have managed to rob 53 million people of their culture, to impoverish an economy which supplies one-third of the Soviet Union's food and one-fifth of its industrial products, and in effect to destroy the largest nation in the world without its own state. They aren't apologising, they aren't going to take the blame for whatever new civil war or famine or nuclear disaster results from the latest games. Even Alexander Solzhenitsyn, in his first essay to be printed in the motherland since he was expelled from the Soviet Union, writes that Ukraine does not exist at all: 'Ukraine is a product of Mongol invasions and Polish colonialism.'

The Ukrainian economy, which shares its problems with the rest of the Soviet Union, is only the most recent casualty. At a motorcycle factory in Kiev, the Director for Socialist Development sits up straight in his chair and explains how well he fulfilled last year's central plan, how up-to-date are his motorcycles, how good things look for the future. What he doesn't say is that the central planning system has ceased to exist, his motorcycles are outdated copies of the German wartime BMW (complete with sidecar) and about 800 of them are sitting on his shop floor, incomplete. Parts are not arriving from Leningrad, from Kazakhstan, from Poland, from Sweden. The Soviet Republics, afraid of shortages, no longer ship anything outside their own jurisdiction, Comecon trade has ceased to exist, no Western firm wants to trade with Ukraine, knowing it will be months before it sees any money, channelled via Moscow. 'We are not interested in a joint venture,' says the Director for Socialist Development. 'We are so successful, we do not need joint ventures.'

In Kiev, national pride takes many other unusual forms. At an open meeting of Rukh, the Ukrainian independence movement, the speaker reads out a list of demands: close the remaining Chernobyl reactors, bring in a free market economy, establish Ukrainian currency and Ukrainian banks, establish sovereignty over Ukrainian borders and ... take charge of the Ukraine's nuclear weapons. 'So why shouldn't we control them?'

Behind the speaker's podium lurks a Lenin effigy of obscene height. Midway through the speeches a troop of makeshift cossacks marches across its pedestal. The cossacks seem to be wearing theatrical costumes from a production of *Arabian Nights*: no self-respecting, sabre-carrying, 19th-century Ukrainian cossack would have worn pink harem trousers. The crowd cheers anyway.

In the countryside, things ground to a halt long ago. Looking for relief from the irradiated city, I show my driver a place on the map with a pretty name: Baleya Tserkev, 'White Church'. She shakes her head. 'It is not nice village. No more white church.' I say I want nice, old and nice. She nods vigorously.

We arrive in Obuxov. The driver waves her arm across the flat central square. 'Old and nice,' she says. An empty grocery store, a town hall with boards over the windows, and another unidentifiable building, probably the party headquarters, make up the square. All of the buildings are rectangular, flat-roofed, without decoration or windows, built of the same whitish-grey brick, probably from the 1930s. The driver waves her arm at another Lenin, this time lifting his arm above the square, deserted at mid-day. 'Old and nice,' she says . . .

Just a short walk from Obuxov there is a collective farm. The path is paved with cobblestones, and lined with linden trees. The remains of an estate? From one of the grimy outbuildings, a peasant appears, ears of corn protruding from the apron she holds up over her chest.

'What was here before this *kolkhoz*?' She is blank-faced, incredulous.

'Another *kolkhoz*. There has always been a *kolkhoz* here.'

'And before the Revolution?'

'Always a *kolkhoz*.' She smiles curiously. Memory reaches back no further.

In the fields, piles of hay are rotting in the autumn sunlight. No one has collected them because the combine has broken down and there are no parts to fix it. Nearby, the skeletons of ten vast greenhouses stretch over acres of weed. There is no glass to fill in the skeletons, and the greenhouse generators are going to rust.

No, I explain to the driver, returning to the car, I want a real Ukrainian village. Wooden churches. Peasant cottages. Women in flowered headscarves. 'Yes, yes,' she nods, 'I know just where to find that.'

We visit a *skansen*, near Kiev. A *skansen* is a special park, a place where 'ancient Ukrainian culture' has been preserved for the enjoyment of the urban proletariat. Exhibits of charming native architecture – wooden churches, peasant cottages – are lined neatly in rows. They have been uprooted from places like Obuxov, and reassembled here. Samples of Ukrainian 'Folk Art' – mass-produced wooden spoons and crudely painted *matrushka* dolls – are for sale at exorbitant dollar prices, despite the notable absence of dollar-carrying Western tourists. Elaborate signs describe the geographical and socio-economic origins of the peasants who once lived in this style of hut or that version of thatched cottage. In one of the churches, there is even a real service. A renegade sect of the Ukrainian autocephalous Orthodox Church, fed up with the intimacy between Orthodox patriarchs and communism, has decided to meet here. It is the closest thing they can find to authenticity. Children run back and forth outside, shouting to be given ice-cream.

There is a television equivalent to the *skansen*. At a hotel restaurant in Kiev, I watch a balalaika concert, brought to the airwaves courtesy of the Ukrainian Ministry of Culture. Fat factory workers in synthetic flowered skirts play baleful tunes, all the time affecting the 'cultured' facial expressions of an opera singer. The barman curls his lip at the low-grade prostitutes and wants 14 dollars for a beer. If Solzhenitsyn is correct – if the Ukraine is no longer a nation – it means that the Russians who invented this system have no right to call themselves a state, or at least not a European one.

On the surface, things seem better in the western Ukraine, the strip of land which the Red Army took over from Poland in 1939 and never gave back. Like the Baltic States, the western Ukraine has suffered only 50 years of Soviet communism instead of 70. There is something left here, an occasional graceful curve to the road, the odd onion dome on a village church. Opposition has a different flavour too, both more radical and at the same time more realistic. And the last round of local elections was democratic, whereas Kiev lies under the shadow of the Communist Party, as well as Chernobyl.

In the city of Lvov – once half-Polish and half-Jewish, now all-Ukrainian – the new town council has already removed Lenin from the central square, expressly against the wishes of the Parliament in Kiev. Five days later, crowds of nervous onlookers still stand clustered around the empty pedestal, as if waiting for something to happen. The pedestal itself, the wreckers have discovered, was made from gravestones taken from a Jewish cemetery, destroyed by the Nazis.

'The statue was blocking the view,' explains Ivan Hel gleefully, deputy mayor of Lvov, a member of Runkh, another Ukrainian who spent 18 years in prison camp. The Lvov town council is now planning to take down all the city's Lenin statues – Lenin sitting, standing, walking, speaking, reading – put them in a park, and make their own *skansen*. Money earned from gate fees will be used to build flats. In Lvov, there are 850,000 people on the waiting list for flats.

In case this doesn't work, the town council has another plan: develop trade links with the West. That is, barter Ukrainian eggs for Polish bricks. So far the Poles are cool towards the idea. The Ukrainians want two eggs to one brick, the Poles want three. Meanwhile, in a chemist's shop in central Lvov, a sullen saleslady rings up an order on an ancient cash register marked 'National Cash Registers, Inc, made in Dayton, Ohio'. Once upon a time, Lvov was part of the big, capitalist world.

At the turn of the century, American petroleum companies even drilled for oil south of Lvov, creating a small boom in the town of Drohobycz nearby. Bruno Schulz, a Polish-Jewish writer shot by the Nazis in 1942, also lived in Drohobycz. Schulz was not kind to his home town. He once wrote that he had discovered its dark secret: 'Nothing ever succeeds there, nothing can ever reach a definite conclusion. Gestures hang in the air, movements are prematurely exhausted and cannot overcome a certain inertia . . .'

Failure still hangs over the town's dusty streets. Schultz's house is marked with a plaque. A woman walks out of the front door, and says she has never read his books, they aren't translated into Ukrainian. But at the old Polish Catholic Church, a small man – born in Drohobycz, expelled after the war, now resident in Poznan – shouts in Polish that he knows another secret about Drohobycz. Babbling inconclusively about soldiers and 1939 and blood running into his garden, he leads us round and about the city until we arrive at the back of the old Austrian courthouse.

There are holes in the ground, marks of digging. Along a low bench nearby, the locals have set up a row of skulls, dozens and dozens of them. Many have a small bullet hole in the forehead. A few have a rusted axe blade sticking out the back. Around this macabre display, the citizens of Drohobycz have hung street signs which they recently removed from their town's walls: Lenin Street, Lenin Square, Lenin Place.

A grinning 'forensic scientist' gives us a tour. Here is the pile of skulls, there is a leg bone with elastic still attached, the remains of a ladies' garter belt. Most would have been Poles, or anyway local bourgeoisie. It doesn't much matter any more. When Soviet soldiers took over the western Ukraine, they shot everyone who was pretty, everyone who was rich, everyone who might possibly have any talent at all. The idea was to make the western Ukraine look as bleak and impoverished as the east, as impoverished as Russia itself, as fast as possible.

The digging still goes on, with approval of the new, democratically elected town council. Nothing much has been said about the find – probably one thousand corpses – outside Drohobycz. Mass graves, after all, are common in the Soviet Union.

But the people standing around the half-uncovered graves in nervous groups, craning their necks to hear what is said, do not seem to consider Stalinist crimes passed. They seem to be afraid, just like the people in central Lvov who stand near what used to be Lenin, waiting for retribution to come from somewhere.

'This happened once,' they are whispering to one another, 'it can happen again.' One mistake with the control levers and the heat will rise, one hundred times higher than normal in less than four seconds.

6 October 1990

'The Russians are coming!
The Russians are coming!'

DIARY

John Wells

Lord Home's gentle recollections of the Thatchers not laughing immoderately at themselves in *Anyone for Denis?* ('The last nice Prime Minister', 6 October) brought back memories. At the time of the Thatcher visit to the Whitehall Theatre there were fairly heavy bets backstage amongst us as to whether Mr Thatcher would come at all. The show was on a Sunday night, and earlier in the week, the news was that the Prime Minister was coming on her own. At the end of the week, Toxteth erupted, and it seemed unlikely we would get either of them. We had underestimated Mrs Thatcher's unswerving resolve to do what had to be done, and in Mr Thatcher's case her unswerving resolve that others should do the same. Half an hour or so before curtain up my dressing-room door burst open and an enormous dog came in, dragging a small security man. He said 'Sniffin' for bombs', and was dragged out again. Then chants of 'Thatcher out!' came drifting over the rooftops from Whitehall, and I knew that I had lost my bet. I was going to have to go on and be cheeky about the Prime Minister to her face. I think the worst thing from my point of view was seeing the rims of Denis's spectacles glinting in the middle of the stalls. I did feel very sorry for him. There had been fears that their presence would inhibit the audience from laughing, and Robert Fox, our producer, had packed them round on all sides with what Shakespeare called Rude Fellows of the Baser Sort, bankers and City figures, most of whom had money in the show and who understandably roared all the way through. As if that wasn't bad enough, Denis also had to put up with two rows of hacks sitting at the front of the stalls, whose heads swung round in unison at every laugh to see how they were taking it. The same degenerates, I was told afterwards, swayed up to Mr Thatcher during the interval, tapping their noses, winking and indicating his glass, saying 'G and T, eh Den?'

I don't think it's true to say that satirical comment has been stifled in the last ten years under Mrs Thatcher. Politicians have never been too keen on that kind of thing, and when Lord Longford asked Harold Wilson if he'd mind him going to see the stage version of *Mrs Wilson's Diary* the then Prime Minister said of course he wouldn't mind himself, but he thought it might upset Mary. On television *Spitting Image* has boldly gone a good deal further than most of us had gone before, whether with the puppet Mrs Thatcher unzipping in the gents or in its jocular picture of everyday life at Buckingham Palace. But my latest experience with the BBC makes me think that, balance or no balance, the old girl may have got them rattled. Or at least indecisive. When an independent producer encouraged me some years ago to collaborate on a script about the Thatchers in retirement, ante-dating William Douglas-Home's more charitable stage comedy on the same theme, I was not too optimistic. I then attended one of the funniest meetings I have ever been to, at which the very young and serious lawyer representing the BBC read out things like 'Overbearing wife: pages three, five, seven'. 'Intemperate husband: pages one, two, three, etc.' I think I may have annoyed him, and he finally became very cross indeed and hit the table with the flat of his hand, spilling everybody's polystyrene cups of coffee. This the Head of Comedy sagely allowed to soak into the papers on the table. Scripts, to my surprise, were then commissioned, and we wrote them. Weeks went by, then the BBC said they didn't feel they could make a decision on mere scripts, and commissioned a pilot programme. This was made, and more weeks went by. Then the BBC said they didn't feel they could make a decision on that either, but suggested that if the characters of Mark and Carol could be made more palatable they were keen to go ahead and at considerable further expense commissioned a second pilot programme. A cynical agent tried to dissuade us, saying it was all to do with knighthoods: they might possibly be wasting the Corporation's money but we were definitely wasting our time. Rejecting this kind of talk as absurd, we set to work turning Mark and Carol into two wonderful human beings. The programme was recorded, and the series turned down. I am toying with a post-Armageddon scenario with Ronnie Corbett as John Major and Charlie Drake as the Queen Mum, but I think the time may have come to leave it to the puppets.

13 October 1990

MEAN STREETS

D. J. Taylor

It was my wife's idea that we should respond to an appeal for help in this year's Oxfam Week collection, she who made the arrangements for registering us as collectors and she who unpacked the large parcel which arrived a few days later. Nothing could be more straightforward than the system which Oxfam proposes to its volunteers. They are provided with a badge of authorisation, an instruction leaflet enjoining politeness and forbidding the harassment of the unwilling, a bundle of leaflets explaining the purpose of the collection and a pile of self-sealing envelopes. Having made an initial sortie to deliver leaflet and envelope, you return after a decent interval to collect donations. That is the theory.

We live in a large mansion block down by the river in London SW6 and it was here, conveniently enough, that we arranged to collect. The block looks out over a quiet suburban sidestreet, bounded by tennis courts. Porsches and Jaguars lie drawn up on the verge. There is a combative residents' association which monitors the deficiencies of the managing agent and the atmosphere is studiously genteel. Prime territory, one might have thought, for donations to a widely respected, non-denominational charity, and it was in the not quite conscious assumption of easy pickings that early one evening last week, as the light began to fade, we set out.

There are about 150 flats in the block, divided into mini-blocks of six. We decided to take these alternately, convening every five minutes or so on the pavement to check on progress. Half an hour later it had become clear that things were not going according to plan. I should say at the outset that we encountered several impressive instances of generosity – people who presented us with pocketfuls of change or who had filled envelopes waiting on the sideboard – but nothing in the instruction leaflet had prepared us for the three other categories into which those residents who bothered to answer their doorbells began to fall.

Category one was the very large number of people – perhaps eight out of ten – who simply claimed not to have received the envelopes. A succession of vague-minded people shuffled across their door-steps to protest that, no, they hadn't seen it (the envelopes are bright yellow and practically unmissable on the mat) and, no, they knew nothing about it. It was frequently useless to explain that one had delivered it personally 36 hours ago. A small proportion of this group could be cajoled into making a donation.

Category two – small but insistent – had somehow got it into their heads that the purpose of Oxfam Week was to solicit old clothes. At several flats, in fact, the owners had assembled these garments in carrier bags and placed them ready in the hall. They seemed strangely put out when we did not want them, I noticed, and there was a wistfulness about their protests which suggested that disposing of old clothes is a more or less impossible task.

Category three was merely offensive. 'Good evening. I am collecting for Oxfam.' 'How did you get into this building?' 'I am a resident and I have a key.' 'Oh, I see.' Door closes sharply. At one highly polished portal I was confronted by a suave and saturnine looking middle-aged man. 'Good evening, sir' (my politeness is of a particularly scrupulous sort), 'I am collecting for Oxfam.' 'Ah yes,' said the man with equal politeness. 'Thank you.' I smiled expectantly. The door slammed shut.

Gradually, as the progress continued, other sub-categories declared themselves. There were, of course, the people who had Strong Views About Oxfam ('Yes I read your leaflet,' an elderly lady said severely, 'and I notice all the money seems to be going to the frontline states in South Africa'). There were the people who quite reasonably claimed that they gave money to other charities or to private covenants. One thing interested me above all: my wife and I were volunteers who had given up a couple of hours of our time, but it was commonly assumed that we stood to benefit personally from the collection or, at the very least, were employed by Oxfam.

Two thirds of the way along the block I stopped and watched through the glass doors where Rachel was having an animated conversation with the unseen inhabitant of a ground-floor flat. A moment later she came out onto the pavement. 'I didn't know people could be so horrible,' she said. Then she burst into tears. Abashed and dispirited, we decided to go home.

This, of course, was a single excursion undertaken in a single block of flats, but several facts stood out. The most generous donors, I should say, were people under 30, the most tight-fisted the middle-aged. Elderly people seemed completely baffled by the whole enterprise and unable to understand any explanation that was offered to them. And despite several high points – an old man who quietly and almost apologetically wrote out a substantial cheque – the chief impression was one of deep, unrepentant meanness. It is worth pointing out that, collecting at the recommended time and counting flats where inhabitants were out, we retrieved 15 envelopes out of a possible 102. In all, 148 flats produced a total of £42.61, an average of 34.7p per flat.

Apparently, I later discovered, this is what charitable collectors in prosperous suburbs should expect: according to a recent report in the *Economist*, if you really want to fill the bucket in a charity collection you should go to a depressed part of the North-East.

It goes without saying that those who collect for charity should never assume too much. After all, they are intruding upon people's privacy and sense of security – it is a fact that in London flat-owners tend not to know their neighbours and consequently a ring at the door is often a cause for alarm – and even standing upon someone's doorstep with a collecting tin is, I suppose, harassment of a sort. But I had never before encountered the British bourgeois in these circumstances: staring fatly from his hallway and peevishly affronted by a docile request to help starving children. And I have met better manners – and greater generosity – in a down-and-outs' hostel in Liverpool than here in this well-heeled suburb where expensive cars lie on the verge and opulence shrieks from each briefly glimpsed interior.

13 October 1990

*'I wish you wouldn't bring your unemployment
home with you!'*

SPORT

STEVE TAKES THE LEAD

Frank Keating

One autumn seven or eight years ago, I poured a succession of stiff nightcaps and, heaven help me, began counting the Christian names of all English League footballers listed in soccer's irresistible *Rothmans Football Yearbook*. Gary won hands down, routing Terry and Gerry, Warren, and Dayle. I've been at it again this week. The newly minted, first *Rothmans* of the 1990s shows a real turn-up. There are now 92 Garys playing league soccer; but they have surrendered a healthy lead and fallen into third place after an astonishing surge by Steve (134), and a dashing run from midfield by Mark (112). The Darrens (46), Deans (29), and Waynes (25), who looked so eager to go the whole way around 1982, are now slipping down towards the clapped-out relegation zone where languish those 1970s title-chasers like Barrie and Kevin, Terry and Gerry. My tips for the mid-Nineties: watch out for sustained attacks by Lee, Craig, Jason, Shane, and Shaun: they are already each massing confidently around the half-way line.

The late-night, small-print swot leaves you punchy and drunk. But still sober enough to realise suddenly where the Mills & Boon romantic novelists filch those magnificent monikers they award their heroes and villains. Well, want a strong, silent, evenly gazed, gleaming-toothed *non pareil*, who strides across moors, and sorts out trouble at t'mill before enfolding virgin heroine in his strong arms in the final paragraph? How about Christian McLean (Bristol Rovers) for a start? Or Jason Longstaff (Leeds Utd)? Certainly Wakeley Gage (Crewe Alexandria) foots the bill. So too Zac Hughes (Rochdale), Craig Shakespeare (West Brom), or the well dressed Dean Crombie (Darlington). And Scott Sellers (Blackburn Rovers) has a genuine paperback butchness about him.

I am afraid, however, that Darren or Gavin Peacock (Bournemouth and Hereford Utd respectively) would never bed the belle by the end – much too *smooth*. Also exposed right down to their correspondent Hush Puppies by the last chapter would surely be Jade Sinclair (Hartlepool), Romeo Zonderan (Ipswich), Dale Jasper (Crewe), Rufus Brevett (Doncaster), and Clayton Blackmore (Manchester Utd). If the Misses Mills or Boon wanted, say, a bibbing Celtic poet with unrequited love in his heart of gold, how about Sean Reck (Wrexham)?

Or a real, hairy-scary Caliban-type? Step forward Kenneth de Mange, of Hull City.

No supremo of the squad can over-fancy his chances of promotion with a centre-forward named Iffy Onura (Huddersfield Town). Or a full-back called Andy Flounders (Hull). Or have too much faith in these three goalkeepers – Gary Leake (Huddersfield), Andy Leaning (Bristol City), or Laurence Batty (Fulham), though the latter seems nominally at least in the great Fulham tradition of eccentric custodians of the rigging, like Teflon ('Non-Stick') Macedo, and dear old 'Snowdrop' Mellor (who came out but once a year, and then only after Christmas).

Mum's mid-Sixties Hollywood yearnings could be responsible for Marlon Beresford (Sheffield Wednesday) and Mitchum Ward (down the road at United); and most certainly, I should say, in the case of Gary Cooper (Maidstone) and Jeff Chandler (Cardiff City). Talking of stage names, surely Bristol City's physiotherapist sports one? In *Rothmans* this mystic masseur is listed as Buster Footman.

13 October 1990

'Come on guys! I can't run in these. They're my trainers.'

LOW LIFE

LIGHTS OUT

Jeffrey Bernard

So that's it then. The gravy train is going to be derailed tonight. I might go along to the Apollo to see my name in lights for the last time. When they turn them off it will be like seeing my own life-support system switched off. Then I really will be unwell. The road to obscurity is looming up ahead and I am reminded of the morning after a brilliant one-night stand. As I was leaving the lady's flat I said, 'I'll see you tonight then?' She said, 'Tonight? Today is Tuesday. You were Monday.' Ouch.

If I didn't think that very nearly all of life was totally absurd then I suppose I would be feeling a little down. As it is I can only marvel at the fact that the play just crept into its second year. As I have said here before, I thought Keith Waterhouse was stark mad when he told me that he was going to turn this column into a play. That was one afternoon in the Groucho Club nearly two years ago. Then I thought no one would put it on and if anybody did it would come off after a couple of nights. But a year in Shaftesbury Avenue utterly amazes me. And it does so because not a day goes by without my remembering awful aspects of the past, like living in that ghastly dosshouse in Camden Town. I had lunch up there with Anna Haycraft yesterday and we both said that we still think of getting a taxi and going to a decent restaurant to be no less than luxuries.

I just wish it hadn't taken Keith 57 years to get around to me. He, Peter O'Toole and Ned Sherrin have been the Orion's Belt that has lit up my narrow horizons for a long time. My only regret is that Tom Conti seemed to me to disapprove of the character he was playing. A hiccup in the run. I would rather be disliked intensely than disapproved of. If I have to be judged then I prefer to be up before the beak in Bow Street magistrates' court. And now there is talk of a film of the play, but only talk, mind you. If they do do it who on earth will they get to play Norman? His lookalike, Walter Matthau, would be far too expensive.

Meanwhile there are matters of much more import occupying my mind. For instance, last week someone told me that Jill Tweedie and Midge McKenzie have just gone or are about to go to Iraq to speak to Saddam Hussein. If anybody had told me a few weeks ago that I would ever end up feeling sorry for that lunatic I should have damn nigh fainted. I could even have felt a touch of sympathy for Hitler had Andrea Dworkin or almost any American feminist paid him a visit. There are people who should be kept aside in cases of political or military emergencies just to be dropped, parachuted that is, on to various countries. Terry Wogan would act as a permanent curfew in Beirut once he opened his mouth.

Another thing that gives rise to some speculation is the fact that Lord Howard de Walden could have changed the course of history. A man in Newmarket told me on the blower yesterday. It seems that Lord Howard was motoring through Germany just before the war and winged a pedestrian just enough to knock him over. His passenger told him that the victim was Hitler. Lord Howard then sought him out to apologise and later reported that Hitler was a 'terribly nice chap, thoroughly charming'. Funny people the English aristocracy. What might have been if the car was a couple of inches closer? I still wonder about that when I think of the Royal Mail van that struck me down. Anyway, now it is one more walk down to the theatre and then it will be as my prep school headmaster would shout at 9 p.m., 'Lights out'.

27 October 1990

CITY AND SUBURBAN

NIGEL MARKS HIS ANNIVERSARY WITH A FAREWELL FROM AMBUSH

Christopher Fildes

Nigel Lawson's resignation caught me with steam up on the Watercress Line. It was and is a day to remember. I had been happily chuffing along some preserved railways on the *Daily Telegraph*'s business, and on getting home was surprised to be rung up by Max Hastings, the editor. 'Lawson's resigned,' he said. Shaken to the buffers, I asked what he wanted me to do. 'Put down that telephone', came the word of command, 'and start writing.' In the year that has followed, Nigel

Lawson has, contrary to his nature, remained almost silent. Even his old enemy Sir Alan Walters was left to make a fool of himself without assistance. Now he has marked the anniversary in his old style, which runs to surprises and, preferably, ambushes. He turned up in the Commons to ambush the Prime Minister, without needing to name her – how pleased he was that she had taken his advice about the European Monetary System, what a pity she hadn't taken it when he first gave it, how much trouble she'd have saved . . . A parting shot from ambush, for he has told his constituents that he will not stand again. So ends the extraordinary political career which I saw at its beginning, 20 years ago, when he was motoring past the playing-fields of Eton in a loudspeaker van, broadcasting his patchy campaign song: 'Eton and Slough, Eton and Slough! We want Nigel, we want him now . . .' Eton and Slough didn't though, but, by the 1974 election, he was the candidate for a safe seat, had written much of his party's manifesto, and, I think, had been promised that he would go straight into office. On election night, learning that he was in Parliament but that his party was out, he rushed across the polished hall of his new house (now for sale) at Stony Stanton, and had the misfortune to tread where his secretary's spaniel, Lupin, had left a turd. He suffered a crash landing. The secretary, with marked presence of mind, cried: 'Oh, don't you realise, Mr Lawson, that's a sign of good luck!' He was not persuaded.

27 October 1990

'Happily, I don't have a social or personal conscience.'

RED IN TOOTH AND TYPE

Paul Johnson

Long interviews with personalities in the news – this week it's Jimmy Goldsmith – are the top current fad in British journalism today. Indeed they are in danger of getting out of hand, with the star interviewer elbowing the subject out of the frame. The ideal interview, like good prose, should be a sheet of perfect glass, through which the person under scrutiny is seen clear and whole. The outstanding practitioner used to be John Freeman, whose *Face to Face* series still makes matchless viewing 30 years later. All you saw of John was a back view, and Kingsley Martin, who was fearfully jealous of John's celebrity, used to say, 'He is the only man who has ever made himself famous by turning his arse on the public.' Such self-effacement is rare nowadays, though one who comes close to it is Valerie Grove of the *Sunday Times*. This week she was getting a fine performance out of A. S. Byatt, whose selection as this year's Booker Prize winner goes some way (though not much) to justify the existence of this gruesome institution, which has done more harm to English literature than anything since the Leavises. It is always a pleasure to enter the London Library and find Miss Byatt scribbling away, head bent industriously over her books. Mrs Grove, by simply listening and noting, brought out the subtle flavour of this civilised writer, who comes close to making Eng. Lit. Crit. intellectually respectable. Another excellent interview, this time with Keith Waterhouse, was published in the *Times Saturday Review*. I could almost hear the old boy, who never says quite what you expect, holding forth, or rather muttering, but the interviewer, Candida Crewe, was invisible and unheard. That is as it should be.

With a heavyweight interviewer, of course, it is inevitable that his/her personality will be felt, if only in the questions beginning 'But . . .' That is what you expect, indeed want, from the *Independent*'s Terry Coleman, whose highly original mind, attacking topics from oblique angles, makes him Britain's best interviewer today. What I object to is the type who begins (in effect): 'I am the famous interviewer, and what have we on the menu today? Oh–*ugh!*' The archetype of this approach is Lynn Barber, also of the *Independent*, who is said to be the journalist most admired by the younger generation. If so, flattery has pushed her over the top. Last week she was upstaging Kirk Douglas by pretending to go to sleep. If she finds him dull, why interview him?

This week she was telling us that Frank Warren had sued her for libel, but that she had forgiven him, sent him a get-well card when he was shot, etc. I knew about the shooting and that he had something to do with boxing but we were 1,200 words into the interview before Miss Barber told me exactly who he was.

With feminine needle at work, the interview itself is liable to become the issue. I can't now recall a word of the notorious chat Barbara Amiel of the *Times* had with Germaine Greer, but Miss Greer's riposte in the *Independent Magazine* was a minor classic of scorned-woman fury. Why must clever, likeable ladies have such rows? Miss Amiel has a fresh line of comment about almost everything, and I could listen again and again to her account of how her parents abandoned her when she was 14 – it is the best thing since *David Copperfield*. So I found Miss Greer's account of her behaviour during the interview unrecognisable. Greer's mind is first-rate and on most literary topics she has more illuminating things to say than anyone I have heard since C. S. Lewis. How, then, can she stoop so low as to accuse Miss Amiel of having big feet? Supposing I were to write that she conjures up for me, as she does, the handsome but heroically embattled figure of the wife of an ex-convict living in Paramatta, circa 1820? She would rightly dismiss this as a piece of sexist impudence. So is not sauce for the chauvinist gander sauce for the feminist goose?

Miss Greer says she only agreed to be interviewed by Miss Amiel in the first place because she was under pressure from her publisher, and that as a result of it he will not put pressure on her any more. That, dear lady, is a cop-out. Writers are just as keen on peddling their wares as publishers. I don't recall Lord Weidenfeld ever having been obliged to twist my arm to submit to journalistic interrogation, though I am very careful indeed about whom I allow across the threshold. There are some operators who are not interested in your books at all and are simply looking for an opportunity to attack an exposed flank. Foreigners, in my experience, cause little trouble. I have had a lot recently, mainly from Spanish-speaking countries, Italy, Scandinavia, etc. They are often pretty young women, very polite – one might almost say gushing – and agreeably uncritical, and they dispose of what seems enormous amounts of space. It is true they sometimes ask difficult questions: 'Who would you say, Señor Johnson, is the most significant post-Peronist president of Argentina? Please give reasons.' There are occasional culture gaps too, especially with the Japanese. One journalist from Tokyo said he was particularly interested in my views on Larrup. It was not quite as funny as Kingsley Amis's account of getting to conversational grips with his Japanese translator, but the interview had its moments, as we roamed over Larrupean unity, the Larrupean Community and related topics. He may have been taking the mickey, but I doubt it. It is only in the English-speaking world that being interviewed is like entering a minefield. My advice to any celebrity, be he pop-star or racing-driver, is to ask himself a simple question: What's in it for me? If the answer is: Nothing except vanity, then refuse. I took a risk myself this summer when I agreed to be put in the Psychiatrist's Chair by Dr Anthony Clare. Friends begged me not to. But I made a careful calculation that if I could get in plugs for, say, two of my books and keep the rest of the conversation mainly on religion, the operation would just be worth it. And so it proved. But I would not recommend it to all. The Doctor is no fool. As for exposing oneself to A. N. Wilson or Miss Barber, they are the Scylla and Charybdis of reputational oblivion.

27 October 1990

'Ring any bells pal?'

AFORE YE GO

Leaves from the commonplace book of Wallace Arnold

Like Paul Johnson, I am very careful indeed about whom I allow across my threshold, and, again like Johnson, I favour interviewers from Finland, Brazil, the Isle of Wight, Tierra del Fuego, Malta, New Zealand, Bromley (Bromley, Peru, forsooth) and many of the Latvian-speaking countries. These past few days the world's press has been banging on my door begging to interview me about my venerable tome, *Le Monde Agréable Du Wallace Arnold*, published in this country as *The Agreeable World of Wallace Arnold*, in the States as *Wallace Arnold's Kooky Planet*, and in Latin America, where his name counts for so much, as *Wallace Arnold: El Amigo de Pablo Johnson*.

I summon the name of Paul Johnson to my aid not simply to lend this column a goodly dash of gravitas, but to rally his support to the Arnold flag. In last week's look at the guttersnipes of the 'press', Johnson wisely proclaimed that the ideal journalist was 'a sheet of perfect glass through which the person under scrutiny is seen clear and whole'. Well put! Paul's own doughty journalism is itself a model of clarity and self-effacement. Never one to parade his own opinions, ever deferring to the thoughts of the person under scrutiny, Paul is a veritable model of impartiality, as his recent articles in the *Mail* ('Certify Kinnock Mad Or Risk World Destruction', 'John Smith – Hard Left Bully-Boy In Sheep's Clothing' and 'I Say Jail All Eggheads NOW') surely prove. But many of those 'star' journalists who queue night and day outside my portals know nothing of fair play; they are, as Paul suggests, simply 'looking for an opportunity to attack an exposed flank'.

Mr Smellysocks

Like Paul, I have suffered at the needle-bearing hands of the dread feminine 'star' journalists, witness recent profiles of myself in the *Independent on Sunday* ('Lyn Barber Meets Mr Smellysocks', 17 October 1990) and the *Times* ('Amiel on the Burping Wallace Arnold', 22 October 1990), and I will in future be employing a very long spoon when inviting journalists, especially those of the female variety, to break bread in my mansion. Any scrivener worth his salt must be prepared to peddle his wares in the marketplace, but it is, to my mind, absolutely essential that no interviewer comes away with anything other than the title, price and pagination of one's tome, one's full name and title (if any) and a couple of well-spun sentences, correctly quoted, on the subject of one's choice. Anything more represents not only a distasteful invasion of one's privacy but a foul slur on one's professional reputation.

I took a risk this summer when I agreed to be put in the Psychiatrist's Chair by Dr Clare. Friends begged me not to, but I reckoned that a plug for two of my books would render the slog of countering his impertinent questions worthwhile. 'The mother of the young Arnold was, I believe, a formative influence?' said Clare. 'Without her, I could never have penned my best-selling *Pardon My Swahili: Arnold Abroad* or even *The Un-Fairer Sex: Wallace on Women*, both still available,' I countered. Touché! Clare retired defeated and truth (dread word!) remained firmly under lock and key!

3 November 1990

*'I'd always assumed they'd be more
intelligent than us.'*

SPORT

RACING DEMONS

Frank Keating

Mercifully, the banshee din of Grand Prix cars won't be juddering Sunday afternoon television sets for a few months. The snarling racers (the drivers, that is) have been dicing since well before Easter. The season ends in Adelaide this weekend. The sombre, bilious Brazilian, Ayrton Senna, is already world champion, having driven straight up the backside of his closest rival, Alain Prost, at the first corner in the penultimate race a couple of weeks ago. Senna plays dangerous dodgems out there. They say the only time he smiles is when he spies a shunt in his driving mirror.

Careering along in the slipstream of Senna and Prost has usually been Nigel Mansell. Our Nige is the most unlikely lead player in this conceited, glitzy, girl-greedy jet-set. When he puts his affable gormless oar in at the beautiful people's parties it's like hearing *La Dolce Vita* jarringly dubbed all through with a nasally thick Brummagem accent. It irks the svelte, languid Gucci-poochies of the circuit that Mansell – always with nice little wifey in tow – is far more audacious behind a wheel than the lot of them except Senna and Prost. *Le paysan anglais*, they sneer, may be fast, but he's slow on the uptake.

Don't you believe it. Mr Mansell – *sir!* – had me, as they say, a treat last year. I still quiver with fear at his name. I am not enamoured with motor sport – the unspeakable in pursuit of the unapproachable – and know nothing whatsoever about gearbox ratios or double declutching. But because someone was sick or something I said, sure, I'd help out and cover a couple of Grand Prix races as best I could. At the Mexico GP I filed back that Mansell had been left at the starting-grid because he'd muffed getting into first gear (which was true) and had been left looking a stranded lemon like you and me at traffic lights. Then, on the way home, the tiresome stewardesses got in a tizz because there was nowhere in first class to dock the whopping great, gaudy, diamanté-speckled 6-foot-wide spaceships which were the pair of corny souvenir sombreros Nigel was taking home for his kids; and also that he'd scraped off the Béarnaise sauce or whatever from his main course and demanded tomato ketchup instead. Just matey, patronising, observations. A couple of weeks later, like a clot, I agreed to pen a piece of the usual waffle for some editor or other who wanted Nigel to be dead-heated in first place with Nick Faldo and Steve Davis as Britain's most colourless, boring sportsman.

Just before the Silverstone GP the phone rang. How about Nigel giving me a spin round the course in his new Ferrari F40, a 202mph two-seater, and so the nearest any passenger has ever been to simulating a racing driver's experience? Thanks, nice wheeze, I thought; good ol' Nige, he'll just gently pootle me around, amiably pointing out the curves and the cambers. I only began to twig when he insisted in the pits that I be zipped into a flame-proof suit, and that I was found a decently tight fit of crash-hat. As he checked my seat-belt, twitches of a diabolic grin began to lick around his lips. Then the thing erupted into an excruciating howl of revs and we catapulted out of the pit lane on to the track. Had I ever touched 200, he shouted? 'No, my Ford Escort is regularly overtaken by tractors,' I simpered. It was absolute, ultimate, scarifying hell. Three laps: hurtling, full-pelt petrification, every smidgin of every sense stampeded with fear, with this bloody Brummie beside me, chortling as he corkscrewed the blood-red, kamikaze capsule up this crazy corridor to, I was certain, the very doors of death. I had lockjaw, and couldn't speak for two and a half hours afterwards.

Delicious revenge. Terrorising revenge. And fair dos.

3 November 1990

GETTING TO MEET THE EMPEROR

Michael Lewis

My invitation to meet the Emperor of Japan came this summer, as I sat alone in a squalid hotel room in Tokyo, eating a McDonald's hamburger and listening to the theme music from *Rocky* on US armed forces radio. The caller, a young Japanese friend of mine, put it simply: 'Do you want to get an award from the Emperor?' I saw no reason to refuse. 'Hang up,' said my patron, 'and my friend will call you in ten minutes with the details.'

Ten minutes later another young Japanese man, whom I'll call the

Boss, phoned with the details. The Boss explained that each year the Osaka Junior Chamber of Commerce invited ten foreigners between the ages of 25 and 40 to tour Japan for a week, meet the Empress and Emperor, and receive the coveted 'TOYP' award. TOYP stood for Ten Outstanding Young Persons – one of those naturally ironic concepts that could form without irony only in the hierarchic mind of a Japanese. The point of the award, said the Boss, was to promote World Peace and Harmony right into the 21st century. I stress, the Boss knew nothing of my credentials for the task except that I was a) American and b) a friend of his friend. That was enough, since he was the head of the selection committee. To win I had only to follow his instructions in filling in a few forms. The only firm requirement, apart from youth, was that the candidate must never have set foot in Japan.

'But,' I said, 'I'm already in Japan.'

'Can you leave?'

Three months later – having left and returned – I sat staring into the middle distance, in the coffee shop of an Osakan hotel, wondering how I was going to survive the next week. I'd just seen our schedule. Before pressing the Imperial flesh the ten outstanding young people had to survive five days of meetings, speeches, conferences, discussion groups and more meetings. Never in my life have I seen so many meetings squeezed into so little time. I offer one morning as a small illustration:

9:30 a.m.: Guidance for Pre-meeting of TOYP Osaka Conference.
10:30 a.m.: Pre-meeting of TOYP Osaka Conference
11:30 a.m.: Meeting of TOYP Osaka Conference
1:00 p.m.: TOYP Osaka Conference Post-Meeting

As I pondered this, a young man approached, introduced himself as the German representative, and sat down. 'So you are an outstanding young person also,' he said, as if we two had just pulled off the hoax of the century. I nodded. He pulled from his breast pocket a thick document filled with fine print. 'Have you seen this?' he asked, shaking it violently. It was our schedule. I nodded again. My new friend said he had taken a few days off from his steel company in Düsseldorf because he liked the idea of a vacation in Japan. 'But this isn't wacation,' he said. 'This is verk!'

And so it was. The telephone call the next morning came at 5:45 a.m., from an apologetic Japanese man who wished to inform me that the first meeting of the day had been moved to 8:45 a.m.

from 9 a.m. Just as I had stopped wondering why he hadn't waited until dawn to announce this stunning fact, and was drifting back to sleep, the man rang again to announce that the meeting had been moved back to 9 a.m. I thought it was a joke, until it happened the next day and the next. Every night, without fail, our busy hosts met late into the night to discuss the next day's events. (More meetings!) Every night they shifted the first meeting forward 15 minutes. Every morning, 20 minutes after telephoning with the news, they moved it back again.

By the time we reached that first morning meeting most of the outstanding young people were spent. We – two Americans, two Britons (one of whom was a Labour MP), one German, one Pole, one Czech, one Thai, one Spaniard and one Belgian – sat jet-lagged and sleep-deprived around a long conference table. Surrounding us were about 25 members of the Osaka Junior Chamber, all of whom wore the same bright blue dayglo polyester sports-jackets. They wore these jackets everywhere, creating the impression of an international golfing committee that had become lost on the way to the tournament.

This first meeting began with a lesson from the Boss on how to behave in the presence of the Emperor, whom we wouldn't be seeing for nearly a week. Once inside the palace we would form an arc and wait quietly for His Majesty. We would not speak to him until spoken to. We would not test his divinity by, say, asking him to cause a hailstorm or to fix a parking ticket (the Boss could be droll). We would not be put off by the Imperial manner. 'The Emperor when he talks to you comes right up close to your face,' said the Boss. 'You will be like a frog looking into the eyes of a snake' (the Boss could be melodramatic, too). The Boss then ran through the list of other people we would visit: the Mayor of Osaka, a famous Japanese anthropologist, an executive at the Kobe steel works, the managers of several well-known sites in Osaka and Kyoto, and the Prime Minister, Mr Kaifu. At each stop one of us would be asked to make a speech of gratitude, and present to our hosts the gifts we had brought from our homeland.

Problem. None of us had thought to bring gifts. We instantly realised the threat to World Peace and Harmony – being, as we were, especially alert to such matters. After the meeting we conferred, then ran off to our rooms to ransack our luggage. The German returned with a collection of beer steins, the Thai with some beads, the Pole (an economist) with a stack of literature about investing in Poland. As we were throwing into a pile various second-hand articles I believe I heard the Labour MP say, 'Here, give them this – me mum gave it to me last Christmas,' but perhaps I misheard.

Thus the pre-Imperial leg of the tour began. There is not the space here to do justice to the comic horror of those five days; it was, I suppose, the price of the ticket to the palace. The goal of World Peace and Harmony quickly gave way to a kind of forced march through Japanese culture. The Japanese anthropologist tried to persuade us – as we nodded around a table – that the Japanese economy was becoming more Western, that its régime of lifetime employment had collapsed, that the Japanese people had at last become true individuals. The next day a senior executive of Kobe steel was offended when I asked if any of his 26,000 employees ever quit. 'Never in history,' he said, as he made his selection from our dwindling and increasingly soiled pile of gifts.

Time and again we found ourselves thrust before crowds of Japanese like a circus act, and asked to give our 'impression of Japan'. Most of us had only just arrived in Japan. On the third afternoon we were led into a hall full of people and seated along a table at the front, beside a local university professor. No one had told us why we were there or what was expected of us. The professor made a five-minute introductory speech in Japanese, of which the only two words I understood were my first and last names. He finished and looked to the translator, who smiled and said, 'Mr Michael Lewis from America will now give us his views on the subject: What Japan should do in Eastern Europe.' I closed my eyes, thought of the Emperor, and did what only the Labour MP did well: bullshit.

Somewhere along about that third day, as World Peace and Harmony drifted from sight, a question began to form in the minds of the group: *What on earth are we doing here?* As we stood one evening on a stage, facing a crowd of about a thousand Japanese, the Spaniard leaned over and whispered to me that the real reason for the programme was to provide the citizens of Osaka with inexpensive instruction in English. The German hissed back that, no, we'd been brought in to rant and rave about unfair Japanese trade practices. It was his opinion, I should say, that Japanese people loved to be beaten. On and on we argued, as we each in turn moved to the podium to invent a speech.

No plausible explanation for our presence in Japan emerged until the final day. Our tour bus sped to the palace. Along the way our Japanese hosts began visibly to swell with honour. Several said that this was quite clearly the best day in their entire lives. *In their entire lives.* I had had a glimpse in Osaka of Japanese emperor-worship, when I cornered a 12-year-old Japanese girl and put to her a series of questions. Who, I asked, was her favourite film star? Michael J. Fox, she replied. Who would she rather meet, Michael J. Fox or Prime Minister Kaifu? Michael J. Fox, she giggled, as though the question were patently absurd. All right: Michael J. Fox or the Emperor? No contest: the Emperor.

So there we were, 20 Japanese and ten outstanding young people, standing quietly in the receiving room of the palace. Everyone at once was trying unsuccessfully not to appear nervous, when an oleaginous man with long white teeth from the Ministry of Foreign Affairs entered to say that the Emperor and Empress would be with us shortly to spend an hour of their precious time. Our arc snapped into place and there was the feeling that the slightest irregularity would be punished. The lives of these people were still swirling, however vaguely, around their Emperor.

It was then that the jaundiced thought struck. It is far easier for an undeserving foreigner than for a deserving Japanese to gain an audience with the Emperor. What better way to get in to see His Majesty than to accompany ten outstanding young persons from abroad? In addition to promoting World Peace and Harmony we were a pass into the palace. All of a sudden I admired the shrewdness of my hosts. In a way, we were in silent league together, as neither group could gain an audience with the Emperor without the other.

Soon came the pitter-patter of Imperial feet. The Emperor and Empress entered, nodded, and began to greet the foreigners. They moved down our arc together, like the Duke and Duchess of Kent inspecting ball boys at Wimbledon. When they came to me, we spoke for five minutes about – what else? – World Peace and Harmony. The Empress pretended to be amused by an invitation to spend her next holiday in my home, and said, a little bitterly, that her movements were tightly controlled by the oleaginous man from the Ministry of Foreign Affairs. Then, having finished with the outstanding young people, the Imperial couple proceeded to greet our hosts. And if only you could have seen their bows.

10 November 1990

PILBROW

AFORE YE GO

Leaves from the commonplace book of Wallace Arnold

Perchance I have already penned a small memoir of my old friend and quaffing partner Michael Heseltine's years as a *Blue Peter* presenter, deputising for Mr Christopher Trace, before, with brilliant timing, ousting him from his job.

This week seems a perfect time to continue these reminiscences of Michael's rise to fame and fortune. Frankly, *Blue Peter* was not big enough to contain his myriad ambitions. I first realised this when, passing through the Peter Jones television department at 4.45 on a damp Thursday afternoon – what? '63? '64? – I chanced to see Michael's striking features echoing all about me in row upon row of dread goggle-boxes. Moving closer – I had promised myself a Shetland woollie, and felt that closer scrutiny of said garment on the Boy Heseltine might pay dividends – I couldn't help but notice that Michael had interrupted his useful introduction to the story of King Alfred and the Cakes with a vehement denunciation of his critics.

'I have said it before and I will no doubt say it again,' he began, 'that I have no intention whatsoever at this point in time of challenging Miss Valerie Singleton for her job as key presenter of this quite superb children's television magazine programme. I really couldn't make myself any clearer.' He then resumed the tale of the cakes, prior to welcoming the boys and girls of Taunton High into the studio to sing a medley of seasonal verses, lanterns all aglow.

Old clothes-brush

Within days of this announcement, the world learnt that Miss Valerie Singleton was indeed facing a challenge of her doughty stewardship of the programme. Midway through an item on how to turn an old clothes-brush into an attractive and unusual Christmas tree decoration ('simply tie a piece of string around it'), Val was visibly irked to find a hand straying into shot bearing a large pair of household scissors. Snap! Within seconds, the old clothes-brush had fallen to the floor, causing the Christmas tree to lose much of its lustre. A vicious trick, and though Heseltine issued strong denials that the hand was his, repeated re-runs of the film confirmed that the flamboyant initials engraved upon the signet ring were the tell-tale 'MH'.

Of what happened in the next few weeks, no one can be sure. Let it suffice to say that Val mounted an effective counter-offensive and, shortly afterwards, an official announcement confirmed the replacement of Michael Heseltine with the then unknown Mr John Noakes.

The next few years must have been hard for Michael. He picked up the odd job here and there – modelling the cover of the Gorringes autumn catalogue, clad in thornproofs, trilby on head, duck-quack in hand; a stint as Captain Troy Tempest's number two in a short-lived stage production of *Thunderbirds* at the Yvonne Arnaud Theatre, Guildford; the role of Sinister County Squire in an episode of *The Avengers* – but none of these roles lent him quite the weight he needed for a full-blown career in politics. However, Lord Luck was soon to tap him on the back (*to be continued*).

17 November 1990

WHY WERE ALL THE TORY WISEACRES SO EXTRAORDINARILY STUPID?

Auberon Waugh

When, after the time of Mrs Thatcher's tenth anniversary in office, I observed that she had never asked me to luncheon and was obviously not going to do so at that late stage, and then proceeded to urge the Tories to find a new leader, I was, of course, being facetious. It was over a year earlier, at the time of the Gibraltar shootings on 6 March 1988, that I personally decided she was no longer a fit person to continue as Prime Minister. My judgment was based on little more than gossip (what we writers call personal information) about her role in the matter, but it was confirmed by the almost unqualified support she received – not just from the *Sun* and *Sunday Telegraph* but from *The Spectator*, too – in her putative James Bond role as executioner without trial of suspected terrorists. The country's opinion-formers, it seemed to me, had been gravely corrupted if they were prepared to accept that the best way to uphold the rule of law in Ulster was to counter murder with murder.

I was almost alone, on the Right, in my fine pompous stand. The general feeling was that shooting was too good for them. Never mind that our only justification in Northern Ireland is that we are the legally constituted government, responsible for upholding the rule of law against murderers and terrorists. Mrs Thatcher's popularity soared, for possibly the last time until her resignation last Thursday.

Brooding about this in my loneliness, I decided that all my colleagues had been corrupted, to a greater or lesser extent, by the proximity of power. They had come to think of themselves as part of the ruling caucus. Some of them, of course, actually became part of it, like Ferdinand Mount. Others may have got no closer to it than a luncheon invitation to Downing Street, where the Prime Minister flattered them to the extent of pretending to be interested in their opinions and eliciting their enthusiasm for her own.

Perhaps, as has been suggested, the accumulated resentment of all those back-benchers who had never been invited to lunch at Downing Street, and had never received the treatment, had some influence on the final unfolding of events, but on this occasion I am more interested in the influence of those journalists who were invited and who were prepared to indulge the illusion of being part of it all.

For the last two years it was painfully apparent to anyone living in Britain – unless keeping company only with a handful of right-wing journalists mesmerised by the glamour of Downing Street – that Mrs Thatcher, from being the Conservative Party's greatest asset, had become its greatest liability. Her achievements were magnificent – winning three elections, smashing the unions, seriously reducing direct taxation, etc – but, in the course of time, she had become a national and electoral disaster. 'Loyalty, loyalty,' cried the bread-and-butter brigade, but loyalty has nothing to do with it. You do not feel loyalty to the plumber who, having successfully unblocked your drains, proceeds in a fit of demented conceit to smash up your house – least of all if he declares he has earned the right to do so.

For the last two years, as I say, it was painfully apparent to anyone of the smallest intelligence that Mrs Thatcher had to go before the next general election. Her obstinate adherence to the poll tax was only a symptom of the malaise which had overtaken her. The War Crimes Bill was a more worrying manifestation of it, as far as I was concerned – due to return to Westminster for reconsideration any day now. But what worried me most was the denial of natural perception. It is a feature, as any countryman will tell you, of mad, broody old chickens who refuse to leave their clutch of addled eggs, that they are peculiarly vulnerable to foxes. This one was guarded by serried ranks of otherwise intelligent soldiers for truth: Moore, Mount, Worsthorne, Anderson, (Frank) Johnson, Hastings, even young D. Lawson, as well as by the Murdoch pack of Bushells, Wyatts and Littlejohns.

There was never the slightest chance of Thatcher leading the Tories to victory after the poll tax. But the saddest thing is that they really believed what they said. Many, if not most, of that list have laid bets with me that the Conservatives would win the next election under Thatcher. I hope I do not have to send round reminders. But they put their money where their mouths were against all the evidence of by-elections, local elections, opinion polls and common sense. Undeterred by that, they solemnly sat down to convince themselves that she was right about the Common Market, joining their voices with the moronic yelps of those for whom the issue reduced to defence of the Good Old British Banger against foreign sausages. Every time Thatcher spoke of 'national sovereignty' in relation to currency control they breathed ecstatically about Thatcher as the last great patriot. Yet it was abundantly plain to those of us who had not lunched at Downing Street, and did not share the lower-class preference for English sausages, that all Thatcher meant by national sovereignty was her own unfettered discretion to screw up the economy once every four years for electoral purposes. Even as they applauded her patriotism, reckoning they had some shares in this national sovereignty, they

'I was kicked a good deal further upstairs
than I had anticipated.'

failed to consider that the same unfettered discretion would devolve on Hattersley and Kaufman next time round.

Thatcher had become a menace and we are well rid of her, although there can be no doubt she was a magnificent scrapper. Not least of her qualities was the ability to brush aside the myriad pressure groups which attend upon the governmental process. That Douglas Hurd was deficient in this quality became apparent after the Hungerford massacre, when he allowed the police lobby to push him into his fatuous gun-licensing legislation.

If last week did nothing else, it provoked a wonderful article from Bernard Levin in the *Times* pointing out the deeper lunacy of Mr Heseltine's ambition. There were those who complained that John Major was a humanoid, and it is true that he does not seem to resemble any human being I have ever met, but perhaps we needed to be governed by a humanoid, if only to prevent reasonable men from losing their senses. But the final consideration must be that Berkeley and Home, the two dim politicians, have achieved more for the Conservative Party than their philosophical namesakes ever did. These leadership elections should be held every six months while the party is in power, if only for their entertainment value and to stop Prime Ministers and journalists alike from infecting each other with the same hysterical self-importance.

1 December 1990

THE MAKING OF A PRIME MINISTER

Bruce Anderson

On Saturday 17 November, John Major went into hospital for an operation on a wisdom tooth. The trouble had first flared up in September, but this had been the first week that could be cleared in the Chancellor of the Exchequer's diary.

Mr Major was informed that it would take him about ten days to recover from the operation. During that time, he should have a complete rest, and should try to speak as little as possible. It was not then expected that his ten days' convalescence would culminate in his accession to the Premiership.

Three days later, however, Mrs Thatcher narrowly failed to eliminate Michael Heseltine's challenge. Throughout Wednesday 21 November Margaret Thatcher's position slowly crumbled. A number of erstwhile Thatcher loyalists approached John Major and asked him to stand against her, or at least to refuse to sign her nomination papers. He brusquely rejected both requests: if the PM wanted to run, he regarded himself as honour-bound to support her.

Meanwhile Graham Bright, Mr Major's Parliamentary Private Secretary, was also being lobbied. During Wednesday, nearly 100 Tory MPs approached him with offers of support for Mr Major should Margaret Thatcher withdraw.

Within the hour, Mr Major had decided to let his name go forward for the succession. Norman Lamont, Peter Lilley, Michael Howard and John Gummer met in the Treasury to begin planning his campaign. A campaign headquarters was needed. William Hague, Mr Lamont's PPS, suggested a house in Gayfere Street just off Smith Square: it belonged to a friend of his called Alan Duncan, an oil trader and Tory prospective candidate.

Mr Hague telephoned Mr Duncan, who turned out to be at his tailor's. When Mr Duncan returned to his office, he found a message to ring the Chancellor's office, and assumed, as most people would, that someone was pulling his leg.

William Hague, meanwhile, had grown impatient with the delay. He had a key to the Duncan residence, as he sometimes used the spare bedroom, so he simply took it over. When Mr Duncan arrived home, he found Norman Lamont and Richard Ryder in full command, moving furniture around and reorganising all the rooms, while British Telecom engineers were installing extra telephone lines.

Fortunately, Mr Duncan is a political addict of considerable resilience with a matching sense of humour. So when he was welcomed to his own house, and they said 'So glad you can join us, and who exactly are you?' he contented himself with pouring his visitors a drink. It was a couple of days before everyone in the Major team realised that the self-effacing, endlessly helpful and amenable character who was constantly volunteering to do whatever needed doing was actually their landlord.

The speed with which the Major campaign sprang into action was impressive. By Thursday evening almost everything was in place. Messrs Lamont and Ryder had already created a structure, while the volunteers to man it poured across from Westminster. Your correspondent, debarred from his usual journalistic outlets by some little local difficulties, joined up as a foot-soldier.

Within hours, over 50 Tory MPs had signed up to work for the Major team. They were instantly divided into two groups. One lot were assigned parliamentary duties: their job was to patrol the House of Commons, listening, lobbying, persuading, eavesdropping, and to feed back every piece of information to the Gayfere Street headquarters.

There the second group met in the basement, in what had been and may in the future become once again Alan Duncan's dining-room. 'The bunker', as it quickly christened itself, functioned as a Whips' Office. Any scrap of intelligence that came from Westminster was sifted, assessed, tested and re-tested. The Major campaign was well aware that Mrs Thatcher's team had been duped into overestimating her support, and they were determined not to make the same mistake.

In charge of the bunker was Francis Maude, who is now a Treasury minister but was formerly a Whip. Mr Maude, a witty, sardonic character, proved a most effective chairman. Several times a day, he and his team ran through their lists, discussing every single Conservative MP; at regular intervals new running totals were issued – but again these bore little relation to the raw data.

One of Mr Maude's principal adjutants was Ralph Hayward, whose *Who's Who* entry lists psephology as his main recreation. Mr Hayward, who looks like a bank manager, is a formidable number-cruncher. Together, he and Mr Maude evolved a method of discounting the pledges they had received, in order to allow for the mendacity quotient.

In any such campaign, a certain number of disgusting, unprincipled characters are known to pledge themselves to all the camps. So, right until the end, the figures for firm pledges published by the Major team were adjusted to allow for this. In the event, the 'disgusting, unprincipled' discount proved exaggerated, as John Major himself always thought it would.

Mr Major, too, is a former Whip. He has often regretted the fact that he never did a stint as Chief Whip. While he was a Whip, he had the reputation of being the office's most accurate counter of heads: so it proved during his own campaign. He constantly twitted the bunker for the timidity of its figures, and used to complain in mock horror when, at the end of a day in which he himself had won over half a dozen converts, he would be informed that the number of firm pledges had only increased by four.

Ideology played little part in any of the candidates' campaigns. Mr Major had the advantage of being thought to be the most right-wing of the available candidates, but Mr Heseltine was doing everything possible to move into Mr Major's natural territory, and to claim that he was Mrs Thatcher's rightful heir.

That, however, was not a successful tactic. Most Thatcherite MPs would have wished Mr Heseltine to understand that matricides cannot be heirs.

Mr Hurd, meanwhile, was reduced to the claim that he would improve MPs' conditions at Westminster. That promise had a ring of desperation to it, and only confirmed the bunker in its view that Mr Hurd was suffering the same fate as the weakest candidate in a by-election – his vote was being squeezed.

The determining factor was personality. A large section of the Tory Party could not forgive Mr Heseltine for unseating Mrs Thatcher. Some Thatcherites, however, were so upset that they could hardly think straight when it came to the choice of successor and were disinclined to vote for anyone. Throughout last weekend, the Major camp was encountering such characters, one of whom, Michael Brown, left a message on his answerphone: 'If that is a candidate, I would like to be Governor of the Cayman Islands.'

Some of these disgruntled Thatcherites clearly felt that their leader had been the victim of an establishment plot, which might even have involved John Major himself. The figure of Tristan Garel-Jones was often cited. Mr Garel-Jones – formerly the Deputy Chief Whip and now a Foreign Office minister – would be regarded as a cunning fellow even in his native Wales. At Westminster, he is widely credited with diabolic powers.

No use explaining to the enraged ultra-Thatcherites that Mr Garel-Jones was working for Douglas Hurd (the outcome of the Hurd campaign puts the diabolic powers in perspective). Anyone in the present Cabinet was blamed for being insufficiently supportive of the PM, while Mr Heseltine was at least given the credit for stabbing her in the front.

Mr Heseltine, meanwhile, did everything possible to appeal to the Right, and succeeded in gathering up a few misfits, mainly thickos and hysterics, who were so shell-shocked at the removal of Mrs Thatcher that they proceeded to vote for the man who had destroyed her. Margaret Thatcher herself, horrified at the thought of a Heseltine victory, appealed to the right-wing defectors to vote for Mr Major. She even saw some of the more bovine spongiform cases individually, to no avail. Protesting their undying admiration for the Prime Minister, they proceeded to ignore her wishes.

But their behaviour was straightforward compared to that of Nigel Lawson. The Major camp was determined not to allow the campaign to destroy friendships, and by and large succeeded in their objective. In Mr Lawson's case, however, matters are more difficult.

Those who worked with him at the Treasury can remember his spending hours denouncing Mr Heseltine's entire approach to government. Mr Lawson has never been known for his tolerance, but even by his own high standards, his intolerance of Mr Heseltine was striking. Yet here he was supporting Mr Heseltine against Mr Major, who had been Mr Lawson's loyal deputy when he was Chancellor, and for whom Mr Lawson was known to have a high regard.

In recent months, Mr Lawson, formerly so cosseted by the Tory Party, has suffered grossly unfair treatment. In particular, his stance on inflation has been ignorantly and maliciously misrepresented. But those who know and respect him would have thought him well able to brush aside belittlement from little men. In the light of his recent behaviour, however, the Major camp reluctantly concluded that his judgment had been undermined. A great man now allowed himself to be turned into a dancing bear in Mr Heseltine's menagerie: the only hope is that the aberration will prove temporary.

Neither Mr Lawson's nor Sir Geoffrey Howe's adherence to the Heseltine camp worried Mr Major's supporters. It was not felt that either man had much in the way of coat-tails. By Monday night, the Major camp was having difficulty in restraining its optimism. The total of firm pledges was approaching 180, while the press coverage reflected our own belief that we had the 'Big Mo': political momentum.

However, on Tuesday morning we were less confident. First, the *Independent* story about Mrs Thatcher's professed intention to do some 'backseat driving' caused anxiety in the tea-room, and was heavily exploited by both Heseltine and Hurd canvassers. Then an ITN poll of backbenchers – which correctly identified Mr Heseltine's vote of 131 – gave us only 158.

Our canvassing gave Mr Hurd no more than 60, but suppose we were out by 15? If his vote were higher, that might well be at Mr Major's expense. If lower, the defectors could switch to Michael Heseltine.

The final hours of most election campaigns are a nerve-racking business, as John Gummer reminded the team at lunchtime on Tuesday. We had been in danger of walking out of No. 11 with depressed faces, which might have been spotted and commented on. Mr Gummer called everyone to order, assured us that he had no doubts as to the result, and reminded us all of the innumerable previous occasions when we had had unjustified anxieties on the eve of a poll.

By then, of course, there was nothing further to do except feel anxious. Press briefings were prepared, to cover every contingency from an outright Major win to an outright Heseltine win. As to the latter contingency, Peter Lilley commented that it was now established practice that anyone coming top in a Conservative leadership ballot should promptly withdraw. But we did not really think that Mr Heseltine could win, so a list of Mr Hurd's supporters was compiled; discreet enquiries began as to their second preference.

No second preference was necessary. Francis Maude's final, un-revealed, figure – which Mr Maude himself showed no sign of believing – gave Mr Major 194 votes. As margins of error go in a secret ballot, under 5 per cent is not bad.

So, early on Tuesday evening, a weary, ecstatic throng drank champagne, cheered, sang 'For He's a Jolly Good Fellow' and swapped stories of our opponents' iniquities and our own superior cunning. All agreed that it had been a tremendous campaign – whose success had no relevance whatsoever to the problems of government.

1 December 1990

'Not another broken home!'

SO FAREWELL THEN, DENIS

John Wells

I shall miss Denis Thatcher. So, no doubt, will my bank manager. But impersonating anyone it is impossible not to feel some affection for them, even Hitler. There is something very basic about watching the way they wiggle their nose and trying to imitate it that must, I suppose, go back to early childhood.

The first person I imitated, apart from my father, was a master at school who was very fat, perfectly poised on two tiny feet, and who spoke like a ridiculously affected, upper-class maiden aunt. He came in quietly when I was 'doing' him one morning and asked me to stay behind afterwards. I imagined the cane at least, but instead he asked me whether I'd like to play Mrs Candour in *The School for Scandal*. From then on I impersonated him to his face all through rehearsals and the local newspaper said it wasn't fair bringing in one of the master's wives to play a female role.

After that it was John Betjeman. I can't think of anyone I've ever admired more: I loved the way he smoked a cigarette, the way his front teeth rested on his lower lip, and most of all the way he talked. Impersonating him was more an act of homage than any attempt to ridicule him, and when he came to see the show at the Edinburgh Festival and we swapped hats afterwards for a photograph it was one of the proudest moments of my life.

I can't imagine swapping hats with Denis. Under the rather trying circumstances of our only meeting, the Thatcher ménage did not give off waves of that magnanimity I had encountered in my old master or in the Laureate; or, after an initial chill, in Mary Wilson and Harold. I sensed the same lack of readiness to suffer professional fools gladly in Ted Heath, and I think it may be to do with what the Germans call feeling happy in your skin. Neither Heath nor the Thatchers seemed socially confident enough to laugh at themselves – perhaps, on the contrary, it was because they were too regal – though Mrs T did manage a grim chuckle in Parliament at Geoffrey Howe's broken cricket bat joke.

But Denis is nonetheless an endearing figure. Whatever the exact nature of his relationship to our greatest peacetime Prime Minister since records were kept he had, in the role of consort, huge virtues as a comic character. His appearance was in his favour, and he had

just enough observable quirks to fit him into a simple Wodehousian context of golf and fags and the banter of the Club or the Saloon Bar.

Soon after they moved into No. 10, he was observed 'ashing out', flicking a couple of inches off the end of his untipped Senior Service into the flower arrangement. A photograph sent in by a reader to *Private Eye* showed him at Twickers, swilling down champagne out of the back of a Roller in the company of two wonderfully seedy figures, one tall and burly, wearing what looked like a tam-o'-shanter, the other small and in a leather hat, with dark glasses and discoloured teeth, the Major and Maurice Picarda to the life.

Another picture I was sent showed him enjoying lunch at a new hotel in South Africa in which he might or might not have had a professional interest, and another time there was a particularly good snap of him pulling the string at an unveiling ceremony. The plaque to be unveiled was on a wall, flanked by two RAF men standing rigidly to attention. As the shutter clicked, Denis had wrenched the string practically down to the ground, and the wind had blown half the curtain across the face of one of the RAF guards, so that his features just showed through in the manner of a veiled statue. From the expression on Denis's face he looked as though he had done it on purpose.

But having given us such clues, his great contribution to creative satire lay in his silence, apparently enforced. Unlike any other spouse of a public figure, Denis was under an absolute Trappist ban. Very occasionally he was allowed in to play a supporting role, improvising for the cameras a few informal comments on Margaret's holiday plans; and once during the Tamanrasset saga allowed to take centre stage as he grunted his way through the Prodigal Son scenario, urged by pressmen to embrace the boy Mark and doing so with as much enthusiasm as he would have embraced the Fatted Calf.

Why was he not allowed to talk? This was the incitement to imagine what he might have said if he had, and I shall miss the fortnightly sessions in the windowless cubbyhole behind reception at *Private Eye* – when Richard Ingrams and I for 11 years worked him like a ventriloquist's dummy – a great deal more than I shall miss the elegant old toper himself.

Over the past week I have been studying the candidates' mannerisms. I have already had a crack at Hurd's Old Etonian Nose and Throat Effect when I was playing Justice Overdo in *Bartholomew Fair,* and I don't think he'll ever bring the house down. Major, for all his father's skill on the high wire, does not seem sufficiently at ease in front of the cameras to risk any of those winning mannerisms beloved of the clowns. My wife suggests I should have a go at doing Mrs Heseltine.

1 December 1990

THE ART OF THE DOORSTEP

John Simpson

Michael Heseltine's head jerked, and something came to his eyes. He had been planting acorns, surrounded by cameras, when the news of Margaret Thatcher's resignation reached him. It meant that he was no longer the certain victor, that he now had a fight on his hands. He found the right words, but not the right manner. He sounded as though he was grieving for his own chances. Michael Heseltine's undoubted abilities do not include a mastery of the art of the television doorstep interview. He shakes his leonine head at the first hint of a question, or retreats into some carefully rehearsed formula which may look good on the printed page but sounds wrong to the ear.

This is the first time any campaign for the leadership of a British political party has been fought out primarily on television; one forgets the speed of the changes which have come to British political life since the 1970s. The three candidates for the Conservative leadership wandered embarrassed and aimless through the English countryside, feeding the wildlife or even feeding themselves in full view of the watching millions. And yet of those millions only 372 were eligible to vote – the electors of a strange form of rotten borough, attempting to second-guess the views of the nation as a whole. It was for them that the candidates were play-acting in front of the cameras: a difficult art to master.

Last week, clumping across an Oxfordshire field alongside Douglas Hurd and asking him those brief, waspish questions which produce the best results, I reflected that he was the only one of the three candidates who understood that the art is to conceal the art. Michael Heseltine was too controlled, John Major too tense. You must possess the appearance of frankness. You must seem to take this irritating questioner, this kind of burr, into your confidence – and through him or her, the unseen watching millions.

Formerly, a British prime minister would give public answers to journalists' questions only in a television studio. Throw an impromptu question outside and you were in trouble. One day in the early summer of 1970 I stood, young and gawky, halfway down platform 7 at Euston Station on my first reporting assignment. Harold Wilson swept down the platform towards me, a portly god in a cloud of aides and civil servants. I gripped my radio microphone tighter. The lobby correspondents had been authoritatively predicting an election soon, but there had been no announcement.

Harold Wilson approached the coach labelled 'Huyton'. I looked round: clearly, none of the reporters and cameramen beside me was going to tackle him about this. Instead, they wore the vacuous smiles which journalists put on in the presence of the powerful. I stepped forward, microphone out, tape turning. 'Excuse me, Prime Minister: when will the election . . .?' The transcript from the tape then reads, 'Simpson: Urgghh.' Harold Wilson had sunk his fist into my stomach. 'You know I never do these things,' he snarled, close enough for me to smell his breath; 'I shall ring the Director-General and complain personally.' 'You'll hear more of this,' hissed Gerald Kaufman, at that time a Labour Party press officer. Then they all swept on, leaving me. I had been mugged by the Prime Minister on my very first story. The journalists and cameramen were still laughing. 'You don't doorstep the Prime Minister, sonny,' said one of them. No one reported what had taken place. There was no complaint to the Director-General.

You didn't doorstep the Leader of the Opposition either. In Strasbourg in 1975 Margaret Thatcher, on her first visit abroad after deposing Edward Heath, stared haughtily at the journalists who presumed to throw questions at her as she arrived at the European Parliament. Even at her press conference she replied in hostile monosyllables. 'You can see she'll never make Prime Minister,' someone said. Maybe it was me. And yet over the next four years she learned to stop resenting the cameras and the questions; they were, she realised, as potentially useful to her in this strange symbiosis as she was to them.

And so she began saying more than just, 'Good morning, good morning,' and answering the dreary, 'Are you optimistic?' with an equally dreary, 'I'm always optimistic.' Head forward like an athlete swooping to the tape, weighed down by that heavy handbag, she would make for the television lights while giving the impression she was heading in that direction anyway. She revelled in the awkward, barbed question. 'Did you enjoy pressing the button?' I asked her once, on the cold North German plain, after she had climbed out of a Challenger tank whose gun she had been firing. Her political enemies were calling her a warmonger at the time. A chilly flash of the blue eyes, then a seraphic smile: 'British tanks are marvellous.'

She learned that there was more to television than the meretricious message that appearance counts; that politicians are at their strongest when appearance and intention fully coincide. Her doorstep interview with John Cole in the immediate aftermath of the Brighton bomb was a powerful statement in itself of the fact that her determination was undiminished. Catch her before or after some big occasion and you would get the full mood of the moment: triumph, carefully controlled scorn, all of Elizabeth Tudor in a sound bite.

It was in Downing Street, to my one-time colleague Michael Cole, that Mrs Thatcher first properly exercised the art of the doorstep interview; his shouted question the morning after the election was answered with the famous, heavily prepared quotation from St Francis about bringing healing and harmony. It was in Downing Street that she instructed the nation, through television, to rejoice at the success of British arms in the Falklands war. And it was in Downing Street that she called out her last, defiant words before the decision to resign: 'I fight on; I fight to win.' She used the cameras like someone in a Shakespearian history play. There could be high comedy too – perhaps intentional, perhaps not. After some malcontent threw a hand-grenade at the building in Luxembourg where an EEC summit was droning on, she emerged clutching Sir Geoffrey Howe's sleeve like a mother with an unwilling teenager. 'Geoffrey was speaking when it went off, weren't you, Geoffrey?' He nodded miserably; she beamed. 'It was quite a good speech, too.'

Her press secretary, Bernard Ingham, seemed to detest these moments. Obliged to stay out of shot, uncertain what was being said, unable to step in and shape or control the message, he lurked in the background, ear cocked, red face glowering. His view of television seemed fixed in the Wilson era: he gave the impression he couldn't quite see what it was *for*. Mrs Thatcher could: it was for talking to ordinary people, as directly as a British politician can. In this, as in more important ways, she has changed the job of being Prime Minister. Her successors will have to learn to master the doorstep.

1 December 1990

RESTAURANT

THE TERRACE AT THE DORCHESTER, PARK LANE

Nigella Lawson

There are, as the novelist Paul Bailey's mother might have said, hotels and hotels. And the Dorchester most definitely belongs to the latter category. True, it doesn't have the hushed splendour of the Connaught, but nor does it have the parvenu vulgarity of its nearer neighbour, the Inn on the Park. The vulgarity of the Dorchester is of a different order. It reeks of confidence and camp, of kitsch period glamour: a Thirties Hollywood mogul's dream of a cruise liner, forever moored to Park Lane.

Having been draped in scaffolding for what seems like years now, while mysterious chippings and blastings took place within, it is now restored to us. The tree outside is once again hung with bulbs, resplendently, elegantly ablaze. Enter into a foyer dripping with crystal-filtered light, dotted with banquettes as plump as a diva's breast. Trip your way through the florid swirls of the deep pile to the Terrace, once the domain of Anton Mosimann and now in the hands of one Willi Elsener.

Vince Prince and his orchestra welcomed us to this eau-de-nil and jasmine temple, all Chippendale-chinoiserie and mirrored columns, with a huskily muzaky rendition of Air on a G-string which effortlessly, harmoniously, drifted into the 'Girl from Ipanema'. From there to 'Something Stupid', to 'Edelweiss', to 'Top of The World', to 'Cuando, Cuando, Cuando, Cuando', to 'Lady In Red'. By this time you will know if this is the place for you or not. If it is, I would advise asking for a table on the perimeter of the dance floor – all six square feet of it – rather than in the gazebo. Brought up in a time when dancing had stopped being a contact sport, I revelled in my ringside seat. What prowess was on show – the floor a whirling blur of fuchsia silk palazzo pant, the gold strap of a spindly sandal glinting as it caught the chandeliered light.

Anton Mosimann is a hard act to follow, and it perhaps would have been wiser not even to try. As it is, 'executive chef' Willi Elsener cooks very much in the same mode. Only it ain't quite as modish as it was when Anton was in the kitchen. There is something, let's be frank, faintly *provincial* now about the spectacle of food carved and chiselled, moulded and prinked, unsensually denatured: as Muriel Spark has it, 'the wild asparagus made into Snow White's house'. Anton Mosimann was, in truth, never that precious. If you have real talent, you can't be precious. Willi Elsener is not without talent, but he doesn't have It, and he comes perilously near the precious with formulations such as 'les Trouvailles du Marché' (the every-other-daily changing surprise menu) and his little orange peas hewn out of carrot. I also think that to boast a 'menu léger' and a 'cuisine légère' without any reference to Anton Mosimann, who made his cuisine naturelle famous in these very premises, is completely lacking in grace.

My tastes lead more towards a surprise than a light menu, so I ordered the trouvailles du marché. A salad of fanned duck breast and Jerusalem artichokes was ceremoniously delivered, then superseded by an amber-coloured beef consommé in which floated crinkle-cut juliennes of root vegetables, then a little plait of sole with a chive sauce, followed by a mouth-cleansing Gewürztraminer sorbet (a vulgar touch, but not necessarily an unwelcome one), then a little round of pink lamb encircled in gold fat nestling up to a little round of beef topped with diced ceps, a selection from a breathtakingly (when I remember the trolley Mosimann used to keep) unexceptional cheeseboard, and finally three little lozenges of praliné mousse, unwelcomingly reminiscent, in its orangey chocolateness, of nothing so much as a pile of whipped-up Matchmakers. Except for the last two courses, all was good, all was fine. But apart from the fact that it was rather like being in a time warp, I think at £48 it could be a *leetle* bit more than just that.

M. Elsener may resent the constant comparisons with Anton Mosimann, but it's difficult not to make them. Before its closure, and it has been a long one, the Dorchester was a place to eat in because of Mosimann. He made the menu, and the restaurant, his own. What you eat now in the Terrace is not in itself inadequate, only you feel you could eat it anywhere.

The wine list, or book, is in the main prohibitively expensive, though the young sommelier cheerfully administered a fabulously smoky chablis (Van de Vey) for £27 and a half bottle of velvety Pomerol (Château Plince) for £14. These are cheap by Dorchester standards.

In full, with tip of 12-ish per cent, the bill for dinner for two, for the above plus a vodka martini, two glasses of champagne and coffee with now obligatory petit fours, came to £165. I can hear you catch your breath, but wait. If it's good food you want, go to Pierre Koffmann, say, or Marco Pierre White. But for pure spectacle, the Dorchester wins. Baulk though I did at the absurdity of the price, I adored my evening. But then, I've always had a weakness for kitsch.

1 December 1990

COMPETITION

A DIFFERENT STORY

Jaspistos

In Competition No. 1654 you were asked to take a recent headline from a newspaper and write a news item attached to it that tells a wildly different story.

Either you were in particularly good form this week or you were lucky in finding ambiguous headlines; whichever it was, the entry was thoroughly entertaining. I'm awarding as many prizes as space permits, and I'm sorry that Katie Mallett, D. A. Prince and Chris Tingley miss getting one. The winners printed below take £12 each, and the bonus bottle of Chivas Regal 12-year-old de luxe blended whisky goes to Simon Rodwell, who pleasantly admitted that his suggestive headline was culled from the *South China Morning Post*.

VIRGIN
BIRTH
CLINIC

DANGERS OF ADDICTION TO PREGNANT WOMEN

A recent study reveals that many middle-aged males develop insatiable yearnings for the company of pregnant women. 'The condition, known as gravidophilia, is a form of phobia,' the report warns. 'Sufferers, who are invariably obese and unmarried, see themselves as social failures. Associating with unmistakably fecund females boosts their self-esteem. Typically, a gravidophiliac feels thinner when next to a bulky pregnant woman, and he is able to indulge his greed without guilt by sharing in her irrational food cravings.'

Dangers include bloody brawls among gravidophiliacs competing for single mothers-to-be outside ante-natal clinics. And new mothers, no longer attractive to their partners, suffer stressful trauma when suddenly and inexplicably deserted.

(Simon Rodwell)

FARMHOUSE DATES FROM ELIZABETHAN TIMES

It is not widely known that date-palms were once a prominent feature of the landscape in the fruit-growing districts of Hereford and Worcester. Date stones have recently been found in a cesspit near Palmistone, carbon-dated to *c*. 1588. The diary of a Tudor farmer's wife mentions the boxing of 'dayts' in oval containers made of date-palm wood with the inclusion of a walrus ivory 'harpoune' in each box.

Elizabeth I never travelled further west than Worcester, despite her Welsh origins; because, it is now thought, she broke several teeth on date stones, requiring Dr Dee's attentions in London. When her remaining teeth turned black she had all date-palms felled and their wood used for the fleet against the Spanish.

(Caro Fendall)

MAJOR TRIES TO SQUARE THE CIRCLE

Retired RE Major John Sweetman of Warminster has come up with a remarkable solution to the source of the mysterious crop circles which appear regularly on the Wiltshire Downs. Major Sweetman has made a careful series of measurements of such circles over several years and, after feeding these at weekends into the powerful computers at the nearby School of Artillery, claims he has proof that the circles come from Mars. The square of one continually recurring dimension is exactly one thousandth part of the polar diameter of Mars – and this is only one among several similar coincidences.

(John Sweetman)

RUSSIAN SUB 'SANK TRAWLER'

Oleg Zendimov, perpetual Number 12 on Dynamo Vladivostok's tour of Britain, finally made his mark last night. In the dying minutes of the 'dockside special' fixture against Hull City, the transfer-seeking striker was sent on to level the score.

Zendimov responded to the call by unleashing a fierce right-foot volley that might have severed the post – had it been travelling in that direction. Instead, providing ample evidence why he's been sidelined this season, the ball rocketed towards the nearby fishing flotilla and went smack into an arriving smack. Skipper Harry Mitchell, shocked by the ball's arrival, jammed the steering into a fatal collision course with a quay. He escaped moments before the boat sank. The question in Humberside last night was: will Zendimov wind up in the dock, too?

(Will Bellenger)

TWO-TON LAMB

A report from Australia suggests that the spectre of famine which has haunted man since the beginning of time has at last been banished from the earth. For many years a team of research scientists in the Faculty of Agriculture of Melbourne University has been investigating the genetics of the growth hormones in animals. The team concentrated on sheep, as these animals are particularly abundant in Australia. Yesterday the scientists published their findings and put on public display the result of their final and astonishingly successful experiment – the two-ton lamb! According to the report the growth-enhancing technique can be applied to any of the animals or birds which have for centuries fed the hungry masses of the world.

(J. Hennigan)

NIGHTMARE OF A TIED POLL

The fall of Mrs Thatcher has brought problems for a parrot scheduled to appear in Esther Rantzen's *That's Life*. The parrot, owned by Jeffrey Archer, used to say, 'Pretty Poll Tax'. Now it has been deprived of food and tied to its perch until it learns a new greeting: 'Morning Major.'

(Simon Cotton)

JAPANESE HEDGE ON CONCRETE SUPPORT

The latest work to arrive at the Bretton Hall Sculpture Park is Akiro Mitsubishi's 'Dragon of Creation'. The basic structure is fifty metres long, and made of concrete – a medium whose essential plasticity Mitsubishi exploits to the full in the way that it sinuously hugs the contours of the park. The dragon's fins are bonsai trees densely planted along the top, each of a different species. Decoded in accordance with the ancient tradition of 'say it with trees', the sculpture is simultaneously the text of a Daoist creation epic.

(George MacDonald Ross)

8 December 1990

THE THATCHER YEARS

Vicki Woods

Eleven years ago, when we first saw the cottage on the Hampshire-Berkshire borders in which we still live, it was a warm, golden afternoon in late summer. Roses grew round the door and sunshine filtered through the dusty windows. The thatch, about four foot thick, sat heavily on the roof like a home-baked pound loaf, and my husband, a rather metropolitan Scot, nearly wept with excitement and the romance of it.

When we moved in, on the eve of Mr Callaghan's 'winter of our discontent' of 1978–79, it was a stone-cold December. We moved in a hurried muddle. I was four months' pregnant with our second child, there was no hot water (only a cold tap in the old scullery), no drainage, no sewage, no floors (they had been dug out in order to put in damp-proofing) and no internal plaster on the brick walls. As the year turned, lorry-drivers, dustmen and gravediggers went on strike; sugar, salt and babies' disposable nappies disappeared from the shops; copper piping and cement were in short supply. Electricity came and went. It's like the war, my mother kept moaning. I slept in my clothes, and in the early hours of the morning I would grope for some of my husband's clothes and sleep in them, too. On the coldest night of that freezing winter, I picked my son out of his cot at four o'clock in the morning and ice tinkled on his (old-fashioned, towelling) nappy: it was the night a baby froze to death in Basingstoke.

The cottage was damp, and where the damp lay, it froze, in the floors and in the walls around the rotting window-frames. The man from the mortgage had poked into the walls and floors and window-frames and given us a list of works to be completed without fail within six months of said date. Gangs of men would come and crack the ice off their buckets and go home again by lunchtime, saying it was too cold to set concrete and anyway, there was no cement.

The only part of the house that wasn't damp were the bedrooms, tucked up under the massive roof. I quite liked the roof, although it didn't look so much like a teatime loaf once the autumn sun was off it. Moss lay on it, and small trees struggled to grow in it, and it reminded me of Hest Bank, a bleak and muddy estuary off Morecambe Bay. Estuaries at low tide look like natural disasters: banks of shiny mud with green and brown bits sticking valiantly up and trying to grow, and rivulets of water meeting and separating round the banks. My roof looked like a natural disaster, and it frightened the man from the mortgage. He said, You must rethatch within six months.

I looked in the Yellow Pages for thatchers, but they lived five counties away and were booked up for two years. We asked in the pub. Peter the landlord said, Does it leak? and made helpful noises about a man he knew who had a tarpaulin, and I said No, it's never leaked; it's just that the mortgage people don't like the way it goes up and down like that. There was a short, baffled silence, which I took to mean, If it ain't broke, don't fix it, and I continued, after my stupid townie fashion, to try to find numbers to ring. Eventually, one of the brickies working on my damp-proof course asked his mate, who knew a man in Micheldever, who said he could start as soon as the cold weather broke.

This is not how to look for a thatcher. I know that now. You don't look for a thatcher, you look for a thatch. You drive round and round in wider and wider circles, down past Laundry Cottages and up into Old Burghclere and along the back roads towards Whitchurch and Overton and then back towards Poundisford and Monk Sherborne, and when you see a roof you like you ask the owner a) how long it's been up, b) what materials it's made with and c) the name of his thatcher.

We are two miles over the Hampshire side of the border here. If you sit on my roof you can see Watership Down and the rolling acres of my neighbour Andrew Lloyd Webber, who occasionally leaves them, in a black BMW, to drive half a mile to the pub with his latest wife. (The village is fondest of the first Sarah, was mildly scandalised by the teentsy ra-ra skirts and pink tights of the second Sarah and has offered a guarded welcome to nice, horsy Gurdey.) Here in Hampshire, the traditional thatching material is 'long straw'. Very few houses in Hampshire are now thatched with long straw, and the ones that are look a bit like mine did 11 years ago: dark and wet-looking and streaked with green like Hest Bank.

On a long-straw thatch, you can see the great fat ears of corn lying visible because it's worked downwards. Nowadays, the commoner straw thatch is 'short straw', which is worked upwards, so the ears of corn are tucked underneath and not visible. There is also reed itself – Norfolk water-reed – which you don't see around here too often because it costs the most. Long straw is the easiest to work. Thatchers have to be neat, laying each bundle of straw on to the slope of the roof as uniformly as possible and overlapping them as uniformly as possible in order to make clean, straight lines so that the rain will run sheer, and fall off the end like a curtain. Good thatchers get their eaves and window-eyebrows so clean-cut and sharp that the whole roof looks as though it's been cut from scone-dough with a bread-knife. If thatchers work unevenly, the wind and weather will work hollows into the roof and the rain will eventually carve little channels and rivulets into the slope, Hest Bank fashion, that go green and noisome and rot the straw beneath. Bundles of long straw, with their great floppy ears of corn hanging at one end, are not so uniform as the stalks alone – 'short straw'. Water-reed, of course, is the most uniform of all.

Which is why reed lasts the longest (these days, 80 years or so, but there's an old reed thatch in Norfolk that's 100 years old and as sound as a bell). Short straw is next: the master thatchers' associations usually reckon on 25 years or so. And long straw has the shortest life: ten to twenty years; which is why, only 11 years after we moved in and rethatched, we are having to rethatch again.

Perversely, I like long straw best. It's the boskiest-looking, long straw; rougher and hairier and less raffiné than short straw or reed: Donegal tweed compared to slick mohair suiting. There is a lot of tarting-up goes on in Hampshire. A lot of 17th-century cottages that don't boast a single straight line or right-angled corner sport shiny new faux-18th-century front doors and faux-Edwardian glasshouses and faux-Tudor leaded lights. When you pop a razor-sharp, short straw thatch on the top of these, the effect is artificial, as though the straw were

'He appears to have drastically reduced
his carbon dioxide emissions.'

made from lengths of yellow plastic tubing. (I believe that in Sweden, thatch *is* made from lengths of plastic tubing, and you can buy fake thatch in eight-by-ten sheets in this country, like giant toupées. Each toupée is guaranteed for 90 years, but the *joints* aren't.)

So we thatched, 11 years ago, with long straw. The man arrived from Micheldever on a brilliant, icy day in February. He introduced himself as Mr Whitcher-the-Thatcher and said he'd leave the straw in the garden and start up when the weather broke. For the next fortnight, horses had to be urged into a trot past the tempting haystack and their riders' cries rang out in the steely air.

By the time he started work, I was seven months into a difficult pregnancy, longing for London and taxis and wall-to-wall carpeting, and sick unto death of the cold and the wet concrete and the plaster dust. As I shuffled about the cottage trying to keep up with my toddling son, I could hear Mr Whitcher-the-Thatcher's thump-thumps as he banged in the hazel rods, and the soft thuds as he threw down his bundles of straw. But mostly I lay like a mole in a hole and took very little notice of Mr Whitcher-the-Thatcher, except when he climbed off the roof with straws hanging off him to warm his purple claws on the Rayburn and drink tea. He was a Hampshire native who said 'him' for 'it': 'He's getting on well' (of the roof) and 'He's going down a bit' (of the haystack). He pronounced thatcher with two As: thaatcher; making a drawn-out short A as in Baa-baa, Black Sheep, not the drawled long A that smart Catholics use for Mass ('We're orf to Maass').

As March turned, and the daffodils began to poke out, the ambulance-drivers joined the gravediggers and the dustmen on strike, and on the day after my second child's estimated date of arrival, Mr Whitcher-the-Thatcher and I got to know each other rather better. After only one rather out-of-the-blue and bafflingly fierce labour pain, I became acutely aware that my baby was going to be born right now – *this minute* – and I sank to the floor, dragging the telephone down with me by its lead. Eight fairly crowded minutes passed, during which I gabbled for help on the telephone, shrieked aloud, tried not to 'bear down' (midwives' language) and made efforts to divest myself of the heaps of my husband's clothing I'd been living in since Christmas. My mother, wearing gardening gloves and holding a trowel, ran about moaning horribly and fetching electric heaters and blankets, while I struggled to persuade the only ambulance in Hampshire, which was working emergencies only, to bypass a coronary in Whitchurch and stop off for me. Seconds later, the baby was born, with the right number of eyes, ears, legs, arms, fingers, and toes, though I never thought to look what sex it was. In these situations, you gotta prioritise, as the

Americans say. And, as the walls began to come in and out around me (from shock) and the baby turned pink and began to breathe, I saw Mr Whitcher-the-Thatcher marching manfully into the room, eyes averted. He was dripping, as usual, with stalks and ears of corn, and he said, bafflingly: I've brought him a straw. I was filled with rage. Birth and near-death crowded the room like lowering giants, and here was this *stupid Hampshire peasant* trying to persuade me into some *farcical arcane loony rural ritual* involving thaatchers and gifts of straw and God knows what – like *kissing a sweep* on your wedding day – and I made efforts to drive Mr Whitcher from my presence with the sort of foul language that pupil midwives are well used to hearing. The thatcher, still with his eyes averted, said primly, I've sterilised it. It's a soft plastic straw. From the *kitchen*. In case he needs his passages clearing; in case his breathing's blocked.

O Mr Whitcher, how I maligned you. As it happened, the baby didn't need his passages clearing. My new daughter breathed like a good 'un from the first seconds of life. And, as it happened, the emergency ambulance arrived like the cavalry, and by the time my husband ran in, minutes later, Mr Whitcher was back on the roof with his hazel rods, thumping and thudding away. Much later, he told my mother that all his children had been born at home, with only him to assist the midwife.

I don't know whether it was the excitement that caused Mr Whitcher's long straw to sink and settle into muddy banks and channels over the next 11 years, or whether it was the problems endemic in the material itself, but my roof began to look very much like Hest Bank last winter, and one of the dark green rivulets is beginning to ease damply into my bedroom. My new thatcher, a master thatcher, is libellous and ribald about his predecessor's job, but thatching is a jealous craft.

Anyway, we have chosen short straw, and be damned to boskiness. Every other roof in the village is short straw (except one), and all of them have outlasted mine. The exception is a little low cottage at the end of the village that has razor-edged eaves and sharply-cut brows over the windows. I braked to a halt outside it a few years ago and called to the man in the guernsey up the ladder: 'Who are you and where are you from?' The guernsey was a giveaway: this was not a thaatcher, but One of Us: an ex-army major. He said he was from Marlborough ('Mawlbrah!') and answered briskly: yes, he was using reed, not straw, but it wasn't exactly Norfolk reed; wasn't from Norfolk, no. It came from Kenya ('Kenyah!') in a container ('Containah!') and he imported it from there because it was cheaper ('Cheapah!'). It's lasted well, but

I don't like those Swedish-looking razor-edges.

Hampshire County Council sent me a brisk letter lamenting the decline of 'the traditional Hampshire technique of thatching using long straw' and offering to stand me 20 per cent of the cost of a rethatch if I use the hairy stuff with the ears of corn downwards. My splendidly-named thatcher, Barrington D. Hicks, and I thought not, in the end, though it's £3,400 I'm chucking away, and I fretted for some time at the thought of what the price will be to do it all again only 25 years from now.

And then I saw, in the poor unfortunate *Sunday Correspondent* (in the very last issue, in fact) that the Prince of Wales has been quietly and greenly growing organic thatching straw on the Home Farm at Highgrove. 'We've still got a couple of tonnes left,' said his farm manager Mr Wilson, 'so if anyone's interested in some superb thatching straw . . .' Mr Wilson was quoted as saying that organic thatching straw was so terrific, so strong, so sound, that it would last for 40 years. Forty years! I rang Kensington Palace first thing on Monday morning, and went from telephone number to telephone number until I got a chap who was in a position to sell the Prince's couple of tonnes. Then I rang Barrington D. Hicks ('Call me Barry') and asked him if I was doing the right thing. Barry was very excited about using organic straw. It's wonderful stuff to work, he said: it works itself. 'When you butt the ends down, it's like glass rods in your hand.' He used it on the barn over at Compton Beauchamp ten years ago and it's still as sound as a pound; he bought it off an organic farmer in Oxford who's dead now. Pity it's only a couple of tonnes, he said. What do you mean – a pity? Well, it'll just about do your ridge, he said. Lord above! How many tonnes of straw does this roof need? 'Six to eight,' said Barry, and I almost ducked at the thought of that weight of straw above my head. Eight tonnes!

Well, the Prince of Wales has come up trumps, and scrabbled around for another six tonnes of his best organic from somewhere, and Barry is whisking off to Tetbury on his motor-bike to tap the ends down and see if it's like glass rods in his hand. It's wonderful weather for thatching if the wind keeps off and the frost's not too hard, and two months from now, I'll have a roof as round and golden as a risen batch loaf, and a very large hole indeed in the bank balance, and the satisfaction of knowing that the daughter, now aged eleven and a half, will be pushing 50 before she needs a new roof over her head.

So ends my thatcher era.

22/29 December 1990

A DIP INTO TOKYO

Harriet Sergeant

I have just moved back to Tokyo after two years away. Distance made the heart fonder. Clean, safe and orderly, Tokyo had appeared the antithesis of London. I recalled a 'Never-Never' city where window cleaners wore white gloves, taxi drivers refused tips and dog shit was collected even as it fell. Was Tokyo still Tokyo or were there some things I had just forgotten?

In my absence Tokyo has changed. Before, the richest metropolis in the world left its citizens to take care of themselves. Now Tokyoites are demanding better things of their city. Playgrounds have started to appear and trees are being planted. Would I see workshops and consumer associations next? Was civic indulgence the first step to Western decadence? My local swimming pool seemed the place to find out.

The sports centre is a large, modern building surrounded by cherry trees. A bent, old man sold me a ticket and showed me where to leave my shoes. In the women's changing room a recorded voice issued instructions and encouragement. I found myself in need of both. Undressing is a serious business in Japan. Like every Japanese activity it requires the right equipment and a proper attitude. Around me Japanese women performed a series of twists, shakes and jerks beneath towels designed to conceal. Elasticated at the neck and reaching to the knee, they stopped me discovering exactly what about the Japanese female so excites the foreign male. Perhaps it is the quantity of Japanese underwear. In a hot, humid month where even a short walk drenches shirts, the girl next to me had on one petticoat, one slip, a bra, two girdles and a pair of support tights. The matrons drew in their breath as I removed my T-shirt. A pair of Marks & Spencer knickers does not win you friends in a Tokyo changing room.

Neither did my one-piece swimming costume. The matrons glanced at me and nudged each other. My neighbour baffled me: her underwear folded and put away, she wriggled into yet another bra and pants. Over this she slipped a polka-dot bikini. An old lady came in and stared at me. 'Why is that foreigner wearing nothing under her costume?' she asked the others. 'She doesn't know any better,' said one, shaking her head.

Under-dressed but still undaunted, I followed Miss Polka Dot to the swimming pool.

Even a Tokyo rush hour had not prepared me. In the shallow end children splashed, women stood in groups gossiping while old men stared into space or at the nearest pretty girl. In the deep end young men queued up to swim a length. At their turn they threw themselves into a brief spasm of butterfly before joining another queue for the swim back. I could barely glimpse water for people.

I had just reached the steps when a volley of whistles filled the air. Four young lifeguards in red caps and brief, red costumes (the underwear rule does not apply to Japanese men) glared at me from their high chairs. Why was I not wetter, they demanded. Obviously I had not showered properly. I walked back to the showers and returned, dutifully wet.

There is a certain etiquette to swimming a length in Japan applicable to Japanese life in general. You do not queue-jump, you cannot overtake and, if you do collide with someone else, both swimmers must stop and tread water while executing a bow. I broke all three rules when I swam into the stomach of a Sumo wrestler. He was playing ball with two other Sumo wrestlers in the centre of the pool. Each weighed about 25 stone, wore capacious trunks in bright colours and had his hair smoothed into a top-knot. Round them floated shoals of children in rubber rings. When I tried to swim around the wrestler he bounced the beach ball on my head. I looked up over the stomach to the moon face above me. The moment had come, I decided, to practise my first aquatic bow.

In between waiting my turn and apologising I had accomplished three lengths in ten minutes. I was on my fourth length when the pool started to empty. People climbed out and sat on benches lining the walls. Soon I was the only person left. For the first time I began to enjoy myself, when the whistles shrilled. One of the guards climbed down from the high chair, swaggered over the pool's edge and jerked his head at me. Without looking at him, I swam on. At the other end, a second guard leant forward from his chair. 'Get out!' he hissed. I smiled vaguely and set off on another length. 'Rest Time, Rest Time,' shouted the first guard. He crouched down at the edge of the pool and made a grab at me. I kicked out of his reach. At the other end the second guard was preparing to wade in after me. I ignored him and returned to the first guard who was now in the water and very cross indeed. Japanese officials, however lowly, are unaccustomed to disobedience especially from women. 'Rest Time!' he spat out. I stopped, stood up and said that if I wanted to rest I would have stayed at home. The crowd sucked in its breath. 'Out. Out,' shouted the guard. I thought he might hit me. The crowd, still silent, pretended not to look. The guard now jabbed at me, as one might a beast of uncertain temperament. Reluctantly I turned towards the steps, adjusted my costume to compensate for my lack of underwear then climbed out of the pool. An old lady made room for me on a bench. She said, 'This is Rest Time. The guards stand in for our mother. When they see we are tired they tell us to rest.'

Tokyo is for ever Tokyo. I had just forgotten what makes it a dream city.

22/29 December 1990

MONEY FOR OLD ROPE TRICK

Alistair McAlpine

Away for a day from the new gloom of the sale-rooms – a gloom that mostly seems confined to the sales of Modern and Impressionist paintings – a gentleman from Sotheby's grandly announced, after their sale of mediaeval manuscripts, that the market was firm. It had been firm for some years; there had, however, been a hiccup in the early 19th century and things had looked a bit dicky at the beginning of 1530.

Escaping this gloom, I visited Curiosita e Magica in Rome: a shop dealing in magic, and worth visiting whether you have any interest in magic or not. Its only drawback or, for that matter, advantage, depending on your point of view, is that most of the tricks on display are not for sale. The tricks are, for the most part, the ones you used to find in the magic shops of London – Gamages and Ellisons, both closed, or the magic department of Hamleys, reduced now from its former glory, complete with resident magician, to a poor collection of practical jokes, no size, no style. This shop in Rome has the equipment to saw a lady in half; empty frying-pans that after a burst of flames release clouds of doves or a couple of rabbits; a multiplying box two feet square and four feet high that can produce several hundred alarm clocks; dead chickens, rubber for convenient packing and bunches of flowers made of feathers; a mirror that objects disappear through; large cards, a foot or so long, on which the hearts, spades, diamonds and clubs appear and disappear at the will of the conjuror; a milk churn with a dozen padlocks for escapologists who must have been terribly small; and a box for placing over the head of someone from the audience whereupon ten or so of its members push large carving knives through slots and, I suppose, the head of the victim – and hey presto, the box is removed and all is well.

Conjuring, I suppose, is a matter of just how each one of us sees things. I remember one night sitting in the restaurant the Château de Madrid high above the town of Beaulieu in the South of France looking out at the coastline with its lights and moving traffic far below, when the gentleman at the next table – a gentleman from America – said to his wife, 'Look at that view, it's just like a giant sirloin steak.'

Shops that deal in magic face a problem of shop-lifting, or so the Roman proprietor explained to me, not because magicians or those interested in magic are less honest than the rest of the population, just that they are better equipped than the rest of us to remove the stock without the shopkeeper knowing. The proprietor's assistant greeted me with some scepticism as I entered his premises. I suppose I do not look much like your average magician, but after a purchase or two he had coloured sponges appearing out of my ears, bunches of flowers from the waistband of my trousers and rabbits from my collar. Cards walked across the counter, coins multiplied, handkerchiefs appeared and disappeared and then changed colours, pints of milk were poured into my left-hand pocket and bottles of beer taken from my right-hand pocket. It all seemed so easy. What wonders I would perform at Christmas! I have been practising for the last two weeks and either my magic show or Christmas has to be postponed for it has now become clear that there is very little chance the two will coincide.

Sales of magic are rare events. There was, in the mid-Seventies, one at Sotheby's: a large and splendid sale of conjuring tricks, books on conjuring, playbills and other conjuring ephemera. The sale went very well, but collectors have had to wait 15 years and no sign of another proper sale. There was just one lot this week, a lot that belonged to Tommy Cooper, the group of tricks that he used on the night he died – on the stage of Her Majesty's Theatre in the middle of his act. Now Tommy Cooper was my sort of magician. His tricks, always failures, were, in the end, spectacularly successful. He played the humour of failure to the limit with his seemingly off-hand and clumsy performance. The lot before his suitcase full of conjuring tricks was a collection of his old prompt cards, showing the reverse to be true: every move, every mistake in his act had been given the maximum of thought.

It is extraordinary when you look at this sale of theatrical and pop memorabilia to think that works, albeit poor examples, by some of the world's greatest painters are having a hard time in the sale-room, while what appears to be cast-out rubbish is selling like hot cakes. There seems to be an air of desperation in Australia at the moment. On the property page of the *Financial Review*, a page covered in two-inch square boxes advertising such tempting items as Prime Commercial Investment, Auctions by the Banks and Sales by Public Open Tender, there was one box prominently displayed at the top centre. It read, in large print, 'Zebra skins of superb quality offered for sale' and, in smaller print, apologetically perhaps, 'Owner redecorating, no further need'. Such is the fate of dead zebras when the fashion changes.

22/29 December 1990

COMPETITION

INSECTICIDE

Jaspistos

In Competition No. 1656 you were invited to comment, in verse or leading-article prose, on the recent case of a man who was fined £50 for leaving a tarantula without food or water for nine days.

What an odd judgment that was. The oddness of it was well exposed by Pippa Legg in her editorial: 'If someone found a common house spider running over his carpet, caught it, placed it in a container, then forgot about it till it died, would this also be punishable with a fine? Is there not an element of "Size-ism" here? The judge should have stated the exact dividing line between the size of a "protected" spider and an "unprotected" one.' Food for thought on the part of Mr Justice Cocklecarrot. The magistrate in our case reportedly maintained that 'spiders have feelings, just like us'. Fancy being *hated* by a tarantula! I was a mere arachnophobe, now I'm a screaming one.

The prize-winners printed below take £12 each. Bad luck, David Griffin; if you had made the cut, you would have been the second winner on Canvey Island. The bonus bottle of Chivas Regal 12-year-old de luxe blended whisky belongs to Gerard Benson.

> He who the Spider racks with thirst
> Shall live despised and die accurst;
> The starved Tarantula's despair
> Spreads rage and ruin everywhere;
> Who would the dainty web destroy
> Shall be deprived of Heaven's joy;
> He who neglects the Arachnid
> Shall be relieved of fifty quid;
> But she who shares her curds and whey
> Shall in God's coin receive her pay.
>
> (Gerard Benson)

SICK AND PERVERTED! These are the only words to describe so-called animal-loving Britons who betray the trust of dumb creatures.

From the degradation of dogs to the kidnapping of

cats the chronicle of cruelty goes on. Now there has been a case of spider abuse, an act so despicable that one must question the private ownership of tropical animals in this country.

As Page Three Lovely Lisa discovered (see page 6), a tarantula is a friendly beast with an innocent charm and appeal, in no way like the ordinary house spiders which we are happy to swish down the plughole or crush underfoot. In a cold climate it is unable to survive without human aid which makes the DELIBERATE STARVATION of one of these lovable animals all the more disgusting and depraved.

A £50 fine is NOT PUNISHMENT ENOUGH. The *Sun* demands a review of this case immediately, and the instigation of appropriate legislation.

(Katie Mallett)

'Of course I'm disappointed ...' said Alice as the Mock Turtle introduced himself, '... I was hoping it was the MUTANT Turtles that lived here.'

A widower, Sir Jasper Ryders
Knew all about exotic spiders,
And gave his only daughter Jill
A small tarantula, named Bill.
Jill misbehaved – I can't recall
Exactly how or why; at all
Events, her father thought he ought to
Deprive the girl of food and water
For several days, although this meant
Bill sharing in the punishment.

When both were rescued, nearly dead,
The magistrates saw rather red:
They said he should be kind to Jill,
Then fined him heavily for Bill;
'Tut-tut,' they said, 'if Bill had died,
We would have had you put inside.'

(David Heaton)

To the lay observer the recent tarantula cruelty case might seem to smack of arbitrary justice. Did the spider's deprivation not simultaneously ensure survival for the flies which would presumably have formed part at least of its food, so that the neglect merely preserved one life form at the expense (potentially, anyway) of another? Might one not even argue – if somewhat perversely – that cruelty was minimised, since the tarantula was still alive after nine days, whereas the flies would certainly have died?

Yet such reflections are dangerous. Where would it all end? With rescuers of stray dogs, perhaps, locked in litigation with kangaroo preservationists sensing hope for their protégés in diminished dog food sales? In a world of conflicting interests, statute and precedent are our bulwarks against chaos. The spider is protected and the flies are not. It is through such apparent inequities that the equity of law is preserved.

(Chris Tingley)

I had a little spider,
and it danced the tarantella,
And I loved it very dearly
Until it bit my fella.

His arm swelled up enormous
And in his pain he cried,
'Go, kill that bloody spider!'
And then the poor bloke died.

I took my little spider
And hit it with a brick,
But the Animal Rights have got me,
And now I'm in the nick.

                              (Hazel M. Stanley)

Trust British legislation
To furnish this equation,
And ask a non-provider
Two ponies for a spider.

                              (A. D. Gibbons)

22/29 December 1990

BATTLE STATIONS

John Simpson

Baghdad

The cars carrying the British ambassador and his staff turned the corner and disappeared from sight, hooting their goodbyes and their relief at getting out. Silence settled over the embassy. A few ashes whirled about in the wind: they and a heap of confetti on a rubbish heap were all that was left of the embassy's papers. In the inner courtyard the little First World War field gun still stood beside an inscription recording the capture of Baghdad. Several locally employed ladies of a certain age were still doing their clerical jobs. All of them had Iraqi passports. They were much too loyal to complain about being left to fend for themselves. I went round telling the ladies that the BBC, at any rate, was staying; if they had any problems they should come to us. Tears glistened in an eye or two then, and voices were a little husky.

When the Americans left, it was very different. I hadn't much liked the chargé d'affaires, Joseph Wilson IV: he was inclined to tell you over dinner about his successful brokering of international agreements in Africa, and why he had run the Iraqi crisis as he had. From time to time he would spit out little flecks of tobacco from the big cigars he smoked. He was, he said, a child of the Sixties. The day before he left he went round trying out an electronic gadget that insulted people in a squeaky voice. He also told those who planned to stay on in Baghdad that they were going to die. On the morning of the great American departure there was a good deal of studied phrase-making: 'We're leavin' because we don't want to be a pound of ground round.' 'There's gonna be no more level terrain here. There's gonna be only rolling craters.' 'We're goin' to pound these guys so far down you're goin' to have to pipe in the sunlight.'

It wasn't the macho talk of nervous men preparing to bolt. It was part of a deliberate policy to frighten the Iraqis, and to frighten us. The Americans, perhaps rightly, don't want too many witnesses if the last hope of peace evaporates and they attack Baghdad. No matter how careful they are, they are bound to kill some innocent people. The Iraqis are equally bound to use the journalists who stay on here to give the full, unpleasant details to the world. Saddam Hussein bases his strategy on the belief that the United States and its allies have no real stomach for war and no staying-power; people who have seen him recently say he is confident that directly things start to go wrong President Bush will call off the attack. 'We will only have to face two air strikes,' he is reported to have said, 'then it'll be ended.'

As the UN deadline came closer and the unthinkable seemed increasingly likely, many of the journalists here found their editors at home were becoming more peremptory. 'If you aren't out by the 15th I'll regard it as a personal betrayal,' said one. President Bush himself telephoned various American editors to urge them to evacuate their teams. That frightened a lot of people here, and the excuses intensified: 'I came here to cover a crisis, not a war.' 'What's the point in staying if you can't be sure of getting your material out?' 'Suppose the Israelis nuked this place?'

The last possibility worries me too. In fact most of the possibilities worry me. I walk down the empty corridors of our hotel, wondering what damage a missile or a crashing B-25 would do to the structure. I have moved our office from the twelfth to the fifth floor, pretending I didn't want to climb so many stairs in the event of power failure; it was really in order to feel less exposed. A sufferer from claustrophobia, I can barely conceive of jamming with everyone else into the bomb shelters in the hotel basement, their air-sealed doors and low ceilings; disliking the dark, I have supplied myself with torches and candles, books and compact discs.

The sensible thing, of course, would be to return to London, settle into an armchair at the Chelsea Arts Club, and read all about it in the newspapers. But like Vergil's Aeneas, we who stay here are *fato profugus*: driven by fate. I couldn't bear not to be here when it happens. It brings out the Sydney Carton in one, of course.

On a rather lower level many of us exhibit observably similar symptoms: little nervous habits, long abandoned, have a tendency to return, and irritability becomes harder to control. Yet the jokes become better and sharper too. When his offer for an expensive carpet was rejected a friend of mine told the shopkeeper, 'I'd accept it if I were you: the next person in here will be black, six foot six tall, and carrying an M16 rifle.'

Those who are staying on are not, for the most part, the self-regarding heroic types. There are few, if any, medallion men among us. My own group is composed of quiet, thoughtful, rather well-read people. All are volunteers here and they soon became bored with my asking whether they were sure they wanted to stay. They are good company, too. The radio correspondent has the same surname, age and general attitude to life as I do: which confuses the Iraqis and amuses them in equal proportions. Naturally, the gathering crisis is having an even stronger effect on the behaviour of ordinary people. As war seems more likely the old rules, the old duties, the old fears all become a little less exigent.

Our Ministry of Information minders seem preoccupied, their eyes focused on the middle distance, their attention harder to obtain. Supporters of the old system are suddenly showing signs of doubt about the future, and small personal confidences abound. A particularly stern figure whom I have seen every day for two months here suddenly revealed he had a brother in London who was a journalist and knew me.

Corrupt officials have become more reckless in their demand for money. People stay away from their offices and shops longer. The central telephone exchange sometimes fails to answer for half an hour at a time. The staff in our hotel are beginning to melt away. Laundry takes two days instead of one, room service is dwindling, porters are harder to find. Each morning when I labour up and down the hotel swimming pool, the heated water is a little cooler and a little less clear, and fungus spreads between the tiles. On the hotel lawn, sewage appears to be seeping to the surface. A nasty smell of decay hangs around the front steps.

At the same time people are becoming more outspoken, even if only in private. 'Iraq is good car with bad driver,' said a previously discreet friend of mine; 'maybe now we change the driver.' An all-out attack could destroy the government of Saddam Hussein and, having come to like Iraqis, I want to stay with them and see what happens under these circumstances. It is a strange reflection, as I sit here looking out of the window at the darkened city of Baghdad, that by the time these words are printed the war, and everything with it, may have started.

19 January 1991

'Gerald's not taking any chances.'

GROUNDED CHICKENS

Vicki Woods

The haute couture collections taking place in Paris next week will be sparsely attended, especially by Americans. Don't you know there's a war on? Many American fashion editors won't be attending, nor fashion buyers, nor the superstar American models – the six-foot, mostly blonde 19- and 20-year-olds with bee-stung lips and beautiful skin and big wide eyes who say, 'We don't get out of bed for less than $10,000 a day.'

Americans are notoriously windy travellers. In contrast to their gung-ho F-111 pilots who are kicking Saddam's ass in the Gulf, American civilians have yielded superiority in the air. They won't fly to Paris. They won't fly to Europe, in fact. Nor to Thailand either, nor Australia, nor the Philippines, and some of them are even getting a bit leery about shuttling to O'Hare or Dallas, Fort Worth, for fear of Abu Nidal and the Nidalites.

'Couple here want to book a passage on a so-called pleasure cruise.'

Last Wednesday, Terminal 2 at Heathrow stood tense and empty, even for the last businessman's flight out to Paris. Sniffer dogs lolloped about, the knuckles of the Sock Shop girls were white, the strained-looking staff on the information desk were discussing security plans to remove all the letter boxes from the building and flights to anywhere east of Suez were showing CANCELLED or ten hours' delay. I felt a bit windy myself and had to lie across six empty Club Class seats to recover. I got three newspapers, all the Tissus Citron I could carry off and VIP treatment from the CRS riot police at Charles de Gaulle, as did the other 30 or so passengers on an airbus that carries 300. The luggage came up pdq as well, presumably because the loading staff were desperate to get rid of it. Eastern Airlines quietly folded up last week without terrorism to help it along.

'Nobody from the New York office will be coming, of course,' said the American fashion magazine I write for on Day One of the war. Nobody? For the collections? Why? 'Because all employees have been told *that on no account* must they *step* on a plane.' Why? 'Because it's *far* too dangerous; we're in a *war* situation here; it isn't *safe*. Every American citizen is a *target*.' But . . . hang on a minute. What about, erm, me? 'You'll be coming from London, of course. Not from New York.' But I'm a British citizen. I'm a target, too. I mean, we're allies and everything. (Brief pause.) 'Have you considered coming by *train*?' Oh, look, this is mad. I can't believe nobody's going to come from America. What about seeing the clothes? 'Oh, they can have *videos* sent to New York.' By carrier pigeon? 'No, by Federal Express.' You mean, parcels can fly but people can't? But Federal Express has people, too; flying the planes. 'Listen, we're talking about *key personnel* here. The company has to be responsible for their safety.'

There's something about the Americans that differs wildly from me and thee. My neighbour the headhunter was due to hold his annual board meeting in Frankfurt. He had to cancel it when the American contingent squealed about travelling to Europe. 'Bit windy, the Americans.' We reflected on windiness, and how Sylvester Stallone cancelled his visit to promote *Rocky IV* (or whichever it was) at the Cannes Film Festival in 1987 because Mr Reagan, to the fury of Kate Adie, had bombed my old school (it was in the Azizia Barracks in Tripoli, which is now home to Mr Gaddafi). That was the summer no Americans came to London, in case Abu Nidal and the Nidalites got to them. 'The coward dies a thousand times; the hero only once.' Though once is enough, I suppose. Mr Stallone may now reflect that events proved him absolutely right about ducking the Cannes Film Festival because he is still very much with us. But so, I imagine, is every single other star who turned up at Cannes that year, barring the odd cardiac arrest from too much cocaine.

Americans are scared of living and scared of dying. You can't cook breakfast for an American house guest without inducing *timor mortis*. You see prime Suffolk bacon and eggs and sausages, and they see cholesterol (death), saturated fatty acids (death) and high levels of sodium (death). You can't buy champagne in America without the Surgeon-General reminding you not to point the cork towards your eye: It May Be Dangerous To Your Health (blinding followed by death). The Rayburn in my kitchen could not be sold in America, because the handles on the oven doors get hot. I use an oven glove, but the American housewife is protected by Federal law and a four-inch wooden handle from having to work out that anthracite can reach a temperature of 400°F in 20 minutes (severe burning and possibly death).

How does a nation like this ever raise an army? And, having raised it, how does it let it overseas to chew gum, kick ass and bomb the bejasus out of Baghdad? Stormin' Norman Schwarzkopf looks like a robust sort of a bloke to me. Does he stick to a low-cholesterol diet? And why is it that the American army is encouraged to display the sort of matey truculence that stiffens the nerve at this frightening time, while the civilian population is expected to jib and panic and cancel their flights? Sylvester Stallone never hid the fact that he was petrified to fly to Cannes. Americans don't mind admitting that they're panicked. I suppose that makes them a sensible people with wonderful parenting strengths ('I should get on a plane that some maniac wants to blow up? Leave my kids fatherless?' and so forth). But mass panic is a terrible thing to let loose, and it is genuinely odd that an entire nation should be paralysed with fear because of the minute statistical

probability that a Nidalite will get some scores of them.

I'm remarkably scared of dying myself, as a civilian mother of half-grown children. I am as morally hoist as any other former peace marcher about whether or not it's a Just War, and I can panic as well as anybody if I see an untidily parked car outside Harrods or a sweating air hostess; but it's too late to get out of it now. I watched a British nurse this morning on television saying yes, she was scared up here at the front line, but, 'If your number's up, it's up. You can't spend every minute worrying about it.'

One doesn't want to sound like a *Sun* editorial, or Mrs Miniver, but shouldn't we carry on flying and to hell with it? The pilots and cabin staff and loaders still have to get the planes out. I know absolutely that terrorist bombs will come, but I can't know absolutely either that they will or they won't get me. Who can hope to avoid a random fate or 'the inescapable will of God' to quote King Fahd? 'I was thinking about *driving* across,' said a fashion editor I know. Well, I'm going back this week and I'm not thinking about driving across, or getting the train across. I'll damn well keep flying across, and I hope to find lots of Kenneth More types sitting in the airport lounge, making jokes through their stiff upper lips. By Day Five of the war the beauteous (and British) editor of my American magazine had booked her ticket too. Are we downhearted? No.

26 January 1991

A DIFFERENT KIND OF WAR

John Simpson

It isn't what any of us expected. I have seen various wars, from the sudden bush skirmishes of Angola and Rhodesia to the mindlessness of Beirut and the occasional ferocity of Afghanistan; but none of these was remotely like what has been happening in Baghdad and the other cities of Iraq. In the 20 hours between the expiry of the United Nations' deadline to Saddam Hussein and the moment the first air raid started, those of us who were in the Al Rasheed Hotel in Baghdad talked obsessively about the likely pattern of the war. The repeated warnings of President Bush and his spokesmen were deeply disturbing. So was an expression used by an American air force general on American television: the Al Rasheed was to be a 'turning-place' for cruise missiles. These things worried away at us like an infected bite.

By the night of 16 January the main topic of conversation among the journalists was the power of the 2,000lb penetration bomb. A large, unshaven man from one of the American networks who was planning to get out said, 'Man, I wouldn't be down in the shelter when one of those mothers comes out of the sky. I saw them in 'Nam. You'll be dead meat. The vibration's gonna shake the fillings right outa your teeth.' I ran my tongue round my fillings, familiar and smooth: how bad would the vibration have to be to shake them? Finally I summoned up a response. 'Not half as bad as the vibration on the road to Jordan,' I said; 'that'll shake the money out of your pockets, and in your case it's a lot more serious.' He was notoriously tight-fisted, and the going rate for a taxi to the Jordanian border was $3,000.

Other people, also leaving, worked out our margins of safety for us. 'I've seen penetration bombs land in Beirut. One hit by the swimming pool here, you ain't gonna be alive. If it hits away over the street you might make it.' These thoughts penetrated our imaginations with considerable effect and exploded there. I dozed for an hour or two and dreamed of penetration bombs. And yet none of these things came to pass. Our mistake was to associate the destructive capability of the new weapons technology with the hit-and-miss delivery systems of the past. The missiles I had seen landing on Teheran in the Iran-Iraq war were closer to V-1s than to the Tomahawks which the Americans were to use against Baghdad. Only the Iraqis fought the old war of indiscriminate attacks against Tel Aviv and Riyadh with their elderly Scud missiles. If the Americans had used the equivalent of Scuds it would have been another war of military men against civilians. There would have been fearful casualties, yet the economic and military infrastructure of Iraq would have remained largely intact. Instead, the American missiles and smart bombs have worked their way through the centres of population and done the maximum damage, not to life but to Iraq's ability to prosecute the war. When the air force general said the Al Rasheed Hotel was a turning-place for cruise missiles, he meant it literally: one flew across the front of the hotel, turned at the corner and flew across the back of it before striking its target just opposite. No one in the shelters seemed to lose their fillings.

As I looked out from the fifth floor at the skyline it felt like being in the middle of a very big chessboard: every now and then, at apparently random intervals, a gigantic hand would reach down out of the sky and take away one of the major pieces on the board, without touching any of the others. One day the piece might be Baghdad's electricity supply. The next it would be its communications or its stocks of fuel. With great deliberation, Iraq was being bombed back to the age of the Abbasids. Baghdad became a city lighted only by candles and oil lamps, where information passed by word of mouth rather than television or radio or phone. At night the only sources of light you could see from the Al Rasheed were the headlights of a few speeding cars and the fearful glow from some big chemical plant which had been hit earlier. Otherwise there was no light and no sound.

The Iraqi government was plainly taken by surprise. Such evidence as there was indicated that President Saddam Hussein expected a massive onslaught in which thousands would die. This is presumably why he thought the American will to prosecute the war would be short-lived. It may also be the reason why he refused to authorise the evacuation of women and children from the cities. The plan to evacuate Baghdad was made public by the Minister of the Interior, a portly, scar-faced man who turned up at a camp for refugees which we had been taken to inspect. It seemed a very small camp, considering it was supposed to take a quarter of the population of Saddam City, a vast suburb of great barrenness on the north-east edge of Baghdad. A million people lived there; but the refugee camp contained only 80 medium-sized tents, each sleeping a dozen or so. No one could explain where the remaining 249,000 inhabitants of the relevant quarter of Saddam City would stay. Not that it mattered at the time, since all but a few of them had decided to ignore the order to be evacuated, and stayed at home with the curtains closed.

The Interior Minister bustled across the sandy ground towards our cameras, children and dogs scattering in the path of his bodyguards. The bodyguards fought us back while we tried to get close enough to hear what the minister was saying. Next Friday, he promised (it would be the Friday before the UN deadline), there was to be an evacuation drill for the whole of Baghdad. After that the city would be evacuated in earnest. Friday came and went. So did 15 January. On 16 January, the day before the war began, the Speaker of the Iraqi parliament gave a small news conference. A slight, smiling man, he explained there would be no evacuation after all. When their fathers were preparing to be martyrs in Kuwait, he said, the children were equally prepared to be martyrs.

Back in our cutting room we put together our report. We had pictures from a girls' school in Baghdad: the pupils making their way through the early morning mist, the school bell ringing, the girls settling down in their classroom. The camera-work was good, and I looked at the dark, eager faces of the pupils as they started the examinations which the government had deliberately refused to postpone. The girls were in their mid-teens: a little younger than my own daughters. When we had edited those pictures we added on the Speaker's news conference. I was tempted, when he came to the part about children longing for the opportunity to become martyrs, to overlay close-ups of the faces of those girls, rational and earnest, on his words. But the producer had a better grasp of the BBC's principles than I did, so we let the viewers make up their own minds about it, and decided not to load the issue. But it was hard to ignore the suspicion that if an American missile had landed on the school the Iraqi government would have felt it constituted excellent propaganda.

A train was hit in one of the earliest attacks, and people aboard it were killed. But Iraq's own casualty figures seemed to indicate that the number of deaths was remarkably low, given the destruction that was going on by day and night. In Baghdad itself the losses were lower than anywhere else. That, presumably, is the result of having Western journalists in the city. The Americans must have taken especial care to avoid civilian casualties in Baghdad, where they could have reported back to every television viewer in Europe and America.

In the end, of course, we were obliged to leave. We tried hard to stay. Having cracked a couple of ribs during a bombing raid, I did my best to persuade an Iraqi doctor to say I was unfit to travel; it didn't work. Some of us thought of barricading ourselves in our rooms, but we were told politely that the order to leave had come from the President's office and would be enforced in whatever way was necessary. The Ministry of Information, which knew the value of having us there, had fought a spirited rearguard action on our behalf; but the Security Ministry was determined to get rid of us on the grounds that we were acting as artillery-spotters for the allies, informing the outside world which targets had been hit and which were still standing. The decision to allow Cable Network News, Saddam Hussein's favourite viewing, to remain in Baghdad looked like a compromise between the two ministries. When we found that CNN was staying, there was a good deal of anger among my colleagues; but privately I was glad that someone at least would still be there as a continuing protection for civilians.

As our $3,000 car took us through the suburbs of the city in the direction of the Jordanian border, we saw the big communications buildings and the defence installations split like cans of corned beef opened with a hammer and chisel, while the houses and shops around them were mostly untouched. Everywhere was silent and empty, with a few shell-shocked people standing about dully on the street corners. We passed the restaurant which I had visited on New Year's Eve in search of a party to film. It had been a frenetic affair, with people clambering onto the tables and wearing masks and silly hats and squirting one another with foam. Young girls danced with portly old men, and with other girls, and with their boyfriends. Older women made a lot of noise, and pretty women looked at the floor and giggled. When people found out that we were British they gathered round to kiss us or shake hands. There was a lot of very bad champagne and reasonable Scotch, and everyone sweated a great deal. The New Year would bring terrible things, and no one wanted to remember it for a night. When midnight came and the lights went back on and the shouting and laughter was louder than ever, I watched an old man, bald and fat, his face shining with the heat of the room. He was sitting silently by himself, and opposite him at the same table was a woman who looked like his daughter. She was beaming, and bouncing a child on her knees, making it clap its pudgy hands together in time to the loud dance music. The old man sat there in the noise and the jollity and looked at them, the tears running unchecked down his fat grey cheeks.

Now the restaurant was deserted. The windows were taped against blast, the New Year decorations long since taken down. It was just another silent, tatty building in the city which expected its next air raid at any minute. I had been frightened many times during the previous nights and days, but as I looked back from the car and watched the restaurant receding into the distance, remembering the old man and his daughter and grandchild, I knew there was nothing I wanted more than to come back here.

26 January 1991

'As we sit here, day after day, under this pitiless barrage...'

AFORE YE GO

Leaves from the Commonplace Book of Wallace Arnold

It is with no small measure of regret that I announce the rejection by our once-proud nation of a very great female who took us out of recession and into the land of plenty. I speak, of course, of Margaret Thatcher, who has been left to fend for herself in her South London mock-Georgian style maisonette with hob, downstairs 'toilet' (dread word!) and twin garage facility.

As is well known, the name of Arnold, Wallace, is the prime adornment upon the freshly minted writing paper of The Thatcher Foundation, some way above Thatcher, Mark, and one down from Archer, Jeffrey. The aim of the Foundation – to which, I might add, the sum of £235.67 has already been donated from a variety of sources, after a period of only two months – is to promote the beliefs of Mrs Margaret Thatcher, while at the same time providing that magnificent lady with something to 'keep her busy' over the next decade or so. Might I take this opportunity to beg all readers of *The Spectator*, however hit by the present recession, to contribute a little something to this great cause. It would be sad indeed if this country were to allow this doughty warrior to remain in her present state, alone and unwanted, a mere shadow of her former self.

Without going into too great detail, I feel duty-bound to paint a 'pen-portrait' of a visit I paid to the Dulwich homestead only last week.

Viyella Housecoat

I was there to deliver by hand a major gift to the Thatcher Foundation. It was an envelope from a variety of major City institutions who wished to show a token of their gratitude to this remarkable lady. It contained a Boots voucher worth £4.35p, redeemable at over 600 stores throughout the country, plus attractive greetings card with verse. This, I felt sure, would do much to perk the lady up, and I looked forward to glimpsing the lustre as it returned once more to her eyes.

Envelope in hand, I pressed the bell of the Dulwich maisonette. Before the fifth chime had sounded, the door had swung open. Before me stood a forlorn figure clad in Viyella housecoat and fluffy slippers of floral design, one hand clasping the butt of a cigarette, the other clutching lamely at a jar of Windolene. Mis-aimed lipstick lent colour to her left cheek. 'Margaret!' I sighed, my voice faltering. A tear came to her eye. 'Wallace!' she answered. 'Is it really you?' I held out the envelope. 'Take it, Margaret, I implore you!' I exclaimed. 'The CBI have had a whip-round. They would be most awfully upset if you were to refuse!'

She nodded me indoors. Framed photographs of her sharing a laugh with President Trudeau and greeting President and Mrs Reagan in the VIP lounge at Heathrow lay hugger-mugger on the uncarpeted floors. The cobwebbed telephone lent a bleak resonance to a sitting-room, furnished only with a solitary bean-bag. On the kitchen table stood a beaker replete with a lone straw and a double measure of Windolene. A painful visit, hard to recount, to which I shall be returning next week; until then I urge all readers to contribute handsomely to this most worthy cause.

9 February 1991

POP MUSIC

BAN THE BOOM BANG-A-BANG

Marcus Berkmann

War does not bring the best out of pop musicians. Not only will you not see many of them fighting in the Gulf – long hair, persistent drug abuse and Armani clothes rarely being tolerated in today's modern streamlined armed forces – but you won't see many of them over here, either. Tours by terrified American bands are already being cancelled and besides, aren't the studio facilities so much better in the West Indies? Of course they are. It also seems unlikely that many great war songs will be recorded – not least because the BBC would not play them even if they were. Just to be on the safe side, the Corporation has already suggested a number of records its local radio stations may wish to withdraw from their playlists for the duration of the war. The list has prompted much analysis, but on the whole it seems sound thinking. Who could disagree with the removal of Phil Collins' 'In The Air Tonight' (clearly a reference to Scud missiles over Tel Aviv),

The Doors' 'Light My Fire' (a savage indictment of Saddam Hussein's terror tactics, and nothing to do with sex at all) or Lulu's controversial anti-war anthem, 'Boom Bang-a-Bang'? Abba's 'Waterloo' has also been blacklisted, to avoid upsetting any surviving participants from the Napoleonic Wars. And removing all of Cat Stevens' songs from radio is something many of us have been advocating for many years – since he recorded them, in fact.

But why stop there? If the potential for offence is as great as the BBC clearly thinks it is, then many other songs should also be banished from the airwaves. The Beatles' 'Yellow Submarine' is clearly dangerously subversive, and almost certainly a source of valuable intelligence material to the Iraqis, as is John Hanson's 'The Desert Song'. As for Was Not Was's catchy dance hit 'Walk The Dinosaur' (chorus: Boom boom acka lacka lacka boom/Boom boom acka lacka boom boom), it's remarkable that the group's members have not yet been interned for their own safety. And after the BBC wisely considered the sensibilities of our allies, and banned The Bangles' 'Walk Like An Egyptian' – a move that has no doubt had everyone dancing in the streets of Cairo – there can surely be no excuse for Debbie Harry's 'French Kissing In The USA'. The entire oeuvre of the Los Angeles band Guns 'n' Roses, too, must surely be doomed.

9 February 1991

'Oh, it's not the Madonna, then.'

TIME TO GET THE STINKER MURDOCH OUT OF HERE

Auberon Waugh

Last Thursday, 7 February, on the 22nd day of the Gulf War, I was interested to see that the *Sun* had decided it had been going on for long enough. While Our Boys and Girls were preparing to give their lives for justice and democracy, the *Sun* decided to use as its main news story of the day the fact that it had acquired some three-month-old photographs of Lord Linley's birthday party, celebrated in a Soho restaurant which he had opened on the same day. A coloured photograph of the young man, wearing an oriental coat, being fondled by two transvestites, appeared on the front page under the headline 'It's Lord Lipstick!'

The picture was captioned: 'Hot lips . . . painted-up Viscount Linley with two of the transvestite guests at his birthday party rave.' The story accompanying the *Sun* Picture Exclusive was written in the enthusiastic style to which we have all become accustomed:

> This is the Queen's nephew Lord Linley as you never saw him before – wearing lipstick at a wild party. And his two pretty companions are MEN in drag. Princess Margaret's bachelor son painted his lips red and dressed in a glittering kaftan for the bash marking his 29th birthday . . . Linley was seen KISSING and DANCING with transvestite waiters and drag queens from nearby Madame Jo Jo's club in London's Soho.

Further pictures inside do not confirm this, although there is one of him looking terrified at the camera and another of him being ostentatiously kissed by an androgyne. A guest is reported as saying that he later slipped out of the back door to avoid being photographed in lipstick.

This would seem to suggest that he was not keen for such photographs to appear in the tabloid press. An expert reader would also have noticed that no date was given for the celebrations described. He would have concluded that it was quite an old story, made topical only by the fact that the *Sun* had suddenly acquired the pictures, or decided to print them.

Not so the poor, befuddled *Sunday Times*. It devoted a leader of almost unbelievable pomposity to rebuking 'members of the royal family whose behaviour has been less than we have a right to expect', commenting that 'the performance of even the inner circle since hostilities broke out has hardly been faultless'. The other major charge against the wartime behaviour of royals and near-royals concerned Lord Althorp's night of nausea with Miss Sally Ann Lasson. But that, too, had taken place a year before the war started and became of wartime interest only when the *Sunday Times*'s sister paper, the *News of the World*, decided to buy Lasson's account of it.

'Britain's armed forces are waging war against the fourth largest military machine in the world,' intoned the *Sunday Times*, setting the background. Well yes, that would be one way of describing the situation which applied last Sunday. Another would be that Britain had decided to help the largest military machine in the world bomb the daylights out of a desert state (Iraq) of only 16 million inhabitants:

> Lord Linley, the Queen's nephew, decided to celebrate
> his 29th birthday last week by donning fancy dress,
> wearing red lipstick and posing for the tabloids holding
> on to various males in drag.

The obvious injustice in accusing this young man of 'posing for the tabloids' may be excused, perhaps, within the polemical tradition. But to describe him as celebrating his birthday in the previous week, and then draw dire conclusions from it, demonstrates only the sad mixture of ignorance, pomposity and incompetence which has become

'Hello, is that the support group for people
with nothing to worry about?'

the hallmark of New Britain after the proletarian *sorgimento* of the 1960s and 1970s. I would not expect the editor of the *Sunday Times* to have the date of Lord Linley's birthday written in his diary but the merest glance at *Who's Who* would have informed him that Lord Linley's birthday was on 3 November last year – nearly two and a half months before hostilities broke out in the Gulf. If he does not like *Who's Who*, or cannot afford a copy, he might have telephoned the restaurant, Deals West (071–287 1001) where he will be told that the party took place on 29 November. Any cub reporter would have checked his facts before going to town in this way: 'Their behaviour at a time of national crisis is helping to undermine the very role of the royal family.'

Did he not even show the copy to lawyers or were they too incompetent to spot it? Linley is a known litigant, and Althorp suffers from none of the constraints which might apply to members of the royal family (and neither of them is a beneficiary of the civil list). Although I do not normally approve of recourse to the libel laws, except as a last resort, on this occasion, if I find myself appointed member of the jury, I think I may award the plaintiffs £250 million apiece in punitive or exemplary damages. This is because I have come to the conclusion that Mr Rupert Murdoch has delighted us long enough.

One of the least attractive aspects of Mrs Thatcher's later years – and the main reason she was eventually so much hated by her own Cabinet – was the reign of terror imposed by the thuggish alliance between Thatcher, Ingham and Murdoch. Any colleague who displeased her would be done over by the Murdoch press with venom and savagery even while she protested her admiration for the victim.

We have got rid of Thatcher and Ingham. Now the time has come to get rid of Murdoch. His pay-off was to be permitted, as an American citizen (albeit with an Australian accent), to own not only a gigantic slice of our national press, but also an effective monopoly in satellite television, making him the most influential and powerful person in Britain.

Never mind his detestation of our class system. I can see it must be annoying that in any English gathering (beyond his own, paid sycophants) the entire company collapses in laughter at his accent every time he opens his mouth, especially if he thinks he has something important to say. Our class system can look after itself.

What he has now adopted is a sustained campaign against the monarchy and the royal family: 'A growing number of young people, by no means all on the political left, are [sic] also beginning to question the purpose of the monarchy, perhaps encouraged to do so by the behaviour and lifestyles of too many of their royal contemporaries,' intoned the *Sunday Times*. As I have shown, Murdoch's minions first discredit the royal family by bribes and invasion of privacy in the *Sun* and *News of the World*, then come over all pompous in the *Sunday Times*, even accusing their victims of 'posing for the tabloids'.

It will not do. Many of us feel exasperated with the monarchy and royal family from time to time, but when we wish to get rid of them, we will do it ourselves. We do not want an American financier with a silly accent making these decisions for us. I wish to see a simple Order in Council, under the monopoly legislation, requiring Murdoch to sell all his English newspapers forthwith. In mercy he may be allowed to keep his satellite television.

16 February 1991

TWENTY YEARS ON

Sandra Barwick

St Aidan's school in Carlisle still smells much as it did. The assembly hall is still pervaded with the heavy aroma of school dinners, that sickly blend of cabbage, custard and mincemeat of 20 years ago.

In 1970, when I was a pupil there, not much else survived the reformists. That year the brave world of comprehensive education had just obliterated Carlisle and County High School for Girls which had occupied the buildings for almost 70 years, its strong academic standards, its grey and maroon uniform, its highly dedicated and qualified female staff, its competitive, hierarchical – some thought snobbish – discriminatory, old-fashioned system. Its demise reflected the spirit of an age and so, perhaps, do present events.

Aged 16 in 1970, I had just mastered the old system and learned how to poise my maroon beret at what I hoped was a rakish angle which would demonstrate seniority over juniors while irritating seniors. When the change came and replaced my school with a comprehensive named St Aidan's, all I knew was that life had become modern and progressive. Where we were progressing, and why, remained mysterious. Carlisle High School had not taught the questioning of authority. I was one small product on the academic assembly line, and the factory had been re-fitted. No one asked the pupils' opinions. No one asked the parents. No one asked the teachers. A new egalitarian and democratic age was imposed from above.

I see now that this progressive régime was, in its way, a superior preparation for life to that offered by the High School – my old grammar school. From being an ordered, disciplined structure in which obedience and virtue were rewarded, my world became grey, anonymous and incoherent. Survival replaced enjoyment.

There was no shortage of funds. New buildings sprang up for the study of metalwork and woodwork and a vast indoor sports hall appeared.

The new age of equality obliterated the compulsory school uniform, prefectorial offices and prizes for academic achievement. Mass assembly in the morning was gone. The school had almost doubled in size, from 600 to over a thousand: no one room could hold us. We were now a mixed-sex school, but the senior teaching posts were held almost exclusively by men, and strange men some of them seemed. The headmaster startled me by his only remark in three years, as I leaned against a corridor wall: 'You're looking very S-shaped today.'

The head of sixth told me that he was not very concerned for the welfare of the sixth form on the grounds that we were always going to survive. He was more worried about the children in the remedial classes who could not read the writing on a cigarette packet. The idea that we might all be educated to reach our optimum did not seem to be current. This kind of attitude may help to explain why some Cambridge colleges have had to start positive discrimination to help let in state pupils. Under the new system at St Aidan's there was, of course, no tuition for the Oxbridge entrance examination, but there was education of another sort, for through our purple corridors blew a strong political breeze. At compulsory general studies periods we watched a series of anti-war films, where poppies faded, women wept to a backdrop of nuclear explosion, and plaintive guitars twanged a farewell over ranks of military gravestones.

I made my own farewell to the place with relief and anger three years after its metamorphosis. Not much disturbed my efforts to forget it in the years that followed: there was an article in one of the Sunday supplements which compared St Aidan's and Eton as opposite ends of the spectrum; and in 1983 one of the senior masters, seen by other members of staff as 'a brilliant innovator', was given a suspended six-month prison sentence for spanking the bottoms of 13- and 14-year-old girl pupils through their nightdresses with a training shoe. The girls' parents had been present throughout these innovatory spankings, convinced by his authority that he must know best.

Other than from these stories it was hard to tell the successes of the new order, because the headmaster did not publish examination results. It is true that generally the success of the comprehensive movement is hard to quantify. Some comprehensive schools have an excellent reputation; as a whole they have not succeeded in sending more working-class children to university than before, but perhaps that was never the aim. What is quite clear is that the population of this country, relying on the unscientific but persuasive evidence of their own experience and that of children of relatives and friends, has little faith in the present educational system. Only 37 per cent of the British, according to the latest Gallup survey, are confident in the quality of the nation's education, compared with over 70 per cent in Denmark and West Germany. Certainly it was on unscientific evidence that parents, unenlightened on the matter of educational theory, were, in the end, the judge of the régime at St Aidan's.

Parents with ambitions for their children sent them to the old boys' grammar school, which had also gone comprehensive, but retained a higher reputation for an interest in academic standards. The county council further stimulated this trend by announcing three times, as parents debated where to send their children, that it was going to close St Aidan's down. The school now has fewer than 500 pupils – fewer than the old High School days – rattling around the optimistic extensions of the Seventies.

Eighteen months ago a new headmaster, David Kemp, a Newcastle man with degrees from Edinburgh and Toronto universities, was promoted at St Aidan's: his task, to attract pupils back by appealing to parents. St Aidan's Comprehensive is now, despite much obstruction from above, called 'St Aidan's County High School'. The pupils wear a compulsory navy-blue uniform. There is an awards ceremony which celebrates academic and non-academic achievements. The headmaster wears – oh horror! – a gown at assembly. The old girls' High School boards, boasting of scholarships, have been retrieved from the cellars where they have lain for 20 years, polished, mended, and re-hung in the old hall. New boards bear the names of the academic achievements of St Aidan's pupils – those who went on to gain firsts at university or came top in the county in their A-level results. The school's prospectus boasts that it still teaches Latin and sends pupils to Oxbridge – particularly to Downing College, Cambridge.

Last week, their minds wonderfully concentrated by the hung Cumbria County Council's latest decision to abolish the place, the parents of St Aidan's pupils voted by a 97 per cent majority to opt out of county council control and give power into the school's own hands. This time democracy has been extended downwards. So far 114 schools in the country have opted out, and 60 more are likely to ballot soon. St Aidan's fate now lies with the Secretary of State. The teachers and the pupils I spoke to support the parents' decision. They do not want to return to the old selective system, but they would like a chance to give themselves a future which will meet the requirements of the pupils and their parents, and one free from political interference. The place has plenty to work on in pursuit of future excellence: a large sixth form, three computer rooms, technical teaching facilities, laboratories, a swimming pool, its own studies centre in Langdale in the Lake District, a language laboratory, committed teachers, small classes, and an application from a polytechnic in another town to use some of its spare space to teach degree courses.

'I wonder what we'll call ourselves?' the headmaster mused, as we stood outside the old Sixties front entrance. 'Maybe Carlisle and County High School.' Time will tell, I hoped in 1970, as I grieved over the destruction of what I thought was valuable, as well as plenty which needed improvement, and time, indeed, has told.

23 February 1991

'There goes the neighbourhood.'

THE HAIR-RAISING HISTORY OF CHARLES THE BALD

Charles Moore

We in the editorial community, as I am surprised no one yet calls it, have endless discussions about why people read what they do or don't read what they don't. If only we could enter the minds of the people 'out there', we think, we would sell millions upon millions of copies. It was in one of these discussions recently that I heard myself airing the opinion that women liked reading about health and men did not. I never read about health, I said, and I felt rather proud of myself, as if there was something stoical in my attitude.

Brooding afterwards, however, I have to confess that as I pass high-mindedly over all those bits in the newspapers about breast cancer and passive smoking and back pain, my eye does nowadays linger on any item about baldness.

So I am in a position to inform readers that the current situation in the depilation community is as follows. A team at Cambridge, which includes a friend of mine called Terence Kealey, has managed to grow a human hair in a test-tube. The trick, according to the *Independent on Sunday*, was to extract a hair follicle from spare human skin 'without putting these important dermal papilla cells under stress'. So far Dr Kealey has failed to follow the injunction, 'Physician, heal thyself' (he is strikingly bald), but apparently all sorts of experiments can now be carried out on these important dermal papilla cells, and it is only a matter of time before great auburn manes and woolly mops will be sprouting in laboratories, tended, perhaps, by secretaries who at present have to confine their nurturing skills to spider plants and Busy Lizzies.

Meanwhile, at Bradford University, Valerie Randall is isolating these important dermal papilla cells, distinguishing three types of follicle – from the adult, male beard, from the 'non-balding' part of the scalp, and from the pubic area. Perhaps she will soon be able to flood the market with those pubic wigs, known as merkins, which were particularly popular in the Tudor period.

It is difficult to describe the mixed emotions with which an interested party reads of these developments. One would like to think, of course, that one was perfectly indifferent. Who cares about being bald? one asks defiantly; people will still love me *for myself*. There is even a certain distinction in baldness (as people tell one when they are trying to be kind). Shakespeare was bald, and Aeschylus died when an eagle, mistaking his naked pate for a rock, dropped a tortoise on it.

But the truth is that it is quite hard to love anyone for himself and for no other reason, and one therefore does well to give people a little assistance. And although one might accept that baldness is one of the ills that the male flesh is often heir to, one does not want to come into the inheritance too quickly. 'Not too much off the top, sir?' asks the barber considerately. Nowadays I prefer to get the point in first myself. 'Not too much off the top, I suppose,' I say with a merry laugh, but my face in the glass looks a little sad.

When I was a child, my mother used to induce me to have my hair washed (I think this only happened about once a month) by lathering it into the shape of a rabbit or a unicorn. I have never asked my wife to perform a similar service, but if I did she would not be able to make much more than a snail's antenna.

It is one thing, however, to mourn the tresses which lie thick as autumnal leaves that strow the brooks in Vallombrosa every time one runs out the bathwater, and another to scrape them up and try

'That's quite a mane you have.'

to stick them back on, which is what Mr Andrew Neil, the editor of the *Sunday Times*, looks as if he does. Vanity makes one regret one's loss of hair, but an even greater vanity makes one dread the idea that friends would discover that one was trying to regain it.

Outraged nature might wreak some terrible revenge. The re-implanted hairs would grow at a different pace from the surviving originals, or they would turn a different colour, or one's entire head would become an illustration of the parable of the sower. Even worse, some of Dr Randall's follicles might be misplaced, and one would find oneself crowned by a thick pubic wire. *The Spectator*'s High Life correspondent, whose own hair retreats but still clings to the top, like mountain snow in summer, once pressed on me a wonder drug that would make it all grow back. I was too vain to dare to try it.

Besides, even if it *did* all grow back in a perfectly orderly manner, how would one be received during the course of the treatment? Would people notice the change, but be too polite to comment, as most friends do when the opposite happens? Or would they inspect it admiringly as one might a well prepared garden in February? Or would they only mock?

For the moment, then, it is reasonably easy to resist. Safer to stay in the rearguard of technology, and only read about the new possibilities, and sigh.

But the culture does not stay still. The canon of taste changes with surprising speed. Until quite recently, it was regarded as tarty or vulgar for women to dye their hair. Now it is entirely accepted. Presumably this is because the dyes have become very convincing, and because the idea of re-inventing your appearance is considered attractive rather than sinister. The same will eventually happen with baldness. Everyone who goes bald will regrow his hair, perhaps becoming more admired than the man who never lost it in the first place, rather as divorced women over 30 are now considered more eligible than those who have stayed single. The man who stays bald will become defiant, even ill-mannered, like people who refuse to replace their teeth. But my generation will be too late for the fun, and will be interviewed on television by people who laughingly ask what it is like to go round with nothing on your head.

I am writing this at a time when a bald man is making difficulties. Mr Gorbachev is trying to bring 'peace' to the Middle East in a form which would more or less undo the recent achievements of the Western allies. The Editor, who has a full head of hair, has chosen not to publish much about him this week, feeling that everything may have changed by the time the magazine has found its way round our railway and postal systems. So this may be the only comment you read this week on the great matter of the hour.

Mrs Thatcher is blamed for almost everything, and for the most part unjustly. But one thing she is not criticised enough for is her enthusiasm for Mr Gorbachev. Her declaration that she could do business with him probably gave him about two years' breathing space with Western conservative opinion, and recent events show that he knew how to take advantage of it. I do not know why Mrs Thatcher formed the view that she did. These articles that I have been reading say that bald men have a tremendous number of testosterone hormones. Anyway, since she is a woman, she could not possibly have understood the drive for world domination that the trauma of baldness can engender in the male psyche.

23 February 1991

DIARY

Craig Brown

I spent two hours over lunch with Charles Moore a fortnight ago and failed to notice that he was going bald, then last week I read his moving lament to his lost hair. Oddly enough, I have been going bald since the age of 20 (how much longer before going becomes gone?) yet for most of the day I am able to wander around under the happy illusion that I have an almost unmanageably extravagant head of hair, along the lines of an English Jimi Hendrix or even Carmen Miranda. Only when I catch sight of myself in shop windows am I brought face-to-face with the realisation that I more closely resemble Mr Robert Robinson. Though I am grateful to Mr Moore for pushing a new line in baldy propaganda to the effect that bald men are excitingly power-crazed, I'm afraid that it won't wash with the world at large. One of the many upsetting aspects of hair loss is having to read flagrantly baldist fiction in which walk-on characters are described as 'dull and balding' as if the two adjectives went together as naturally as 'happy and glorious'. Those who do not suffer from it suspect that baldness is as much a character defect as a physical defect. This is why Gerald Kaufman, who is really not so bad as politicians go, seems to inspire convulsions of irritation. Perhaps if he were to invest in a Lionel Blair-style bouffant hairpiece, his pronouncements would gain a new authority. Other politicians have gone in for hair replacement therapy, some of it bizarre. The late Mark Boxer had as sharp an eye for hair as he had a nose for gossip. As a cartoonist, he found that when he got the hair of a caricature right, the rest followed. A year or so before he died, he told me with great glee that he had been chatting to a dermatologist at a party. This dermatologist had told him of a new method of hair replacement which involved planting the patient's pubic hair on the bald patch. He assured Mark that a senior Tory politician was undergoing this treatment, but discretion forbade him to reveal which one. Coincidentally, the very next day, Mark visited the opera, and found that the head behind which he sat belonged to Mr (as he then was) Norman St John-Stevas. But even diarists must exercise discretion from time to time, so I think I will close Mark's story there . . .

2 March 1991

'We've got rhythm – who could ask for anything more?'

LOVE AMONG THE RUINS

Guy Kennaway

The striking thing about old houses is how new they look. It is a result of the mania for restoration that has been sweeping Britain. I know a couple who spent their honeymoon up a ladder picking old paint out of a cornice with cotton-buds. It's getting difficult to find any houses that really look their age. Twenty years ago the country was littered with marvellous old broken-down buildings. People in Wiltshire used to live in them perfectly happily. Now you can hardly find a derelict railway station, let alone a barn, and that delicious feeling of chancing upon an abandoned house in a ruined wood is a thing of the past, unless you go to France. It is the fault of the renovators; they are destroying our heritage.

Fortunately, Marcus Dean has just published a Good Ruin Guide, called *Scotland's Endangered Houses*. I believe his intention was to draw them to the attention of the renovators, but there is still time before they 'save' these houses, to experience the delights of buildings that are old, and for once really look it.

I can particularly recommend a couple of houses in appalling condition on the Isle of Skye. The first is an ivy-clogged shell sinking into waterlogged earth in a derelict wood on the banks of a loch. Hebridean storms have blown in the casements and blown off the roof but, incredibly, there is a well-worn path from a side-door to a stream, where an occupant has been getting water. If you stand as I did, imagining the story of the house, absorbing the waves of melancholy in the howling wind, a woman with an educated voice and a desperate pair of shoes will emerge from a hovel beside the house and tell you to go away. But she happily lingered for a quarter of an hour to chronicle the unimpeded decline of her family. The council had tried to rehouse both her and her aged mother, tackling the two of them in the Caledonian Bar, Portree, but the offer had been refused. To pay taxes and debts, everything saleable had been sold, including land on which cement bungalows now stalked the house from behind, but the women were not going to move out. What made them cling so desperately to this disagreeable life? It is impossible to understand unless you have looked out at the loch, with the Atlantic to your right, the magical hills to your left, and heard wild-eyed plans for the future, that resonated with tales of childhood summers in the main house with her cavalry officer father. Then it is easy to see. And although the place is now decrepit and depressing, it evokes truer feelings and deeper longings than any of the sanitised museums of the renovators.

The 18th-century house on the other side of the loch has a roof and window casements, but was abandoned over a decade ago. Yet when I cupped my eyes at the cloudy window panes, I saw that despite the shovelfuls of fallen plaster the place was still fully furnished, down to rotting rugs, mildewed curtains and punctured cushions. I could almost smell the mould on clothes in the cupboards upstairs. On the back of a sunken sofa a James Last LP had been balancing all these years, left there absent-mindedly on the last day. How had things come to this? Why hadn't the furniture been put into storage? Outside, brambles climbed in the pantry gauze, sheep nosed by the leaning sundial, and the garden played Grandmother's Footsteps across the lawn with the house. The place evoked all the pains of a family in terminal decline: procrastination, disagreement and resentment among the older generation, that has more pressing problems and wants the cash from a sale. An avenue of ancient hardwoods leads down to an immense stone boat-house on the seashore. Its windswept, empty interior must have echoed with laughter when the boat was launched in rainy summers past to cruise the Western Isles. Now it stands as a temple to lost causes, with swollen woodwork, bearded gutters and ivy in the harling, a tragic object in the wild landscape, a reminder of the way dynasties decline and riches evanesce.

It is a reminder that you do not get from a newly 'saved' country house. These places have been brought to an evolutionary fullstop by revisionist decorators. And for some reason no one seems to be complaining. What would happen if the iron age settlements on the Orkneys were 'saved' for habitation? Or the Rollright Stones re-pointed? Spencer House, in St James's Park, recently renovated at immense cost by Jacob Rothschild, is a case in point. There's a painted lily if ever I saw one. Each room has been restored to its golden moment, creating a whole that would never even have existed in the past. It is the aesthetic equivalent of a compilation album of Mozart's arias, with a bit of Wagner thrown in for good measure. There is simply no sense of time having passed in its sparkling interiors. If Spencer House could talk it would probably say how embarrassed it was, being, as it is, like a dowager duchess forced into gaudy national dress.

What makes the situation particularly alarming is that the buildings erected today tend to be made of concrete. Concrete may make lousy homes, but it makes even worse ruins. It doesn't even crumble. It holds no secrets. Its stained partitions simply shed their rusting windows and stand like empty boxes before falling over to catch your foot on their sharp edges.

Architectural purists can rebuild to designs from archives, and even go so far as to distress furniture and finishes, but they can never reproduce ageing. It is the one effect that will always be beyond them. Ensuring that some buildings are allowed to decay in peace is one cause that everyone has a duty to rally to. The good news is that all we have to do about the situation is absolutely nothing.

2 March 1991

A PLAGUE ON THE BBC

John Keegan

'I told you so' is not a charitable phrase. In fairness to myself, let me say that I have never before uttered it in print. If I cannot choke it off this week, it is for a simple reason. It is that what I have thought from the outset of Operation Desert Shield would be the certain outcome of Operation Desert Storm now stares us in the face. The Iraqi army fell to pieces in the first hours of the offensive. Saddam is about to be revealed as a paper tiger. The war is nearly over. Allied victory – swift, total and almost costless in life – is at hand.

I can say 'I told you so' because, in an article I wrote on Christmas Eve last year, published in *The Spectator* the week before the air offensive began, I forecast that the Iraqi air force would be eliminated from the war without any significant loss to the allied side and that once the ground war began, with the Iraqi air force absent, the Iraqi army would run away. Not all the Iraqis have run yet. That, however, is only because the majority have not yet met allied troops to whom to offer their surrender.

I take no satisfaction in saying 'I told you so'. I write the words nevertheless with considerable emotion. I did not begin life as a journalist. For most of my years I have been an academic military historian. For the last five years, however, journalism has been my profession. For my fellow print journalists I early conceived and retain a warm affection and regard. But in the case of some of those who practise the profession in the television medium their coverage of the war has filled me with burning contempt.

I except at once the television news-gatherers and reporters. They, it seems to me, have done their job as they should. Peter Arnett, much assaulted in the United States, may at times have recirculated from Baghdad an Iraqi version of events with more emotion than the facts warranted. I would like to be sure that, with an Iraqi minder at my elbow and scenes of the suffering of ordinary Iraqis before my eyes, I would not have done the same. Many of the others, particularly Martin Bell and Michael Nicholson, have by any standards been pillars of objectivity. In the best traditions of British broadcasting, they have patently told the truth as they perceive it without for a moment implying that their loyalties lie anywhere but on the side of the good.

It is the television opinion-makers who have aroused my ire. The Dimbleby brothers and Jeremy Paxman, in particular, seem to me to have betrayed their responsibilities to a contemptible degree. I have watched their technique with mesmerised fascination. I have, of course, often watched them in action in the past. Then, however, it was politics or economics that was their subject and politicians or economists who were their victims. They are fair game. Politics and economics, economics even more than politics, are subjects where opinion is king. It is perfectly acceptable, indeed desirable, that practitioners of those subjects should be coaxed into taking an exposed position, at which the interviewer then chips away by intelligent questioning. When well done, television interviewing of that sort renders a public service. The television grandees who have won their reputations by that technique deserve their high standing, at least as long as they confine themselves to areas of opinion only.

Strategy is not, however, a matter of opinion – not least in the circumstances of the Kuwait war. There is a Soviet concept, 'the correlation of forces', which deserves to be rescued from the wreck of Marxism. What it lays down is that, when two sides become locked in conflict, there is an objective means of determining which is likely to prove the victor. It requires close and careful analysis of all the resources available to the two sides – quantity and quality of equipment, match of types, stocks of ammunitions, size, nature and output of the defence industries, numbers of trained personnel – an evaluation of the operating conditions on the front of engagement and how they favour one side or the other, an assessment of the morale of the forces engaged and so on.

When two contestants are evenly or closely matched, 'the correlation of forces' is not an easy exercise. Had the television opinion-makers been faced with a situation such as prevailed between Iran and Iraq in 1980, they should have been forgiven for confessing bafflement. It baffled all who attempted it. When, however, one side is as overwhelmingly outmatched as the Iraqis have been by the coalition ever since President Bush announced on 2 November that he was doubling the number of American forces in the Gulf, 'the correlation of forces' is an open-and-shut case.

On one side stood a country of 18 million Third World people, without a defence industry and with an armoury of second-hand Soviet equipment which could not be replaced should any of it be lost in combat. On the other stood three of the strongest states in the First World, with a combined population of 350 million, which are respectively the first, third and fourth biggest international suppliers of advanced military equipment. Their armed forces are at the peak of world military efficiency and, by the time the United Nations deadline ran out on 15 January, the army they had assembled in the Gulf equalled in numbers that which Saddam had deployed in Kuwait, while their air forces outnumbered his by four times.

The facts were so stark that the simplest layman could conclude that once battle was joined the Iraqis would be overwhelmed in a few days of fighting. Have the television grandees told us any such thing? They have not. On the contrary: for day after day they have strung us along, turning an open-and-shut case into a cliffhanger. Sober, responsible military experts, many of them retired officers of high rank, have been brought to the studio to state facts and opinions similar to those I have outlined above, only to hear, in the familiar way, their considered advice being chipped away in the condescending, imperious, incredulous tone which is now the received style wherever the television grandees hold sway. In an earlier article I called the refusal of the grandees to listen 'the higher ignorance'. But now I think it is worse than that. It is a petulant determination not to learn, lest learning interfere with the right they have established for themselves over the years to know better than anyone they interview.

If what they were offering were 'just television', as most transmissions are, that would not matter. But a whole nation has necessarily had to hang on the narcissistic grandees' words for the last months. Worse, tens of thousands of viewers who are relatives and friends of our servicemen in the Gulf have had their anxieties stretched day after day by the relentless expression of professional doubt that the grandees have turned on anyone who dared to utter the simple truth that the allies were bound to win and to win without serious loss among the ranks of the soldiers, sailors and airmen who had gone to the Gulf to do their duty.

I do not know Jeremy Paxman, either of the Dimblebys or any of the other television grandees. I do know many of the soldiers who are about to win the great victory. Some I taught as cadets at Sandhurst, many were my colleagues there or at the Staff College. I know their wives and families. I know the lives they have lived during the 20 years when the Cold War reached its climax. I know that they have scraped, on salaries which would not cover a television grandee's lunches, to keep up appearances, pay their debts and educate their children. I know they have spent months of each year living on cold rations in bleak training areas on the North German plain to wear down the will of the Soviet Union in its confrontation with democracy. I know that they have lived under a code of behaviour that the television world would regard as an intolerable restriction of individual liberty. I know that their professional lives have been governed by standards of efficiency so rigorous that a single uncomplimentary report can blight a whole career. I know, in short, that they are people of a quality scarcely to be found anywhere in the kingdom today. What is more, I know that the kingdom values them for what they are.

For the first time since opinions were polled in this century, those questioned state that they hold servicemen second only to the medical profession in esteem. Rightly so; as a letter in the *Times* suggested recently, we may well recognise with hindsight that the most successful national institution of the post-1945 years is the British army – a title that the BBC perhaps deserved when it was the most respected broadcasting institution in the world, but which it has now lost. The army has stoically kept order in Northern Ireland for 20 years without suffering the least taint of political involvement. It has efficiently performed any essential service – fire-fighting, ambulance driving, rubbish collection – left undone by public employees on strike. It won the Falklands war with a despatch that the American army has clearly been at pains to emulate ever since. With the American army it garrisoned the Iron Curtain until the Soviet Union dismantled it in despair.

This wonderful national institution lies under the threat of returning from a historic, just and necessary victory, which will benefit the whole world for decades to come, to face heavy demobilisations under the programme of budgetary reductions known as 'Options for Change'. The British army, 150,000 strong, probably costs some £4.5 billion a year to maintain. The BBC, which employs 23,000 people, costs £1.5 billion a year. Each BBC employee, in short, costs about twice as much as a soldier. Which, frankly, gives to the nation better value for money?

If, from our pockets, we have to choose between paying taxes for the army or licences for the BBC, which do we think better deserves the outlay? If we have to choose between the Royal Scots, now crossing the desert to cut off the retreat of the Republican Guard, and *Panorama*, no doubt already working itself up to point out all the difficulties that peace in the Gulf will bring, to which do we think we should commit future revenue? Is *Newsnight* worth more than the 7th Armoured Brigade? Do the smooth men of our screens better deserve their livelihoods than the quiet and unassuming friends of my youth who are leading their soldiers to victory on the Euphrates?

Marmaduke Hussey, who suffered grievous wounds in the defence of our country, may well feel torn when he next comes to present his budget to the national paymasters. He may well feel that if the grandees cannot contain their arrogance, he at least should moderate the demands of his programme makers. I know, if I were given a free choice, how I would allocate my contributions to the public purse. It would not be to subsidise those lofty and haughty expressions of doubt which have unnecessarily troubled the national mind since the Gulf crisis began six months ago.

2 March 1991

LETTERS

THE BBC'S WAR

Sir: As an admirer of John Keegan over many years I was somewhat taken aback by his diatribe last week against the television opinion makers who, he says, have aroused his ire ('A plague on the BBC', 2 March). I disagree strongly that the Dimbleby brothers and Jeremy Paxman in particular have betrayed their responsibilities as journalists to a contemptible degree during the war. Most certainly, they set out to ask the questions the viewers wanted answers to. But we were insistent throughout the war that we would not speculate, on BBC Radio or Television, in any way that could impede or endanger military operations. All the interviewees on our programmes knew that was our role – and they were happy to use their wisdom and experience to ensure we abided by it.

John Keegan says that we should have concluded that the Iraqis would be overwhelmed within a few days of fighting. The fact we did not report such an outcome was, according to Keegan, because we ignored the sober, responsible military experts we brought into the studio. This is a strange argument – we were there to present the facts as we, and they, saw them, and not to speculate. To do otherwise would indeed have been irresponsible.

As to comparing the cost of the BBC with various units of the army, I think the British public have been superbly served by the armed forces in the last few months. I would humbly suggest they've been well served by BBC journalists too.

Tony Hall
Director, News and Current Affairs,
BBC, Television Centre,
Wood Lane, London W12

Sir: John Keegan's commentaries on the Gulf war were superb. His praise of the British army is well merited. But he is wrong to lay into the Dimbleby brothers and Jeremy Paxman for their work on the BBC.

The enormity of the coalition's enterprise, its political risks, and the scale of its unknown costs – such as the numbers of dead on both sides – were all legitimate subjects for analysis. Certainly the interviewers raised all sorts of questions – that is their task, and they are all of them good at it. No doubt some of the answers were foolish or inaccurate. But that seems a small price for free discussion in a free society.

On another matter, I imagine that Mr Keegan is right that the Soviet concept of 'the correlation of forces' showed beyond doubt that the coalition was bound to win the war. But I am interested as to what that concept would have showed in the Vietnam war – there also the American army possessed overwhelming superiority in technology and equipment.

William Shawcross
East Dean,
Sussex

'*It was eight hours of boredom followed by sixty seconds of frantic activity.*'

Sir: John Keegan is as entitled to his expressions of contempt towards me and the Dimblebys as he is to his extraordinary musings on the relative cost of the BBC and the army.

But for the record, I have not conducted a single *Newsnight* interview with a retired military person on the subject of strategy. Or on tactics if it comes to that. Is that the sort of inaccuracy he had in mind when he mentioned that he was a relative newcomer to journalism?

Jeremy Paxman
BBC, Television Centre,
Wood Lane,
London W12

Sir: Congratulations on Mr Keegan's article. This is something which really had to be written and I am sure that most of the country agrees with him.

M. Fooks
5 Bloomsbury Place,
London WC1

9 March 1991

DIARY

Dominic Lawson

Moscow

For those who can afford it, the best way to endure the horrible length of the British winter is to spend a part of it in the Caribbean. For those who can't, I suggest a quick trip to Moscow. It's vilely cold and inhospitable, and when you return even London in the last mean throes of winter seems warm and welcoming.

This thought occurred to me only when I returned from three days in Moscow, as part of a strangely named Eminent Persons Group – surely it is axiomatic that eminent people never travel in groups – sent to investigate the state of human rights in the Soviet Union. One of the members of our group was Barbara Castle – or Baroness Castle as she does not like being called. As we drove in from Sheremetyevo Airport to our hotel, Mrs Castle (as she prefers to be called) tapped me on the knee with a tiny elegant little hand and pronounced, 'I was here in 1938, y'know. It was so idealistic here then. Not like now.' Young Barbara had been sent, as a member of the Young Socialist League, by Sir Stafford Cripps. Naturally Sir Stafford sent her first class. The time that she recalls as being so 'idealistic' was of course not long after the peak of Stalin's purges. Many Westerners made the same trip at the same time – George Bernard Shaw and the Webbs most notoriously – and were similarly enthusiastic about the fresh-faced idealism of the Soviet new man, as exemplified by comrade Stalin. But I was struck by the fact that Barbara Castle's feelings had not been altered by the passage of time and knowledge. Anyway, in recognition of the more corrupt face of Comrade Gorbachev's Soviet Union, Baroness Castle purchased several tins of best beluga caviar on the black market. She negotiated a very good price, one that fills me even now with jealousy and admiration. Before we parted I attempted to persuade her to give me one of her many tins; while I am too lazy to deal on the black market myself, I am prepared to be parasitical on those who have done the dirty work. But 'No!' said Baroness Castle, 'I won't give one to a right-wing bastard like you!' So she has not lost her idealism after all, I thought, and regarded the lady with even more awe than before.

9 March 1991

'Check the cake's sell-by date.'

BOOKS

THE GREEKS HAD A SWORD FOR IT

Stephen Spender

HOMER: THE ILIAD
translated by Robert Fagles
Viking, £17.95, pp.704
KINGS
by Christopher Logue
Faber, £4.99, pp.96

Reading, during the last week of the Gulf war, this vivid, forward-moving translation of the *Iliad*, it struck me that Homer did not seem dated. Saddam Hussein and General Schwarzkopf fitted easily into the Troy of Hector, with Agamemnon's Achaean fleet blockading it offshore. The Emirs, Princes, Ayatollahs and priests are not far from the world of Agamemnon, Paris, Priam and Chryses. Zeus, Hera, Venus, Apollo and all the other gods, far away on Olympus, enthralled spectators, backing their favourites, sometimes intervening, and sometimes changing sides – a coalition extremely difficult for Zeus to hold together – corresponded well enough to the American and European allies. The Olympians, of course, remained much concerned with burnt offerings, coming from the middle part of the world – sheep, goats, oxen, kids, lambs – in a word, oil.

Compared with the *Odyssey*, which is all imagination, the *Iliad* has something of the authority of a terrifying and wholly pessimistic sacred book which concerns the place of Man within the Universe, and in relation to his own deepest and darkest nature – like, say, the Book of Job. The terrible truth it relates is that the natural condition of humanity is war. Leaders obsessed with power (and perhaps their followers as well) realise their true nature, the objective reality about themselves, only through extremes of violence.

What makes the *Iliad* close to our time is total war in which each side seeks utterly to destroy the other. Reading it, I do not think it possible to imagine any work more truthful or more terrible. Of course one may tell oneself that Homer is concerned with a primitive society of tribes fighting with spears, swords, shields and firebrands for burning down cities. But one only has to multiply the scale of war in the *Iliad* by a factor of, say, a hundred thousand (with weapons capable of destroying several million people) to find oneself in the world of Hiroshima, or of Saddam Hussein setting fire to 300 oil-wells in Kuwait. The end of the *Iliad* will be – the poet leaves us in no doubt – the total destruction of Troy.

It would be wrong to think of Homer's Greeks and Trojans as having very little to lose in the way of what we think of as civilisation. On the contrary, the frail, beautiful, sumptuous indoor existence encasketed in the Trojan walls, and so minutely described in scenes such as the wonderful one in which Helen is weaving a tapestry in her palace in Troy, or that in which Hector, dressed for battle, takes leave of Andromache, seems fully to live up to the kind of classical French paintings of such scenes which we look at in the Louvre. The second of these scenes Fagles rises to beautifully:

> In the same breath, shining Hector reached down to his
> son. But the boy recoiled, cringing against his nurse's
> full breast, screaming out against the sight of his own
> father, terrified by the flashing bronze, the horsehair
> crest, the great ridge of the helmet, nodding, bristling
> terror, so it struck his eyes. And his loving father
> laughed, his mother laughed as well, and glorious
> Hector, quickly lifting the helmet from his head, set
> it down on the ground, fiery in the sunlight. And
> raising his son he kissed him, and tossed him in his
> arms . . . So Hector prayed, and placed his son in the
> arms of his loving wife. Andromache pressed the child
> to her scented breast, smiling through her tears.

Although this is a society advanced in artistic culture, with grandiose architecture, beautiful pottery, art-work of bronze, gold, silver, and even iron, poetry, song and dance, the advanced edge of technology, beyond all else, is the weaponry. Homer describes, in the greatest detail, swords, spears, armour and, above all, shields. He also describes the damage that weapons cause with such precision that the *Iliad* would provide a useful manual to a field hospital having to deal with wounds inflicted upon combatants in war between Greeks and Trojans. The rage of Achilles at Agamemnon, King of Mycenae and leader of the Achaeans, is the force that drives through the whole *Iliad*, giving it unity. The abduction of Helen by Paris is only a pretext for the fighting, like 'Brave Little Belgium', and nothing becomes more obvious in the course of the narrative than that if the Trojans were

'*Freud's* Studies in Hysteria! – *Where the hell is it ?*'

to give up Helen it would not stop the fighting, so long as Achilles
was around. The terrible human truth at the heart of the poem is that
violence transforms the war's heroes by making them transcend their
own subjective natures and become objective forces, revealed as such
to their subjective selves. I am reminded of Ernest Hemingway telling
me in Spain during the Civil War that he had to keep on going to the
front in order to prove to himself that he was not frightened. Courage
is demonstrating to yourself that you are an objective force, mindless
of your subjective feelings. And in this lies the great attraction of war:
that it provides a dimension of objective human reality hardly to be
experienced in peace.

This wonderful translation has the added attraction of an introduction and notes by Bernard Knox. Knox discusses all the fascinating
facts (or the lack of them) of Homeric scholarship and the main

problems raised. He reminds us that no one ever spoke the language of Homer. The *Iliad* is in the literary language of bards who recited the epic, which was not written down until centuries later. The mystery which makes one go on asking 'Who was Homer, or what was he – or they?' persists, surely on account of this being a narrative which has authorial unity. It gives the illusion of being told by one person. And no one dares say, as they do with the Old Testament: 'In lieu of any other author or authors, let us say it was written by God . . .', which is what one feels.

Together with Fagles, I recommend strongly Christopher Logue's *Kings*, a poem following on an earlier volume, *War Music*. This can perhaps best be described as selections from the *Iliad* reflected in the mind and the original poetry of a modern. They are in the tradition of James Joyce, Pound and Eliot. Splinters of the *Iliad* exist side by side with splinters of corresponding phenomena in the modern world. Christopher Logue brings the haunted past to life amid the equally war-haunted present. This is a considerable achievement.

16 March 1991

THE YEARS WITH JENNIFER

Vicki Woods

I always thought Mrs Betty Kenward would die in harness on Ladies' Day, but there you are. She has taken the momentous decision to retire from Jennifer's Diary, having written the curious and anachronistic social pages of *Harpers & Queen* under that name for 50 years (she started the Diary on *Tatler*, and moved it to the *Queen*, which merged into *Harpers & Queen* in 1971). Her announcement caused a puff of valedictory pieces, mostly very rude, to be written up in the papers by gossip-writers ('Vermin!'). And it's not true, as Francis Wheen wrote in the *Independent on Sunday*, that 'the snobbish old fright allegedly found the magazine's new editor too common'. She never gave a fig for any of her editors. She'll be 85 on Bastille Day and is desperate to finish her memoirs. (In longhand, no ghost-writer.)

'You'll be doing Mrs K's pages,' said the production manager of

Harpers & Queen 20 years ago, and I was scared witless. I'd seen her in the lift, in her velvet bows and afternoon frocks and meringue bouffant hair. She barked and snapped in her clipped, pre-war idiolect; her minions toiled slavishly and then she ate them for supper; grown men quaked before her; even Jocelyn Stevens was leery of her, and he was six-foot-odd and an Old Etonian. She stood four-square, like my old Latin mistress, with a steel ruler down her back and her mouth was set in a straight line. She had a killer stare, like the Queen's. Her voice would crack out like a whip. 'Stupid gel!'

The myth was that she savaged an endless succession of terrified little debs called Caroline until they laid their heads on their desks and wept. The myth was underlined with some fact. She savaged softies, but she adored people who 'got on with it'. Her office was crowded with pictures of babies her gutsier ex-secretaries sent her. She once wrote of a South African trip: 'So in one week I met both the best secretary I've ever had and the worst secretary I've ever had!' Both names were printed. The 'best secretary' was snitched from her by Jocelyn Stevens, who exercised his *droit du rédacteur-en-chef* while she was *en vacances*. On her return, everyone quaked, including Stevens, even though he had filled her office with 12 dozen mollifying roses. She is supposed to have stalked in and delivered him a line worthy of Bertie Wooster's Aunt Agatha: 'I've always understood that among people of our class it wasn't done to steal each other's servants.'

Victoria Mather wrote about Mrs Kenward's retirement in last Friday's *Daily Telegraph*. She sniped at Jennifer's gracious – and coded – language, where all brides are 'radiant' and nothing nasty is ever said. 'Omissions were as potent as inclusions,' she wrote. Indeed they are. Victoria Mather included in her piece the fact that she had worked as Mrs Kenward's secretary. But she omitted to say that she'd been one of the girls with her head on the desk, or that Mrs Kenward had snapped at her, 'You look a perfect fright! Can't you look in the mirror before you leave home?' on more than one occasion. She also omitted her dramatic sacking, which we all crowded in to hear about immediately afterwards. 'It was awful, awful.' We passed the Kleenex. Mrs Kenward had come crackling back into her office after luncheon, and demanded to know whether what she had been told by a fellow-guest was true? That her secretary had – had '*streaked*' at Queen Charlotte's Ball? Rather gamely, Victoria stuck out her chin. 'I thought there wasn't any point in denying it. So I said I had. I thought she'd *burst*. And she said, How *could* you? *Whatever* possessed you? And I said, Well, we've always been a betting family, Mrs Kenward, and I was dared to do it for a gold bracelet, so . . . I just did.' More sobs. 'And then she said, Well, in *that* case, gel, you had better look for employment elsewhere! And then she stormed out in a complete rage.' I thought the tale reflected rather creditably on both parties, and I can't see why Victoria omitted it.

Mrs Kenward was as hard on herself as she was on others: that's why I like her. I get nervous when I read in the tabloids about Mr Major's ever-so-tired syndrome. Mrs Kenward's constitution is admirably Thatcher-like. At one royal wedding – Princess Margaret's, I think – she came down with flu; shivering, fever, temperature of 104. 'Bed, Betty,' her doctor said. Bed? Was he mad? He laughed, and agreed that she probably wouldn't die on him during the next 12 hours if she 'sweated it out', so she went to the freezing Abbey in her fever and her furs and 'umpteen pairs of woolly longjohns'. She was 70 when I sub-edited her most famous this-hectic-life itinerary. She had dinner in Caracas one evening and returned the next day (by Concorde) in time for Diamond Day at Ascot. She often slept four hours a night for a week and was 'up before six' for a 'busy type of routine day' barking at the likes of me and Victoria Mather.

Her critics feel that when you dine with the ruler of Dubai you must then write about what a despot he is and not about how prettily his dinner-table is laid. They objected to her glozing over anything 'horrid' – or real – and making everything 'gracious'. I never cared. She was brave enough to make me forgive her breathy prose. Sometimes I would see her, ramrod-straight and unyielding, in the middle of some puzzling 'social' function got up by PRs. She had gone alone, and would leave alone: if her 'hostess', whoever she was, had the grace to introduce her to people, she would blossom and engage herself; if not, she would stand, head up, white hair bravely puffed, solitary and silent.

Mrs Kenward employed the semi-colon erratically, over her 50 years. But it isn't true, as has been said, that she allowed its use only after members of the royal family. Proof-reading her stuff was a nightmare. Her copy was printed, until the mid-Eighties, in 8 point type, which swam before the eyes. I learned not to mind when she commaed off subject and verb: 'The Lord Chamberlain Lord Maclean, accompanied the Queen on the lawn', but I grew to dread race-days, especially from Longchamp, when paragraphs beginning 'Others I met or saw racing included –' were followed by fifty, sixty, a hundred unbelievably foreign names for the printers to muck up: 'Baron Geoffroy de Courcel, the Duc d'Audiffret-Pasquier, the Duc and Duchesse de Noailles, Comte Edouard Decaze, Comte de Leselauc de Kerouara, Monsieur Alec Weisweiller, Mrs Arpad Plesch, and her daughter Countess Bunny Esterhazy . . .' and so on and on. In fact, these were a cinch compared to ordinary society weddings, where, for example, a Williams-Wynne daughter married a Douglas-Home boy and the list of names would writhe like a serpent with the bride's brother Mr William Williams-Wynne (with an E), and her cousin Mr David Williams-Wynn (without an E) jostling for attention with Lady William Montagu-Douglas-Scott, the Hon. William Douglas-Home, Sir Watkin Williams-Wynn and Sir Richard and Lady Williams-Bulkeley. I had to check anything that looked odd. Odd? In a world where Lady Mary Gaye Anstruther-Gough-Calthorp (later Lady Mary Gaye Curzon) looked normal, my blue pencil would hover over 'Mr Sam Plum'.

While it's true that Jennifer would draw veils over many alcoholics, adulteresses, bastard sons, crooked financiers, social climbers and heroin addicts of her acquaintance, it isn't true that her diary was bland. She could be very forthright. She lammed into the slummocky girls at the Berkeley Dress Show one year, lamenting their 'scruffy' hair and 'down-at-heel' shoes. She laid about her right and left at the new fashion for organised gate-crashing. She would speak as she found, grammar and the use of English notwithstanding. 'I was very shocked to see a small number of young men turn up at this charming party, in this historic and respected setting, in open-necked shirts with no tie or even a scarf. This, they may feel, is with it! but in reality it is extremely rude and insulting to their hostess. There are quite a lot of this tie-less brigade at dances these days.'

You couldn't really sub-edit that sort of stuff. Nor her bathos. She did bathos inimitably. Thus, in April 1972: 'The bride, who was given away by her father, wore a cream satin dress and her lace veil was held in place by a diamond tiara. She was attended by Miss Amabel Marten, who had the misfortune to be trapped in the lift for an hour just before the service.' But sometimes she made real mistakes in her copy, which had to be corrected. I bemusedly read a paragraph from Venezuela, where she'd had a blissful time, she said, lying on the Embassy verandah with a cooling drink, underneath the oligarchs. Mmmm. Underneath the . . .? 'Such pretty trees, you know,' she said. Ah, yes. It's 'oleanders', Mrs Kenward.

She was good to me during my pregnancy. I was pregnant at the height of Equal Opportunities, at a time when men on the tube had learned to sit tight in their seats and smile sardonically at one's wearisome bulk and swollen angles with a look in their eyes that said, Equality? You got it. They would only leap to their feet on the rare occasions when I could summon enough energy to threaten to vomit over their briefcases. But you don't always find it in you at the end of an ordinary

Tuesday. *Harpers'* nearest tube was the hellhole of Oxford Circus, a difficult place for human barrage balloons to negotiate. Mrs Kenward made a point of sending a message each day at sixish to say that 'faithful Peter' (her chauffeur) was downstairs with the car if I was ready. I would lumber into the back seat and we would wait for Mrs K to waft down in her afternoon frock. We would get 'comfy', and purr off towards Sloane Square, a much nicer, surface station. 'Now, dear, you can get a bit of fresh air on the platform while you wait for the train,' she would admonish me, 'and put those feet up as soon as you get home and make that old man of yours wait on *you*.'

My son was born in October, and my maternity leave lasted until January. Mrs Kenward's galley proofs were sent over to me in Chiswick to check, before they were double-checked by her secretary and finally checked again by her. One day just before Christmas the doorbell rang. I opened it, and there stood faithful Peter covered in holly. In fact, he was holding two large objects with ribbons and holly attached to them. 'Mrs Kenward sent me, miss,' he said. 'To deliver these. She hopes they'll come in useful.' In one hand was a folding baby buggy and in the other was a portable high-chair. We were living hand to mouth in those days. 'Merry Christmas, miss,' he said. In the background, the baby gurgled. 'Ma'am, I should say,' said faithful Peter politely.

23 March 1991

'I always suspected she was lying about her age.'

OH DEAR, WHAT CAN THE MATTER BE?

Auberon Waugh

I had just finished my piece for this week's *Spectator* – quite a good piece, about the Way Ahead for People Like Us – and was about to send it off on Saturday morning, when the telephone rang. It was the young Editor in a state of great excitement. Had I seen that morning's *Sun*? Of course I had, and was about to pen a few tasteful lines on the subject for my *Way of the World* column in the *Telegraph*, complaining about the front page, which showed as its main news revelation of the day a large photograph of my old Oxford acquaintance, Lord Gowrie, now the Chairman of Sotheby's, at the door of a massage parlour in Camden Town. The photograph, it must be admitted, looked rather strange – at first glance, I thought they had made a terrible mistake and it showed my revered mother-in-law. This might have explained the 'Thought' which accompanied the picture: 'Curious a-peer-ance'.

But I decided it was probably a reference to Lord Gowrie's dusky hue which has often been the subject of comment. If so, it was hitting below the belt, and called for some sort of rebuke. As Great Agrippa explained to the naughty boys in *Struwwelpeter*:

> For if he try with all his might
> He cannot change from black to white.

Whether or not some sort of racial slur was intended, I was certain that Lord Gowrie would think it was – as we all know, these people are tremendously sensitive – and decided on quite a hard-hitting riposte. I decided it might be a good idea to illustrate it for *Way of the World* with the picture of a little 'Indian minstrel' figure, dressed only in underpants with furled umbrella and an earl's coronet on his head, walking up to a massage parlour. But my illustrator, Mr Rushton, thought he might be accused of racism, and agreed to do a portrait of Max Hastings talking on a portable telephone in a restaurant instead.

That, then, was the situation when young Dominic Lawson telephoned on Saturday morning, demanding that I write about Gowrie and the massage parlour. Why so? I asked, explaining my predicament.

'Oh I rather think it would be a good idea,' he said vaguely, 'because so many *Spectator* readers are the sort of people who know Gowrie.'

I wonder if he was being entirely honest in this answer. How many of the *Spectator*'s 94,500 readers does he imagine to be acquainted with the dusky art dealer? Is it a good thing to be the sort of person who knows him? What does this tell us about young Dominic's assessment of the average *Spectator* reader?

It is true that I have known Gowrie for over 30 years, and this scarcely seems the right time to disown all knowledge since for many years I set myself up as a close student of the London massage scene and was, indeed, an expert on its Soho ramifications, just as Wheatcroft is an expert on the country's slimming establishments. But since those balmy days a notorious prodnose on Westminster Council called, I think, Brooke-Partridge, or something of the sort, has made it his business to drive most of the best massage parlours out of the area – aided, needless to say, by endless lubricious exposés in the gutter press – and I have rather lost interest in the matter. Now Westminster City Council are trying to stop people feeding the pigeons.

But Editors, however young, are not lightly to be gainsaid. What, then, are we to decide about the *Sun*'s decision, having been tipped off by a member of Sotheby's staff, to make its main news story on Saturday out of the fact that Lord Gowrie had been seen outside a massage parlour in Camden Town?

First, we must decide why the Editor of the *Spectator* wanted me to discuss Gowrie rather than Iraq, starvation in Russia, or the Way Ahead for People Like Us. Could it be that he supposes *Spectator* readers share the prurient interests of *Sun* readers, surely the lowest and vilest people in the country, at any rate as their tastes are interpreted by the journalists who cater for them? Under those circumstances, perhaps the best thing would be simply to reprint the *Sun* story: 'GOWRIE IN SEX SAUNA: *Spotted making three visits* ... At 4 p.m. yesterday the distinguished Earl calmly strolled up to the parlour, where girls offer hand relief for £20 and full sex for £100 ...'

Gowrie himself behaved with dignity, saying he had no comment to make and that he might be consulting his lawyers – which he has now done. Since the plain innuendo in the *Sun*'s account is that he may have availed himself of the sexual services on offer, and since it will be hard, if not impossible, for them to prove it even supposing for a minute that he did, I should have thought it would be worth a couple of hundred thousand, tax-free, if he chooses to pursue the matter. The judge may have changed, but his case would appear to have remarkable similarities to Jeffrey Archer's, and it should be possible to remove self-confessed *Sun* readers from the jury, since hard things might be said about them.

Should we, in addition, feel indignation on Gowrie's behalf? I think we probably should, and not just because Gowrie, despite his dusky appearance, his strange enthusiasm for 'modern art' and his abysmal poetry, is (very nearly) One of Us. Personally, I could not give a hoot if the *Sun* photographed me going into a massage parlour (although I would not hesitate to sue any Murdoch paper if the report contained a libel), but I might be peculiar in that respect. It would make my enemies happy and give my friends a giggle. Others, of a more secretive nature, might be more deeply wounded. It is the idea that Murdoch's thugs have an absolute right to ride roughshod over anyone's most private activities that sticks in the throat.

Time and again we read of television soap celebrities – almost always unknown to me and to most People Like Us – who have been betrayed by call-girls or rent boys, and it would be easy to decide that this is part of the price of being a popular celebrity. If you make your money by sucking up to these animals and catering for their base appetites, you must accept the risk that they will devour you. But even soap celebrities are human. Prick them hard enough, and they will probably bleed. When we allow Murdoch to send his rats swarming all over their private affections, their marriages, their relationships with their children and friends as well as with their public, we are debasing the whole of English life. I am surprised that *Spectator* readers should wish to consider such matters. In a fortnight's time, I shall reveal the Way Ahead for People Like Us – unless a newsflash intervenes, with the startling intelligence that Mrs Thatcher has been found stuck in the lavatory.

30 March 1991

Linden.

IF SYMPTOMS PERSIST . . .

Theodore Dalrymple

Patients who drink too much are notoriously vague (to put it charitably) about the amount they drink. I have a simple method of eliciting the truth from them: I ask them whether they drink two bottles of Scotch a day. 'Oh no, doctor,' they reply, genuinely horrified. 'Only one.'

These days, when epidemiology has revealed the dangers lurking everywhere, doctors have no choice but to concern themselves with their patients' eating, drinking, smoking, sleeping and working habits. I am so heartily sick of the tepid existence which we doctors are now peddling as the elixir of life that when one of my patients refuses to take my good advice, I want to jump up on my table and give three cheers.

I once practised in a very remote corner of the globe, somewhat lacking in sophisticated medical facilities (other than myself, of course). One day an Englishman appeared, new in the country. No sooner had he arrived than his legs swelled up, and he came to consult me. He was extremely large – what failed dieters call big-boned – and very fat. He lost no time in telling me he was diabetic.

'Do you smoke?' I asked.

'Like a chimney,' he replied.

He was completely unrepentant, so refreshingly different from all those snivelling wheedlers with hang-dog expressions who give you a long story about how they nearly gave up but then their budgerigar died. I got the picture at once.

'And of course, you drink like a fish,' I said.

'Like a fish,' he replied.

'Dieting is out of the question?' I continued, with mounting admiration.

'Completely, I love butter and cream, and meat with fat on it, and rich sauces.'

'Well,' I said, 'I'm sure you know the risks better than I, so I'm not going to lecture you. But if you invite me to dinner, I shall come.'

That was 12 years ago. His wife was, and is, a magnificent cook. I wish I could say the story had a happy ending, but honesty compels me to relate that recently he had two heart attacks which have laid him low. He can hardly breathe, and now he needs cardiac surgery.

Still, I found his refusal to do the sensible thing heroic in its way, and it gave him a dozen years of untrammelled life. He may yet pull through. I know there are medical fascists around – a former President of the Royal College of Physicians, Professor Sir Raymond Hoffenberg is one – who would make such patients pay for the treatment of their 'self-induced' diseases, but this seems to me to come perilously close to the Erewhonian nightmare, in which youths who bash old ladies over the head will receive treatment, but people with heart attacks will be punished.

In any case, patients know their doctors have feet of clay. Last Monday morning, a man whom I know to be a very heavy drinker consulted me because he was feeling ill. I examined him.

'I can't find anything wrong,' I said. 'It must be the drink.'

'It's all right, doctor,' he said. 'I'll come back when you're sober.'

6 April 1991

'Because it tends to trigger certain glands
which release euphoria-inducing endocrins,
I try not to smile too much.'

BOOKS

BILLIARDS IN THE OPEN AIR

Roy Jenkins

QUEEN OF GAMES:
THE HISTORY OF CROQUET
by Nicky Smith
Weidenfeld, £16.95, pp.177

I once had a long audience with the late Emperor of Japan. We had obviously both been concerned to find subjects to keep us going. I had been told that he had written 13 books, mainly on marine biology. I endeavoured to 'show awareness', as editors encourage political writers to do, but he deflected my compliments, at once modestly and grandly. 'No, no,' he said, 'I do not write them myself, I employ scholars to do that.'

He, in return, seemed to have been told that my main private occupation was playing croquet, and with immense politeness had absorbed a good deal about the game. Miss Nicky Smith's current work was not available to him, although he, or his Court Chamberlain, had become as well informed as if they had followed closely her regular contributions to *Country Life* under the appropriate pseudonym of Arthur Mallet. The only trouble was that he appeared to think that I was a world-class croquet player. I could not tell him that I employed professionals to win championships, and I felt it would have been an anticlimax to say that my experience was mostly confined to post-prandial foursomes, often on roughish ground, which was best compensated for by making the hoops a little wider than regulation, after weekend country lunch parties. So both our subjects were founded on elements of misapprehension.

Nevertheless, I did spend a considerable amount of time in the 1960s and 1970s – more so than I do now – on the croquet lawn. This was partly because I often played on my own, having discovered that it was a good form of patience. These solitary sessions could take the form of seeing in how few strokes one could get round the long course of ten hoops and the stick, and sometimes, if everything went right, achieving it in under 20. This was quite good practice discipline, although I always disliked being made to play with others the bastard game of golf croquet with its one stroke a go as opposed to the full game of roquets, croquets and the possibility of long breaks.

More frequently, however, I made my patience take the form of the full game but playing all four balls myself, which at least avoided the tedium of waiting for others. The disadvantages were the difficulty of remembering what point in the course they had each reached, the curious fact that one's loyalties became attached to red and yellow, or less frequently to black and blue, which made it difficult to try equally hard with the unfavoured pair of balls, and at the end of the session the very limited satisfaction to be gained from victory over oneself. However, I suppose it provided good practice as well as fresh air, and improved one's performance for more competitive but still strictly informal encounters.

At least since the 'foot on one's own ball and opponent into the bushes' form of play went out circa 1890, I have never been able to understand the theory of croquet being a peculiarly vicious and bad-temper-producing game, as compared with, say, tennis. It is not exhausting, it has a certain gentle rhythm, and its billiards in the open air aspect, with the verdure of country lawns substituted for the smoke-filled saloon-bar traditions of billiards itself, ought surely to produce calm and benignity. Yet in practice I do recall the most epoch-making row with Anthony Crosland at Ann Fleming's, perversely on an otherwise perfect spring day. I also recall that his wife urged him on

'... Barbara Cartland is already into her second book ...'

with loyalty whereas mine merely commented on the ludicrousness of two allegedly grown-up Cabinet ministers quarrelling over the position of the ball. I also recall a disputatious game, played in a summer twilight, with Teddy Kennedy who was partnered by Senator Tunney, the son of the old boxer. But I think that was entirely due to my irritation as the prospect of victory over a Kennedy, always a good thing to achieve, slipped needlessly away under the incompetence of my partner (who was Kennedy's brother-in-law, so perhaps there was collusion). Happily my games with the literary editor of *The Spectator*, mostly on that same lawn which produced the eruption with Crosland, have never ended quarrelsomely. Otherwise I might not be writing this piece today.

Nicky Smith is very informative about the history and current state of the game, and mostly writes clearly and tautly. She is, however, muddling about dates. Having convinced me that croquet, imported from Ireland, had first become a serious 'garden game' in England in the 1860s, she then announces that it was exported to Australia by settlers in the 1850s,

> whose personal baggage often contained a boxed set
> of croquet equipment – a standard part of the para-
> phernalia of the Victorian middle-class family.

Nor can I decide, fluctuating one way and the other, whether or not she has a sense of humour about her game. At times she assumes a sort of Jennifer's Diary inconsequential glossiness. Thus, of the World Singles Champion of 1989:

> He is a cheerful character whose most singular charac-
> teristic is his relentless control of his game. A trained
> carpenter who also studied for a career in the priest-
> hood, Joe Hogan is a great exponent of adopting the
> 'right psychology'. Like most of the New Zealand
> players, this seems to consist of an undemonstrative
> but unyielding determination to win.

At other times she adopts the moral uplift tone of an old-style preparatory school headmaster whose school is not quite worthy of him:

> Five years later they [the United States] have already
> made great strides towards this goal [of 'strength in

depth'] and in the meantime have invested croquet
with an enthusiasm which has been sadly lacking in
the British game.

My reaction to this is to paraphrase King George V's response to
H. G. Wells's 1917 complaint about an alien and uninspiring court.
'I may be uninspiring,' he said, 'but I'll be damned if I'm an alien.'
I feel that I may lack 'strength in depth', but I'll be damned if I'm
unenthusiastic. I once played in three inches of snow when grooves
had to be constructed between the hoops. Once made, the balls ran in
them remarkably truly.

13 April 1991

THE INSIDE STORY

Roger Cooper

If you are pulled in off the street and thrown into an unheated cell
in winter, your clothes and even your watch removed, as happened
to me in Teheran in 1985, your first thoughts tend towards keeping
warm and wondering what the time is. You quickly adjust to your
prison 'uniform', in my case khaki trousers and a cotton jacket. The
trousers were made, long before, for a man with minuscule legs and
a vast girth, impossible to keep up and cold below the knees, while
the metal-buttoned jacket was uncomfortable to sleep in and far from
warm. I solved the time problem by the angle of sunlight on an
outside wall. After lights out the bars of the cell cast two sets of
hateful shadows on the walls, pockmarked with scratched messages
and squashed mosquitoes, in case I forgot where I was.

My subconscious was desperately trying to do just that, and for
the first few months my graphic technicolour dreams featured mirth
and parties, good food and conviviality. Later, reality intruded and
whenever I dreamed of familiar people and places the programme
would often end with my returning to jail because my 'leave' was
up. To keep warm I started on-the-spot jogging and body exercises,
and was pleasantly pleased to see pounds of flab disappearing. There

was a rota for cleaning the latrines, but I began to volunteer for this in order to get out of the cell more. I was taken to the washing area blindfolded three times a day for four minutes with a quick shower once a week, but after cleaning I could claim an extra shower. As I had expected, one could find useful goodies in the garbage can, which the guards also used: a newspaper, a pair of just-serviceable socks, a not quite empty tube of toothpaste.

My first prison was a barracks for military police trainees. They certainly liked to practise on us and were needlessly harsh and spiteful, perhaps venting their grievances at the square-bashing they were undergoing.

Between interrogations, always blindfolded and accompanied by slaps and punches when I refused to confess to being a British spy, I tried to find ways of amusing myself without books. I made a backgammon set with dice of bread, and evolved a maths system based on Roman numerals but with an apple pip for zero. Orange pips were units, plum stones were fives, and tens and hundreds were positional. This enabled me to calculate all the prime numbers up to 5,000, which I recorded in dead space where the door opened and could speculate on the anomalies in their occurrence.

More practically, I kept track of meals and guards, a habit I kept up until I was freed, so that after a time the personnel would sometimes ask me when they were next on duty or what we would have for supper. I spent a lot of time practising and evolving the rules of Flicket, a game played with plumstones and a blindfold with elaborate scoring rules and tactical possibilities. It is the one game in life I've really excelled at, possibly because I had no competition, but I think even when it sweeps the world, and young Peles are emerging from the slums of Rio to earn Olympic glory with perfect rounds, I will always be a good club-class player.

During most of my time in jail chess was *haram* (religiously unacceptable), but the Imam (Ayatollah Khomeini) had second thoughts and it is now permitted – along with boxing, I was sorry to hear. Chess sets are anyway cumbersome to make and use clandestinely, so I concentrated on bridge once I had made a minia-ture pack of cards. Rubber bridge was not a great success, but I played a lot of hands duplicate-style, in different contracts, and with different defences.

For 18 months I had no books at all, though I did manage to liberate one or two while left unguarded in an interrogation room. I cannot imagine who in Evin had owned a French dictionary of sociology, an Enid Blyton in German, and a manual of chemistry in Bulgarian, but they were better than nothing. Later I was allowed to request some books, *Desert Island Discs* style, and inevitably asked for the Bible, Chaucer, Shakespeare, 'and if it doesn't sound too presumptuous', to quote the old joke, 'a blank exercise book'.

They say there's a quotation in Shakespeare for every situation, and with the Bard's complete works to hand I soon found two relevant passages in *The Winter's Tale* to describe my situation, which I was not allowed to discuss when my brother visited me. So in separate letters to my parents I sent 'coded' messages, praising Hermione's speech beginning, 'Since what I am to say, . . .' and Leontes' '. . . though I with death and with/Reward did threaten and encourage him', to let them know what was happening to me. Unfortunately neither of them looked up the references, so my efforts were wasted.

Before my 'literate' period I developed a wide range of mental games and exercises such as palindromes and anagrams. My inspirations here were the famous 'Flit on, cheering angel' (Florence Nightingale) and I had some reasonable successes with the names of friends, colleagues and public figures, now lost – though three were quoted in *The Spectator* last week by John Simpson.

Although not conventionally musical, I did find I missed music badly and tried to compensate for this with the 'Evin Song Book', all the songs I could remember beyond the first line or two, a pitifully small number. I would sing these quietly when a friendly guard was on duty. This gave me an idea for an anthology of songs, which I hope to develop now I'm free. My grandfather was the Irish poet Alfred Perceval Graves, whose 'Father O'Flynn', first published in *The Spectator* over 100 years ago, is something of a national anthem, so perhaps some hereditary talent and song-writing ability has been lying dormant all these years. Anyway, to my surprise I would often wake up with the most marvellous tunes in my head, sometimes even accompanied by rudimentary lyrics. Since I do not know musical notation, many of these got lost, but one or two have survived through repetition and I hope to present my old army unit, embarrassingly the Intelligence Corps, with a regimental ditty I composed (refrain: 'The Unsung Corps, the Corps that really knows the score. The Corps that no-one's heard of is the Corps that won the War.')

I soon realised that the mysterious joke factories people assume exist somewhere must, of course, be prisons. I found a huge supply of shaggy-dog stories and Irish jokes, even cartoons, although I can't draw, welling to the surface, especially in the dark early days. Clearly some kind of Freudian defence mechanism was at work. One serious party game for gourmets I thought up was to make lists of ten favourite foods (fruit, fish, chicken recipes, etc). The rule is, if there could be only ten of each category left in the world, which would you choose? After hours of anguish I would usually end up with the common workaday species, apples rather than mangoes, and, oddly enough, the ones I often saw in jail (imagine a world without potatoes, onions and rice).

It was over 40 years since I had last studied mathematics formally (for the old School Certificate) although, as a journalist writing on economics and a marketing manager in the oil industry, I always had to be reasonably numerate. I began by trying to remember how to solve quadratic equations and prove Pythagoras's theorem, which took days and consumed many sheets of precious paper (purloined from my interrogators or recycled orange wrappings). Before I could reconstruct the classic solution for the square of the hypotenuse proposition I found two solutions of my own, though I am not quite sure they were both valid. Once I got my calculator back I could explore numbers. I found myself fascinated by recurring decimals, especially reciprocals and their multiples. I noticed that if you divide 1 by 7 and 2 by 7 the digits 28571 occur in both, and it soon became clear that the decimal series were really circles of digits totalling one less than the denominator (so 6 digits when 7 is the denominator). Then I discovered that these circles are in fact geometric progressions, for which I discovered a formula. There were many other interesting anomalies and curiosities. One party trick I evolved was to be able to convert a decimal series back into a vulgar fraction. For example, if you divide 101 by 103 you get a decimal series (0.9805825 . . .). It goes on for 102 digits before repeating.

The trick is to turn that back into the two numbers. When I at last got some maths books I did find a cumbersome method using quite advanced algebra. I worked out a terribly simple way, using an ordinary pocket calculator. In case any *Spectator* readers wish to solve this problem themselves I won't give my solution here. 'Answers please on a postcard', as they say, and I will offer my solution in a future issue.

For almost three years I was totally deprived of contact with other prisoners, and for most of that time had no access to news of any kind. So when I did get my first newspapers, especially non-Persian ones, there was a lot I could not understand. I had no idea what 'the Chernobyl factor' was or who the Princess Royal and Fergy were, and I'm still not sure what Mrs Thatcher said at Bruges. My interrogators realised belatedly that this was a mistake, as it meant the political analysis I wrote for them was often out of date. I should explain here that, throughout my interrogation and even after it had formally ended, I felt it useful to try to explain to the Iranians how Britain, and the West in general, actually worked. Their ideas were often totally at odds with reality: for example, many Iranians believe that the Queen secretly appoints the American president; the officials of the Ministry of Information, as Iran's counter-espionage organisation is misleadingly called, have some equally bizarre ideas. Britain is seen as a sly neo-colonialist, 'an old fox' more skilled in politics than the Americans or Russians, and therefore potentially more dangerous.

In the past year or so I've even had regular copies of *The Spectator*, the Week-End *Financial Times*, the *Economist* and Chatham House's monthly journal, so I'm far less of a Rip Van Winkle than I would have been had I been released earlier.

Nevertheless, I'm still suffering from severe culture shock. The electronic revolution passed me completely by in Evin, where I could not even switch a light on for five years, and in London I'm a real country cousin. I find telephones and electric kettles difficult to use, could not get out of the street door of my flat this morning and feel quite disoriented in the Underground. Already I'm beginning to adapt to the new routines, use a knife and fork, eat at a table and sleep in a bed, although I haven't quite got the courage to drive a car or ride a bicycle yet. Friends are naturally asking me what my plans are.

Whatever I do decide I am sure it will include supporting Prisoners Abroad – the main charity for British prisoners throughout the world, which sends books and magazines, arranges visits and pen-pals and provides desperately needed legal and other advice – and working to improve relations between Iran and the West. Some people are surprised at this and expect me to be bitter at my experience.

Considering I have spent most of my working life in or connected with Iran, I am not going to allow a little thing like five years of wrongful imprisonment to poison my love for a unique country and civilisation; and I think there is still much I can do to bridge the understanding gap between Iran and us (it's mutual). This is not the place for a detailed analysis of where Iran is going or the prognosis for Irano-British relations, but clearly these are questions I shall be trying to answer. Above all I shall do what I can to help secure the release of the hostages in Lebanon and the one Commonwealth and three Western prisoners I left behind in Evin, including another Briton nobody seems to be aware of, and whom I was never allowed to meet.

13 April 1991

'RIDDLED WITH ERRORS, REEKING OF BILE'

Nigel Lawson

Margaret Thatcher was one of the greatest prime ministers this country has known; the Thatcher years were a turning point in our history, with an importance beyond our own shores; and when the dust of the current recession has cleared, it will be seen that the fundamental health of the economy has been transformed.

Sadly, in order to establish this, my former friend and Cabinet colleague, Nicholas Ridley, has felt it necessary to lose all sense of objectivity and to write a work of hagiography, the story of Margaret: saint, miracle-worker and martyr – and of how she was betrayed by the Judases she brought to her table. How every success was hers alone; every failure that of her colleagues. It is a book riddled with errors and reeking of bile.

First, just some of the errors – for they also serve to indicate the character of the Ridley version.

We are told that when I returned to the Treasury as Chancellor in June 1983, unemployment, though high, was beginning to fall. In fact, it went on rising for a further three years, peaking in July 1986. We are told that, faced with the 'perceived deficiency of the various measures of money supply . . . he [Nigel Lawson] began to put greater emphasis on the exchange rate as a possible answer to his dilemma. The first reference to it is in his 1985 MTFS' – shorthand for the Medium Term Financial Strategy the Government has published each year since its inauguration by Sir Geoffrey Howe and myself in 1980.

The first reference?

> The behaviour of the exchange rate can help in the interpretation of monetary conditions, particularly when the different aggregates are known to be distorted. The exchange rate is a route through which changes in the money supply affect inflation. It can also be an important influence on financial conditions . . . the Government considers it appropriate to look at the exchange rate in monitoring domestic monetary conditions and in taking decisions about policy.

That is an extract from the 1982 MTFS, signed in the customary way by the then Financial Secretary to the Treasury, one Nicholas Ridley.

By that time, incidentally, I was Secretary of State for Energy and no longer in the Treasury at all – a fact of which Mr Ridley appears wholly unaware when he erroneously writes that in 1981 Margaret Thatcher 'sacked David Howell and appointed Peter Walker as Energy Secretary to prepare for the inevitable confrontation'. It was of course I whom she appointed. Peter Walker did not become Energy Secretary until 1983.

But to return to the economy, and in particular to the exchange rate. We are told that when Mr Ridley was Secretary of State for Trade and Industry from 1989 to 1990, he argued 'against the "shadowing the Deutschmark (DM)" policy on the grounds that it would weaken industry's competitiveness'. In fact, the policy of so-called shadowing the Deutschmark had come to an end as far back as March 1988. Nor, incidentally, during the period when the Deutschmark was being shadowed in 1987, did I reduce interest rates after the stock market crash, as Mr Ridley argues, because I feared a liquidity crisis. It was a crisis of confidence that was the danger, as business, the markets and the media started to talk in terms of 1929 and the 1930s revisited.

We are told, as part of the background to the alleged 'ambush' of Margaret Thatcher by Geoffrey Howe and myself before the Madrid European Council, that 'there was a European Summit in July 1988 at Madrid. Neither British membership of the ERM, nor Economic and Monetary Union, was on the agenda'. In fact, the Madrid summit was in June 1989 and Economic and Monetary Union was the most important item on the agenda. Hence our insistence on a meeting with her.

We are told that, when I raised interest rates to 15 per cent in October 1989, Mr Ridley was horrified, since 'the money supply was already in heavy retreat'. In fact, narrow money (M0) growth in October 1989 was still above the top of its target range, and broad money (M4) growth was some 17.5 per cent (with bank and building society lending still growing at an annual rate of over 20 per cent): scarcely 'heavy retreat'.

The carelessness with the facts (and examples could be multiplied many times over) extends to carelessness over policy. Mr Ridley makes it clear that he has always been wholly opposed, in principle, to sterling's membership of the Exchange Rate Mechanism of the EMS (which he appears simultaneously to consider both deflationary and inflationary) and writes as if that was the official policy of the Government, at least until the Madrid summit. Of course it was not: the policy, restated on numerous occasions, not least by Margaret

Thatcher, was a commitment to join the ERM, when the time was right. Whatever Margaret Thatcher's personal views may have been (and they may not have been the same throughout), that was the declared policy of the Government; there was therefore nothing in the remotest degree improper in her Chancellor seeking to persuade her (as I did, unsuccessfully, over a number of years) that the time was indeed right.

Again, Mr Ridley makes it clear that in his view we should allow the pound to float freely on the foreign exchanges, since only in this way could Britain benefit from a low and, he hopes, undervalued exchange rate – which he alleges to be the secret of Germany's and Japan's success. In other words, he belongs to the now happily diminished band of those who believe in salvation through devaluation. But that again was never – for good reason, not least the need to combat inflation – the policy of the Thatcher Government. I have already indicated how the exchange rate played an important (though for a very short time not explicit) part in that Government's economic policy, right from the earliest days. And whatever Mrs Thatcher may have said to Mr Ridley in private – and even occasionally in public – in practice she was far from indifferent to the exchange rate: I recall in particular her horror when there was talk, in January 1985, of the pound falling below one dollar.

As for the merits of the case, Mr Ridley wholly fails to appreciate the significance of the new world of free capital movements in which we now live, in which it is capital movements rather than trade which dominate the foreign exchange market. But even on his own terms, his explanation of the success of Germany and Japan is bizarre: whatever has happened to their exchange rates over time is the consequence of their success rather than its cause.

The plain fact is that there is no substance whatever in Mr Ridley's astonishing charge that Geoffrey Howe and I became 'out of sympathy with major elements of her Government's aims and were actively working against her. They were not prepared to accept the meaning of Cabinet Government.' The only issue Mr Ridley can conceivably have in mind was policy over the exchange rate, where, as I have indicated, his conclusion is based on a wholly false assumption about both the declared policy of the Government and the way in which economic policy was carried out in practice throughout most of the Thatcher years.

But then Mr Ridley's concept of 'the meaning of Cabinet Government' is itself somewhat idiosyncratic. In his own words:

> The United States Constitution is quite explicit in stating that the Executive consists of one person – the President ... Britain's practice is not so very different ... The Prime Minister alone carries the responsibility of the Executive, just as the President of the USA does.

Finally, saddest of all to me, is Mr Ridley's picture of how he saw his heroine – perhaps how she came to see herself.

> Life at the top is a never-ending vigil for the leader to safeguard himself or herself from leaks and plots and conspiracies and attempts to destabilise ... The miracle is that she managed to outwit her enemies for so long.

Perhaps I am a political innocent; for, although there were certainly all too many leaks, I was wholly unaware over more than a decade as one of her ministers that her colleagues were contantly plotting and conspiring and attempting to 'destabilise' Margaret Thatcher. Nor do I believe that they were. But what is clear is that, somewhere along the way, perhaps after the departure of the irreplaceable Willie Whitelaw at the end of 1987, the mood changed. The great adventure on which we had all embarked in 1979 to rescue Britain from economic and political decline by charting a radically new way forward and having the courage to see it through, had led, in some quarters, it seems, to a bunker mentality.

Mr Ridley has sought in his book not merely to exalt Margaret Thatcher's achievements, but to explain her downfall. He chooses to do so in terms of 'the enemies within' – the imagined treachery of some of her closest colleagues. But what his account in fact suggests is that one of the main causes of that downfall was an enemy even deeper within. That was the flaws within her own remarkable character, flaws which, no doubt inadvertently, he himself encouraged to the point where, even to her own parliamentary colleagues, they began to eclipse the qualities that had earlier inspired her party and her country, and indeed so many outside it.

13 July 1991